ALSO BY KARL IGLESIAS

The 101 Habits of Highly Successful Screenwriters

Writing for

EMOTIONAL
impact

Advanced dramatic techniques
to attract, enagage, and fascinate
the reader from beginning to end

Karl Iglesias

WingSpan Press

Livermore, California

WRITING FOR EMOTIONAL IMPACT
Advanced Dramatic Techniques to Attract, Engage, and Fascinate the Reader from Beginning to End

WingSpan Press
Livermore, CA
www.wingspanpress.com

Printed in the United States of America

The primary purpose of this book is to educate students on the craft of screenwriting and the emotional impact of great stories. All quotes and script excerpts are offered to illustrate storytelling techniques and are published in compliance with the "Fair Use" doctrine, Title 17, Chapter 1, Sec. 107 of the United States Copyright Law.

Cover design by Bill Graham (www.grahamstudios.com)

Library of Congress Cataloging-in-Publication Data

Iglesias, Karl.
  Writing for emotional impact : advanced dramatic techniques to attract, engage, and fascinate the reader from beginning to end / by Karl Iglesias—1st ed.
      p. cm.
  ISBN: 978-1-59594-028-5 (alk. paper)
  ISBN: 978-1-59594-751-2 (ebook)
  1. Motion picture authorship. I. Title.
  PN1996.I39 2005
  808'.066791—dc22

                        2005026149

        10 9 8 7 6 5 4 3 2

To Tara...
for your love, support, and patience.
All my love always.

ACKNOWLEDGMENTS

Isaac Newton once said, "If I have seen further, it is by standing on the shoulders of giants." I'd like to thank all the screenwriting giants whose work herein proves that greatness in craft is indeed possible.

My deepest thanks:

To all my students at UCLA Extension and the Screenwriting Expo for demanding that this book be written. Without your constant requests, it would still be a series of lectures.

To Linda Venis at UCLA Extension's Writer's Program for providing me with such a fulfilling venue to teach, and to her dedicated staff for running such a smooth operation.

To Rosa Graham for the extra pair of eyes, and Bill Graham for the cover.

To Jeff Coller for the "office" space.

To all my friends and family for their caring and support.

And as always, to my wife, Tara, for her unwavering love, support, and enthusiasm for anything I do.

CONTENTS

INTRODUCTION
The Emotion-Delivery Business

> *"It's not about what happens to people on a page; it's about what happens to a reader in his heart and mind."*
>
> -GORDON LISH

There are three kinds of feelings when reading a script—boredom, interest, and "*WOW!*" Your job as a screenwriter is to create that *WOW* feeling on as many pages as possible. This book is for all writers who want to deliver that *WOW,* and who truly understand that great storytelling is about one thing only—engaging the reader emotionally.

Writing for Emotional Impact is for all the frustrated writers who have spent hundreds of dollars on books and seminars only to realize that the formulaic writing they preach leads to boring reading, a "Pass" from readers, and unreturned phone calls from disappointed executives desperate for exciting material. If you've read the screenwriting books, taken the seminars, and have mastered the rules and principles, you're only halfway there, despite the good intentions of the gurus out there. Although most of them would agree you must write a script that involves the reader, I have yet to see a dramatic increase in script quality. Sure, it *seems* better. We hear new writers exclaim, "Look how well-structured it is... I got my plot points where they belong... My protagonist follows the hero's journey, and he changes at the end." Close, but no cigar. Understand, though, that these structural foundations are an essential part of any screenplay, and some books offer brilliant and valuable insights. But if you want to complete your education, read on.

WHY ANOTHER SCREENWRITING BOOK?

Some of you may be thinking, "Do we really need another book on how to write a great screenplay that sells?" As Robert McKee says, "We don't need another cookbook to reheat Hollywood leftovers." I agree. Take a look at how many books there are on bookshelves and online—my latest search on Amazon.com yielded over 1200 results! It boggles the mind. For the past thirty years, aspiring writers have had a wealth of information devoted to the fundamentals and principles of screenwriting, from books and magazines to seminars and web sites, film school graduate programs, not to mention consultants and screenwriting gurus, all promising you that if you put certain events in a specific order by a specific page number, you'll have a great screenplay that will sell. And yet, nothing has changed. Most scripts being marketed today are formulaic, mechanical, predictable, and therefore dull. Why? Because screenwriting is more than just theories and plot recipes. Sure, you need to know the basics, but it's still a far cry from creating a great script. In my book, *The 101 Habits of Highly Successful Screenwriters*, Oscar-winner Akiva Goldsman (*Cinderella Man, I, Robot, A Beautiful Mind*) says, "Screenwriting is like fashion: All clothes have the same structure. A shirt has a two sleeves and buttons, but not all shirts look alike. Most classes and books teach you that a shirt has two sleeves and buttons and then expect the student to come up with a designer's shirt." Writer Howard Rodman, whom I also interviewed but wasn't included due to the book's length, added that these rules, principles, and theories have become "more tools in the hands of bad development executives. Things like act structure, inciting events, plot points and page numbers are ways in the studio world of taking a script that only one person could have written and transforming it into something anybody could have written."

Might as well come out and say it—there are two reasons for this book. The first is to present much-needed information to the frustrated writer who can't find it anywhere despite the incredible array of screenwriting sources. Aspiring writers are still desperate for valuable information. I hear them complain at workshops and conferences how they're tired of picking up book after book and attending seminar after seminar, and yet not learning anything new. The second reason is a more selfish one: As a busy instructor and script consultant, I'm tired of reading awful scripts. My thought is that if I present techniques used by professional writers, the beginners will improve their writing to a satisfactory level. It may not be great enough to sell, but at least it'll raise the level of writing and make the reading experience and analysis more bearable.

It's time to go beyond the basics and focus on what the screenwriting craft is really about—creating an emotional experience in readers. Good writing is good writing because you feel something when you read it. It's why a great movie can be three hours long and you don't even notice, while an awful ninety minute one can feel like ninety hours. It's why psychologists call movies "Emotion Machines." The experience of emotions is the most compelling reason we go to the movies, watch television, play video games, read novels, and attend plays and sporting events. And yet, emotional response is a subject too often overlooked.

When I became a script reader, I thought it was a great time for screenwriters with all this available instruction we didn't have before. I thought I would read decent scripts, especially since many were from mega-literary agencies like CAA, ICM, and William Morris. Boy, was I wrong. Out of the hundreds of scripts I read over the years, I've only recommended five. Understand, though, that many of the scripts I passed on were *technically* flawless—no spelling or format errors, well-structured, with all the prescribed act breaks on the "correct" pages. The main problem was that they all felt the same, as if they'd been written by a connect-the-dots computer programmed with the same old formulaic algorithm. Not only was I shocked that even agented scripts were mediocre at best, but also annoyed that many aspiring writers were wasting their money on instruction that was getting them nowhere. To this day, a surprising lack of awareness still exists among aspiring writers about what great screenwriting is really about. Emotion, not logic, is the stuff of drama. Emotion is your screenplay's lifeblood.

THINKING ABOUT EMOTION

What if screenwriters took these statements seriously and viewed their product not as a 110-page blueprint bound by two brads, but as the promise of an intense and satisfying emotional experience? Think about how much easier it would be to market your screenplay once you truly understood the reader's emotional needs of great storytelling, why one story grabs them and another bores them, why some words transcend the page and cause emotional fulfillment, and others propel the reader to toss the script away. Emotional contact with the reader is the *only* strategy for success.

To begin, you must shift your perspective. It's time to move from thinking about a movie audience to writing for a reader. Your experiences in a movie theatre are caused by the unified craft of about two hundred artists, whose contributions result in the final product you're watching on the silver screen. You experience emotions from the musical score, the editing, the cinematography, the directing, the set design, etc. Reading is a personal activity. It's just between the reader and the page, one individual connecting with words. A reader will only experience emotions from your words and how you string them together on the page. You're the only person responsible for the reader's emotional response. If it's not the *desired* response, if he's[1] bored instead of captivated, that's it. Game

---

1 *For reading simplicity and clarity, the use of the masculine he, his, and him should be viewed as neutral. It refers to both male and female readers, writers, characters, actors, executives, etc. No sexism is intended.*

over. Still think screenwriting is easy? Sure, it's easy to write 110 pages in proper format with slug lines, description, and dialogue. Keeping the reader interested and moving him emotionally is another story.

It's time to move from worrying about the first ten pages to realizing it's the first page that counts, then the second, then the third... In fact, it's the first beat that counts, the first sentence, the first word. Several readers have told me their bosses are known for reading one page at random. If it doesn't grab them, if it doesn't make them want to turn the next page, the script is tossed away. Try it yourself with a classic script. Pick up *Casablanca*, *Chinatown*, or *The Silence of the Lambs*. Open it at random on any page and start reading. Even if you have no idea where you are in the story, you'll be hooked by the dialogue, characters, or conflicts in the scene, and you'll want to turn the page. This should be your standard of excellence.

It's time to move from fantasies about seeing your script on the screen to building trust between you and the reader. Every time a reader picks up a script, he trusts that you're a professional writer who'll create a satisfying emotional experience. If your writing is not skillful enough to deliver that desired experience, you've broken that trust, and that reader won't be as trustful with your next script.

It's time to move from submitting substandard first drafts because you just can't wait for a producer to hand you a million dollar check to honing your craft and testing every single page of your script for emotion.

It's time to move from superficial rules, page templates, and principles to practical skills and techniques that cause the desired emotional experiences in the reader.

But maybe you're still unconvinced. Maybe you'd like some corroborating evidence that emotion is everything in Hollywood. Not only is the emotional experience the essence of storytelling, it is what Hollywood buys and sells.

HOLLYWOOD IS IN THE EMOTION-DELIVERY BUSINESS

You already know this is a business, but when you think about it, Hollywood trades in human emotions, delivering emotional experiences carefully packaged in movies and television to the tune of ten billion dollars per year. As I said earlier, movies and television shows are "emotion machines."

Alfred Hitchcock, the master of suspense and audience manipulation, once said to writer Ernest Lehman, while they were filming *North by Northwest*, "We're not making a movie; we're making an organ, like in a church. We press this chord, the audience laughs. We press that chord, and they gasp. We press these notes and they chuckle. Someday, we won't have to make a movie. We'll just attach them to electrodes and play the various emotions for them to experience in the theatre."

Look at the way Hollywood advertises its emotional packages—movie trailers and newspaper ads. The next time you see a trailer, disconnect emotionally from it and put on your analytical cap. Notice how each split-second image or brief moment taken from a scene evokes a particular emotion in an instant, the sum of all images promising the viewer a fantastic emotional experience worth the price of a movie ticket.

Take a look at newspaper ads for today's movies and you'll notice most of them have review blurbs, some from established reviewers and media outlets, but most from unknown sources. Don't you wonder why the marketing department would choose to include them, and even sometimes make them up? A reason is that these praises are most often the deciding factor in choosing to see that movie on a Saturday night. Movie marketers live by these statements which are extracted from the actual review written by the film critic. Pay close attention to them and you'll see words and sentences such as, *"will grab you from start to finish, energetically funny, gritty, intense, and unpredictable, a staggering, haunting, and intense movie-going experience, pulse-pounding, highly-affecting, powerfully seductive, superbly gripping, an incredible ride, packs an emotional wallop, hugely satisfying."*

When was the last time you saw a movie ad that said, *"Well-structured, great plot points, fresh dialogue?"* No. What you see more often than not are emotional blurbs, which are promises of the emotional experience you'll feel by watching the movie. They're selling emotions because that's what audiences want.

Can your script match these emotional promises to a reader? Ask yourself why would a studio invest $80 million in your script (today's average cost of producing and marketing a movie) if it fails at the emotional level? Without a thorough commitment to developing this craft—in other words, writing script after script until you're able to evoke strong emotions in a reader, trying to sell your screenplays is a waste of time and money.

I hope you're convinced. Hollywood buys and sells emotional experiences. Therefore, if you want to become a successful screenwriter you must create emotional experiences in your scripts. Previous books and seminars have been helpful in building a solid foundation, but now you need the skills and the tools to create these emotional experiences. You need dramatic techniques. You need craft.

CRAFT MEANS EVOKING EMOTION

You've heard it hundreds of times, how an aspiring writer needs to *hone his craft*. But what exactly does that mean? Generally, craft is knowing how to make things happen on the page. Specifically, it's the technical ability to control language to create an intentional emotion or image in the reader's mind, hold his attention, and reward him with a moving experience. In short, craft is connecting with the reader through words on the page. It's all about, as McKee says, "a good story well told." *Well told* means evoking emotion.

Great writers instinctively use linguistic sleight-of-hand to generate an emotional response in their audience. They're in tune with what they feel, hope for, or are afraid of for every character, at every moment of the story. They don't believe in art by accident. Great writers are in charge of the reader's emotions at all times—from page 1 to 110; every single page. That's craft. All the techniques presented in this book come from highly successful screenwriters who've mastered the craft and created great screenplays that went on to become great films.

YOUR DOUBLE TASK AS A WRITER

"Art is fire plus algebra." –JORGE LUIS BORGES

Your job is to seduce the reader, to make them have to turn the pages to see what happens next, to interest the reader so intensely that they are captivated, taken "out" of themselves into the world you've created. You want them to forget they're actually reading words on a page. In order to do that, you have to find the most exciting and emotionally involving way to tell your story well.

"A good story, well told" has two elements. Therefore, you have a double task: First, create the imaginary world and life of your characters (*a good story*), which is the basic information taught by most books and seminars to stimulate your creativity—how to create concepts, build characters from scratch, develop and structure plots. And second, create the intended emotional effect on the reader (*well told*). We've all been bored by writers and filmmakers who told their stories badly. The same goes for reading thousands of terrible scripts, not because they had mediocre stories, but because they were badly told. As the quote above implies, great storytelling is a mixture of sheer creative talent on one hand (*fire*) and highly skilled technique on the other (*algebra*).

Some of you may be tempted to say, "Well, that's obvious. Every good writer knows that you need to engage the reader." Sure, talented writers know it. But you'd be surprised how many writers haven't bothered to study the craft enough to know how to do it. They're not even aware they're writing for a reader. They constantly look for shortcuts to writing screenplays—easy solutions, character charts, and fill-in-the blanks templates. The overwhelming amount of artificial, cookie-cutter, by-the-numbers, and therefore rejected scripts clearly indicates this is true.

Most people think writing a script is easy, like playing a video game. A proliferation of screenwriting software adds to this attitude. Writing 110 pages in screenplay format is a piece of cake. Everyone does it. Writing 110 pages that move a reader and keep his interest throughout, now that's a lot harder than it looks. That requires talent and craft.

So craft means evoking emotion on the page, but which emotions are we talking about?

THE THREE TYPES OF STORYTELLING EMOTIONS

When reading a script or watching a movie, we experience three different types of emotions, which I call "the three V's:" *Voyeuristic*, *Vicarious*, and *Visceral*. Ideally, your script should engage the reader on all three levels.

Voyeuristic emotions relate to our curiosity about new information, new worlds, and the relationships between characters. These feelings come from the writer's passions and interests, and therefore can't be taught. But you can learn what interests you. Interest, desire to know, to understand, to eavesdrop on intimate conversations are examples of voyeuristic emotions. They're enhanced by our knowledge that this is make-believe—we know we're safe from being "caught" as we "spy" on an intimate scene. Make-believe is the glass wall that separates the intriguing events you've created in your script from the fear of consequences we might experience in real life. For instance, in real life, we wouldn't want to swim in shark-infested waters. But when you sit there in the dark, watching *Jaws*, you imagine yourself in the water, without any fear of being eaten by the shark.

As to **vicarious emotions**, when we identify with a character, we become them. We feel what the characters feel. We live vicariously through them, and it's no longer a story about a character in a struggle; it's about *our* struggle. These feelings come from the emotions your main character experiences, and therefore from the events you've set up. Vicarious emotions are enhanced by our curiosity about human nature and the human condition. If we recognize the emotions the character goes through, and we're connected with that character, we should experience the same emotions vicariously.

Visceral emotions are the feelings we most want to experience while watching a movie, and the ones you want the reader to feel while reading your script. They include interest, curiosity, anticipation, tension, surprise, fear, excitement, laughter, etc., the epic films, the special effects, and the physical thrills we pay good money to feel. If your script delivers a fair amount of visceral emotions, it will give the reader a sense of having been entertained.

The majority of advanced techniques presented in this book are designed to arouse visceral emotions. But before we move on, we have to understand the difference between character emotions and reader emotions.

CHARACTER EMOTIONS VS. READER EMOTIONS

It's important to distinguish these two types. For example, in a comedy, a character may be stressed, but as viewers, we laugh. Or in a thriller, he may be calm and unaware, while we fear for him because we know something he doesn't. This distinction is essential because writers who have a general inkling that emotions are important in a screenplay focus too much on character emotions. They figure if they make a character cry, for instance, we'll feel sadness or pity. If we're empathizing with that character, maybe. But it's not enough. Think how many dramas with strong character emotions fell flat because viewers were bored—no visceral emotions. Whether your character cries is not as important as whether the reader cries. Like Gordon Lish said, "It's not about what happens to people on a page; it's about what happens to a reader in his heart and mind."

WHAT THIS BOOK OFFERS

This book goes right to the source—the craft of highly successful screenwriters, analyzing classic examples, and presenting a smorgasbord of storytelling techniques and tricks of the trade that have one purpose—intensify the reader's connection to the page.

Whereas *101 Habits* explored the working habits of highly successful screenwriters in the hope of learning behaviors that would lead to success, this book presents their specific dramatic techniques in the hope of learning what works in a successful screenplay. Whereas *101 habits* was about the *storytellers*, this is about *storytelling*.

The purpose of this book is not to prescribe but to explore and present. You won't read "must" and "should" here. I can't tell you how to write. No one can. But I'm a strong believer in tools, not rules. I can show you what works in great scripts, how skilled writers capture a reader's attention, and hold it from beginning to end, with a wide range of visceral emotions in between. My hope is that you can apply these techniques, and combine them with skill, talent, and imagination to create great art. The only rule that matters is that the script works, in other words, that it engages the reader emotionally. If fact, it's the only rule in Hollywood which has no exceptions. Rules, principles, and formulas are about what to do. Craft and techniques are about how to do it effectively. No page numbers, just basic storytelling tools. Put them in your toolbox and use them as needed.

This book is intended to complement rather than replace other screenwriting books. It goes beyond the basics. So if you're an absolute beginner with no knowledge of the craft, make sure you read them first to build a solid foundation, and then read this book to complete your education.

WRITER BEWARE

Before we move on, I'd like to offer some caveats: If you love the "magic" of movies, put this book back on the shelf. This book offers advanced techniques that will demystify what you see on the screen. Many of them will seem familiar because you often see them in stories that work. But beware: you'll never experience a movie or read a script the same way again. It's as if you loved magic tricks and were later shown their secret. The illusion is now shattered and you can't see the same trick with the same fascination. In this book, you will be presented with the secrets of great writing. If you don't want the "illusion" shattered, do not read on.

This book assumes a basic knowledge of screenwriting fundamentals. This is an advanced book on the craft of screenwriting and is to be used as a complement to any how-to book on how to write great screenplays that sell. The techniques presented here won't automatically turn you into a great screenwriter. You still need to apply them to your original ideas and keep writing to hone your craft. But they will definitely help you become a better writer.

Okay, so now you know that evoking emotion on the page should be your main focus in drafting a screenplay. Screenwriting means more that writing slug lines, description, and dialogue. It means accepting that your audience is the reader, and eliciting an emotional response in that reader. Emotion means "disturbance" from the Latin "to disturb or agitate." You're literally trying to *disturb* the usual life of the reader; you're trying to *move* them, disturb their hearts and minds, in a sense. It's what readers demand, and what Hollywood is in the business of buying and selling. From this point on, I want you to start thinking, "**I'm in the emotion-delivery business, and my job is to evoke emotions in a reader.**" Write this in big, bold letters and pin it on your bulletin board to remind you of your duties as a screenwriter.

But before we can *disturb* readers, we should get to know them. Who are they? Why are they so influential? And more important, what do they look for in a great script? Let's meet the reader…

THE READER
Your Only Audience

"The reader is entitled to be entertained, instructed, amused, maybe all three. If he quits in the middle feeling his time has been wasted, you're in violation."

-LARRY NIVEN

When a script lies around in a pile, it's nothing but words on 110 pages bound by two brads. It only becomes alive in the reader's mind when it's actually being read and experienced. This may sound obvious, but if today's rejected scripts are any indication, aspiring screenwriters don't bother to see their writing the way a reader does. As writers, we can never forget that we're writing for a reader. Ernest Hemingway once said, "When you first start writing, you never fail. You think it's wonderful. You think it's easy to write and you enjoy it very much, but you're thinking of yourself, not the reader. He doesn't enjoy it very much. Later, when you have learned to write for the reader, it's no longer easy to write." It gets harder because when you think of the reader everything must be examined through their eyes and their potential emotional experience.

Novice writers would benefit from an in-depth look at who these Hollywood readers are and under what circumstances they read. So let's meet a panel of readers, and let them speak for themselves.

WE ARE YOUR FIRST AUDIENCE

Keep in mind that we're your one and only audience, not movie viewers. As you read earlier, it's between us and the page. You don't have the luxury of a cinematographer, editor, or film composer. You're the only craftsperson responsible for our entertainment. Great stories cannot be developed without thinking of the reader. Those who say they don't think of the reader fall into two camps: Writers who write by instinct, who know what works and what doesn't because they have, as Hemingway says, "a built-in shit detector." And those who have no idea what the word "craft" means, who are in the dark about their shortcomings. They keep writing material that gets rejected by the first reader who covers it. The script and the writer go nowhere.

Most successful screenwriters have a strong sense they're communicating with a *someone* when they write. They have an inner reader constantly responding to their words. This inner reader functions emotionally, giving the writer a gut feeling for how the story is experienced. All writing is a two-way street, an interaction between writer and reader in which an effective writer learns what readers respond to dramatically and adapts his material to keep them enthralled throughout the script. In short, the best screenwriters have a deep respect for the reader.

WE'RE THE GATEKEEPERS

Although we're an entry level position, and the lowest rung on the Hollywood ladder, we're the first person to make a decision about your script. We're the gatekeepers. We stand between you and the executive who can make things happen, whether it's an agent, producer, actor, or director. We wield remarkable influence in this town. If we say this is the most amazing script we've ever read, our bosses will read it on their lunch hour. But if we dislike something, that's it; it's over. And since many of our bosses belong to script tracking chat boards, our coverage is shared with other companies, and your script is dead across town.

WE'RE INTELLIGENT AND PLUGGED IN

We're smarter than you may think, and when it comes to analyzing screenplays, we know what we're talking about. We have to. Executives won't hire us unless we prove ourselves first. We see so many TV shows and movies, read thousands of scripts, and are so in touch with popular culture, we can pick out clichés when you think you've come up with something original.

We're men and women, young and old, some in our early twenties, still studying at UCLA or USC film schools. While most of us have at least a bachelor's degree, many hold graduate degrees, most in English, Film or Communications. Our most common trait is our love of movies and of the Hollywood industry, so we're always looking for great scripts.

WE'RE POORLY PAID, OVERWORKED, AND FRUSTRATED

Because this is a coveted entry-level job, we're often poorly paid, sometimes not at all if we're interns. We're overworked, and therefore a bit jaded. Add to the mix that we are frustrated writers who'd rather get paid to write, and you can understand our resentment when it comes to reading scripts. We have to plow through ten or so scripts a week and write coverage for each one, while trying to write our own scripts. We have little patience for substandard material.

WE'RE ON YOUR SIDE

Although we're easily turned off by bad writing, we're still on your side. We're not your enemy, as most often perceived, but your advocate. Why? Because our greatest joy as readers is discovering the next box-office champ, "The One." We want to bring our boss that rare gem, follow it through the executive maze, and see it survive development hell to become a critical and commercial success. It makes us proud to have discovered it. Every time we pick up a script, we hope this is the winning one, the one that'll make us look good for recommending it.

WHAT WE DO

Basically, we're paid to read and judge screenplays. We work through a stack of scripts and turn in our coverage. We either sit all day in silent offices, or like the majority of us, sit at home in a recliner, at a desk, or lying in bed day or night. Not a glamorous process.

Because of the overwhelming amount of submitted material, we're the most valuable time-saver for the executive who doesn't have the time and energy to plow through every script that comes into our office. That's what we're here for—to find the diamond in the rough. True, this is a subjective business; one reader may rave about a script that another will dismiss. But we're paid for an informed opinion based on a thorough knowledge of screenwriting and our ability to recognize well-crafted material. Executives listen to what we say. They depend on our judgments.

For those of you who don't know, coverage is like a book report for a screenplay. It's where we rate elements such as concept, storyline, characterization, structure, and dialogue. We discuss what we see as the story's essential strengths and weaknesses, then give it a final judgment—PASS, CONSIDER, or RECOMMEND. "Pass" means this is substandard writing and the submission is unacceptable. The majority of scripts we read fall in this category. "Consider" means it's a strong script despite some flaws; with some rewriting, it looks promising enough to warrant the executive's attention. "Recommend" means it's a top notch project that should be read and considered. Every element, from superior concept to riveting storytelling to fascinating characters, is solid across the board. We put our reputation on the line with every script we recommend, so we don't take it lightly. This is why only one percent of all scripts we read receive this coveted stamp of approval.

What we look for depends on who we're reading for: for a studio or production company, we look for solid storytelling that can turn into a box-office hit. For literary agencies, we look for solid writing. For talent agencies, we evaluate material for a specific star or director.

WHY WE REJECT SCRIPTS

Every week, hundreds of scripts come into agencies and production companies, and the vast majority of them are turned down. Most of the time, the writer either hears nothing, or if he's lucky enough to get a reply, it's most often, "Not for us." What's the problem with most screenplays? We could go through a laundry list of major factors, like a weak, unoriginal concept, one-dimensional characters, dull story, poor structure, overwritten description, and flat dialogue. But we'll get more specific in the following chapters.

We'd rather reveal the one and only reason we reject a script, if you haven't figured it yet. That's right. Barring amateur blunders such as poor presentation (typos, coffee stains, missing or extra blank pages), improper format, and simply awful writing full of clichés, which just confirm your inexperience, we're more likely to reject your script when we're taken out of the reading experience, when the spell is broken. What is this spell? When you read a great script or book, it's when you're carried along, unaware of the words. It's when you lose track of time, when you're so completely absorbed, you forget you're reading words on a page. You're at one with the material.

So when our attention wanders off, or when we question something, we're pulled out of the story. When our minds add critical commentary, like "This would never happen," "this can't be right," or the most common of all, "God, this is dreadful," the illusion is broken, and the trust we placed in you before reading the first page is destroyed. Your script has failed.

WHAT WE WANT IN A READING EXPERIENCE

"Always grab the reader by the throat in the first paragraph, send your thumbs into his windpipe in the second, and hold him against the wall until the tagline." –Paul O'Neil

We want to be connected with the material, lose ourselves in it, have an emotional experience. We want your script to kidnap us into its world, and turn us from spectator to participant. We want to be interested, be riveted by the page, moved. The word "emotion" comes from the Latin meaning "to disturb or agitate." So we want you to disturb our usual sedated lives, our hearts and minds.

We notice a script when the writing engages us. We immediately get a sense whether the page is alive or dead. Do we like what we're reading or not? Does it compel us to keep turning the pages? You want to hook us with an exciting premise, engrossing characters, a riveting story that escalates in tension, and an emotionally satisfying resolution. The key is to build anticipation, curiosity, and a state of fascination. You'll learn to do this in upcoming chapters.

The writer who can achieve this is skillful with words. After reading so many scripts, we get a feel for someone who has a clear command of the craft. Within the first page, we can tell we're in good hands. In *101 Habits*, Scott Rosenberg (*Gone in 60 Seconds, Con Air, High Fidelity*) says, "You can tell from the first page if someone can write, by its assuredness and its confidence. What this does is allow you to relax immediately and say, 'Okay, you can write, now tell me a story.' If, right off the bat, there are four-inch blocks of text, or it's not formatted properly, I know it's an amateur."

The lesson here? We can tell if we're in the hands of a professional within the first page. So each page needs to be crafted. We expect each page to make us feel tension, anxiety, laughter, anticipation, grief or terror, and to manage those visceral feelings into a satisfying experience by the time we finish reading. That's the industry standard you must meet and even go beyond if you want to be a successful screenwriter. Most of you get so caught up in learning the format you forget that, although a screenplay is a blueprint for a movie, it's still supposed to be an *entertaining* blueprint. Remember that your screenplay will be read a hundred times before a single frame of film is shot, so you'd better make it a page-turner. Others used to say you had thirty pages to grab them. Nowadays, it's ten pages. But the reality is that the first page, and the next, and the next after that, has to catch our attention, and find ways to hold it while you write what you passionately want to tell us. Either way, your pages will either excite us to want to read more, or they'll make us wonder if we're wasting our time. It's all up to you and your craft. Your script needs to pass the one-page test—can we open it at any page and be instantly gripped by the words on the page? Every page should be so interesting that a reader can't put the script down.

The writer has to look for and apply the dramatic techniques that touch the reader. Nothing else matters. So let's look at these techniques. Let's start with the primal essence of any story's appeal—its concept...

3
CONCEPT
Unique Attraction

"A movie is a success or failure from the moment you solidify your concept. Execution is fifty percent. It is the primal attachment to the concept that makes the movie work or not."
—GEORGE LUCAS

Whether you're writing a high-concept, big-budget action script, an intimate character-driven drama, or even a musical western if you're so inclined, it is essential to make your project appealing to producers and agents. I'm always surprised at the extreme bi-partisanship between "commercialism" and "art," or studio vs. independent films. The argument has been debated since the dawn of mass entertainment. The bottom line is about entertaining an audience. Unless you're writing to amuse only yourself, chances are you want millions to be moved by your story. And you'll only become a successful screenwriter if you write what people want to see and producers want to make. This doesn't mean you have to be a slave to box-office statistics. Just that you have to weave your unique soul into the universal themes that have proved to be successful around the world.

THE BASICS: WHAT YOU NEED TO KNOW

I never understood why writers never take the time to make their concepts appealing. Don't they understand that nine times out of ten the concept is the deciding factor in requesting a read? Without fail, every pitch I've heard for a small character-driven, independent project has been dull. I could say the same with concepts the writers prefaced with "This is a high-concept." This may shock you, but most beginners fail at the concept. It's the single most common problem I've found with scripts. Concept is the core of the script. Everything else depends on it. You can create a great hero, write edgy dialogue, and weave in a resonant theme, but if you start with an unmarketable concept, you'll often end up with an unmarketable script.

Although it's true that nobody knows what will make money, the last 100 years have proved that commercial features can flop, while micro-budget independent films can become box-office hits. While some may disagree, I can state with confidence that, putting aside great storytelling and word of mouth recommendations, most of these small movies had a *unique attraction* that was brilliantly marketed. How to make your concept appealing to a reader, no matter the genre or scope of your script, is the focus of this chapter.

For those who claim that concept appeal is an entirely subjective opinion (and you're partly right), I urge you to read on. We have enough audience feedback and a century of data to discover some interesting factors that contribute to appeal.

Most books and seminars advise the aspiring writer that they must create a *high concept* (I'll expand on this soon) because it's the only kind of idea that appeals to Hollywood. Their bottom line is that if you spend six months developing your first screenplay, it'd better have a unique hook, or else you're wasting your time. There's a bit of truth to this. What they seem to ignore, though, is that there are ways to make *any* idea appealing, no matter its genre or topic. I'll focus on these ways in the "Craft" section.

IN HOLLYWOOD, THE IDEA IS KING

Most screenwriting students are no doubt aware of Jeffrey Katzenberg's internal memo to executives while he was at Disney. It's quoted in many screenwriting books and seminars because it preaches the following: "In the dizzying world of movie making, we must not be distracted from one fundamental concept: the idea is king. If a movie begins with a great, original idea, chances are good it will be successful, even if it is executed only marginally well. However, if a film begins with a flawed idea, it will almost certainly fail, even if it is made with 'A' talent and marketed to the hilt." The Los Angeles Times also quoted Katzenberg a few years ago, when he said, "Hollywood is about the marriage of art and commerce—with the accent on commerce. European filmmaking is about art. Period."

CONCEPT SELLS

As I said in the first chapter, Hollywood filmmaking is a business that sells packaged emotions. Concept is the packaging—the cover. It's what sells the viewer to the product. Distributors and exhibitors know a great idea attracts viewers to a dark room where they'll sit immobilized for two hours to experience a range of emotions they wouldn't have experienced otherwise if the film's concept was unappealing. The reality is that no one knows your script may have the greatest dialogue, brilliant scenes, and most fascinating characters ever until after a reader has read and covered the script. And what convinces them to read that script is its appealing idea.

There are notable exceptions, of course, but even for artsy, high-quality, character-driven screenplays, producers know they live or die by the appeal of the concept in a cut-throat market. They know they need a great idea to sell it to higher-ups in the studios, or raise independent financing. This is not about "selling out," just acknowledging the reality of the business for the aspiring writer. A great idea opens minds and hearts to your story. But a great idea doesn't necessarily mean catering to the lowest common denominator and creating an empty, soulless, special-effect summer extravaganza.

THE CRAFT: ENERGIZING YOUR IDEA

A script with an appealing idea will always be read. The reason someone will take the time to read it in the first place, and thereby discover your great dialogue, fascinating characters, and riveting storytelling, is that a script with a good idea has potential in the marketplace. There shouldn't be any reservation that to succeed as a screenwriter, you need an idea that will generate excitement in every person that hears it. You want your idea to be noticed, be attractive, in other words, to appeal. Thus, the key question is, "What makes an idea attractive to the reader?"

IDEAL EMOTIONAL RESPONSES TO A CONCEPT

A way to answer this question is to explore concept at the emotional level, and ask yourself what you want to feel when you read or hear a movie idea. Personally, I want to feel excitement and fascination at the uniqueness of the conflict, with a pinch of familiarity. I want to be curious about a compelling situation, and anticipate how the conflict will turn out. Bottom line, an idea should excite, energize, and electrify anyone who hears it. You want faces lighting up, not eyes glazing over. And you definitely don't want them thinking, "So what?" or "Not another cop on the trail of a serial killer script!"

WHAT MAKES AN IDEA APPEALING

There are only two simple requirements for an interesting idea—not necessarily great, this gets more complex—but appealing enough to convince a producer to give a screenplay an honest read: A great idea should be uniquely familiar, and it should promise conflict.

AN IDEA MUST BE UNIQUELY FAMILIAR

You may have heard producers say this before, but what do they mean exactly by this seemingly contradictory phrase? How can they say they want something different, and yet the same? Isn't "uniquely familiar" an oxymoron? Not quite. What they mean is they want something unique but with familiar events and emotions viewers can relate to. Let's explore each word in detail:

UNIQUE = NEW, FRESH, COMPELLING

This is obvious. A concept that's unique and fresh is always enticing. Some element of it is so inventive, so alluring, it has producers salivating at the potential box-office. Originality of vision—a unique voice or point of view, material that breaks away from the formula—is important. Successful screenwriters always ask themselves, "How can I make this story unique, imaginative, and exciting enough to hook and hold the reader from start to finish? How can I avoid what's been done a million times and really write a powerful story that stands out?" When *The Usual Suspects* was making the rounds years ago, it was more than just a regular crime ensemble piece. It was surprisingly fresh, yet comfortably familiar, and its twist ending was a knock-out punch that made executives take notice. *The Sixth Sense* and *Se7en* had the same impact.

You could call the uniqueness of an idea a *hook*, a *gimmick*, or a *twist*. It's the core of the concept's appeal. For instance, "Dinosaurs brought back to life for a modern theme park" is the hook for *Jurassic Park*. "A lawyer cursed to tell the truth for 24 hours" is the hook for *Liar, Liar*. The hook is how studios will sell the movie, and what viewers will talk about at the office water cooler.

No one will deny that uniqueness is appealing. It's in our DNA. It's a need we have for new information. A unique concept satisfies that need, whether it's a new setting that hasn't been explored before, like how does it feel to be an astronaut (*Apollo 13*) or a fighter pilot (*Top Gun*), or discovering fascinating, idiosyncratic characters, like Forrest Gump. Most great films take us into exciting worlds and let us experience other people's lives, making us insiders for two hours. Find the uniqueness of your concept and you enhance its emotional appeal.

To illustrate hooks, here are three examples of successful movies with appealing concepts. I've bolded the unique hook in each concept:

1. A teenager is mistakenly sent into the past, where he must **make sure his mother and father meet and fall in love, or else he won't exist** in the future. (*Back to the Future*)

2. A group of ex-psychic investigators start **a commercial ghost extermination business** in New York City. (*Ghostbusters*)

3. Kidnappers nab the wife of a rich man and threaten to kill her if he doesn't pay a ransom. But **he's delighted**, and urges them to go ahead! (*Ruthless People*)

When thinking about your own idea, see if you can do the same. Highlight its unique hook. If there isn't one, this exercise will force you to include it in your concept. If you can't highlight the unique situation within your description, it'll just make it tougher to attract readers to your script.

FAMILIAR = HUMAN EMOTIONS

A unique hook is always an appealing element of the concept, but it should also be interesting within the universal framework of emotions. In other words, you could write about anything as long as it can be measured and evaluated on the basis of emotional experiences we're all aware of. Walt Disney and Pixar have built an animation empire by creating stories about animals and other non-human characters with familiar emotions. If we look at the mega-successful animated film, *Finding Nemo*, for instance, a fish and other sea creatures are the main characters. We experience unique information since we don't live at the bottom of the ocean or experience life as a fish. Under normal circumstances, we wouldn't understand the life of a fish and its conflicts. But if the fish goes through *familiar* events, such as losing a wife, searching for an only son, or having to escape a hungry shark, in other words experiencing a specific range of *human* emotions, we relate. And although the fish's emotions are caused by events in his unique sea world, they are nonetheless the same emotions we can all measure and evaluate, and therefore understand. Bottom line, it doesn't matter who or what you write about as long as your characters experience emotions we understand and relate to. That's the universal appeal executives speak of.

To illustrate emotional familiarity within a concept, here are three other examples of successful films, only this time, it isn't their uniqueness that makes each one appealing; it's the emotional journey of the character. I've highlighted the main emotion. See if you can do the same with your concept.

1. A radio talk-show host tries to **redeem** himself after his comments trigger a murderous act by a psychopath. (*Fisher King*)

2. A dowdy bookkeeper reluctantly **falls in love** with her fiancé's brother, and must **choose passion over superstition**. (*Moonstruck*)

3. A working-class single mom **outwits** high-priced lawyers to win a huge class action lawsuit. (*Erin Brockovich*)

A NOTE ABOUT "HIGH CONCEPTS"

I can't talk about the uniqueness of an idea without mentioning the term "High Concept." Everyone in Hollywood speaks about, dreams about, and pays good money for it. Basically, for those who are still unsure about its aspects, it simply means that the concept is the highest appeal of the script. It's the star. It's so exciting, fascinating, and intriguing that viewers can't wait to see the movie on opening day. For a more complete understanding, here are some definitions I've heard from Hollywood executives: *It's easily understood. You get it. When you're told the idea in a single sentence, you relate to it and are excited about it the moment you hear it. You*

immediately see a movie. It's provocative and big. It has legs. It can stand on its own without stars.
It provides an original twist to an already-successful idea, a fresh take on an established genre.

If someone hears your idea and asks, "What's the movie about?" you don't have a high concept. If I pitched the idea, "A woman divorces her husband," it's easily understood, but how many of you will stand in line and pay ten dollars to see this movie? If I described the movie *Speed*, however, as "A bomb on a city bus will go off if the bus travels under 50 mph, and rush hour has just begun," everyone knows exactly what it means, what the movie is about. It arouses interest. The keywords here are intriguing, provocative, unique, fascinating, exciting. Something you don't see every day. That's high concept.

The reason aspiring writers are advised to pick a high concept for their first screenplay, and others until they established themselves in the industry, is that the higher the concept the more forgiving readers will be of the script. A low concept requires flawless craft that takes years for beginners to master. Also, a high concept makes the executive's job of selling it to his superiors and the marketing department easier. Think about how many levels a script has to go through to sell, let alone be made into a movie. The clearer and more exciting the idea, the better the chances your script will be read.

AN IDEA MUST PROMISE CONFLICT

Because we love stories with conflict, an idea that offers a clear and compelling conflict within its logline, whether unique or not, should also have instant appeal. The clearer the conflict, the better. Who's fighting whom about what? Why should we care? What's at stake? Most scripts are rejected because the stakes are not compelling enough. If you write a story about a female rebel in a corrupt third-world country who leads her people to independence, and a friend writes an intimate look at the rebel's relationship with her dying cat, which one would you pay to see? The first idea has built-in narrative drive and conflict. The second doesn't. The promise of conflict in the first idea compels the reader to learn more about how the conflict will be resolved and is therefore more attractive than the second idea.

DON'T WRITE WHAT YOU KNOW

The best way to create something exciting is to write about what excites you. Never second-guess your instincts. The common advice is to write what you know, but I feel it should be more like *write what makes you feel, what intrigues and fascinates you*, because ultimately, the only thing you really know are your emotions. After all, doesn't everyone feel in the same language? Emotion, which equals great writing, transcends genres, ages, economic classes and political boundaries. William Faulkner once said, "If you are going to write, write about human nature. That is the only thing that doesn't date." You shouldn't worry about trends, and you should definitely not write what you just saw in the theaters, because by the time you start, you're already two years behind. All you can do is be true to what you want to do and hope other people will respond. In *101 Habits*, Akiva Goldsman says, "The trick is to be connected to the material of your imagination, thematically and concretely. Write what interests you, because if you're not fascinated and excited by the writing of the script, the reader won't be fascinated and excited by the reading of it. Try to find something in the idea that speaks to your own life, something you think is authentic and true and compelling in the story you want to tell. People are too focused on that 'High Concept' idea. Write what excites you. If it's well written, it will sell more than the stuff written by writers who think they know what will sell."

So what are you excited about? What are you passionate about? What are you obsessed about? What do you love, hate, or fear the most? What gnaws on your bones? What do you value? What events or discoveries made a huge difference in your life? The answers to these personal questions belong to you, and only you. Since you are unique, the answers should be unique and inspire you to develop exciting stories.

12 WAYS TO INCREASE YOUR IDEA'S APPEAL

Some of you may be thinking, "That's all fine and dandy if you happen to come up with an exciting high concept, but what about the rest of us with so-so ideas?" When it comes to character-driven scripts, you face an interesting paradox. Producers say they want great character pieces. Actors choose a script for its well-drawn characters. But Hollywood generally won't look at a script unless it has a highly marketable concept because they have to sell the movie in one-minute trailers, one-page ads, posters, and Internet banners. The solution is to make your low concept appealing enough.

As I said earlier, it doesn't matter what you want to write about as long as you develop a great story around it. Though I cannot tell you what to write about, I can share with you various techniques that can raise the marketability of your soft concept, character-driven story. By themselves, obviously, they won't guarantee a script sale, but if you have written a great story and are having trouble generating interest in it because of its low concept, I recommend applying the following techniques to your idea, and see it if they can make a difference.

1. FIND THE UNIQUE HOOK IN YOUR STORY

If a hook is not apparent in the initial concept, try searching for it within your story. Ask yourself what is it about your story that makes it unique and fascinating? What has never been seen before? What's the most interesting part in the story? Whatever the answer—and you should have something unusual or compelling, see if it can be included in the logline. Maybe it unfolds within a unique setting, like *Top Gun*, *Titanic*, or *Broadcast News*. Maybe your story is about a distinctive character, like *Forrest Gump* or *Psycho*. Maybe it has an interesting twist. Even if the most unique situation happens in the third act, and it's the only fascinating hook in the entire story, try to include it in the concept.

2. WHAT'S THE WORST THING THAT HAPPENS TO YOUR CHARACTER?

Another technique is to ask yourself what's the worst thing that happens to your character in the story? Stanley Elkin once said, "I would never write about someone who was not at the end of his rope." If you're still developing your idea, pick any job or activity and ask yourself what's the worst thing that could happen to a character? For a lawyer, it would be telling the truth (*Liar, Liar*); for a firefighter, it would be facing a backdraft (*Backdraft*); for an adulterer, it would be having an affair with a psychopath who won't be ignored (*Fatal Attraction*). If your character goes through hell and back, mention it in your concept.

3. CONTRAST CHARACTERS (ODD COUPLES)

Most buddy actions and romantic comedies take advantage of this device. It's simply about creating two opposite characters who are forced to work, live, travel together, or even fall in love with each other. Examples abound: *When Harry Met Sally, The African Queen, Annie Hall, The Odd Couple, Lethal Weapon, Thelma and Louise*. The contrast between the two main characters promises entertaining sparks, and it's therefore appealing.

4. CONTRAST ENVIRONMENT AND CHARACTER (FISH OUT OF WATER)

This is similar to the above technique, except here you contrast a character with the environment in which most of the story takes place. This is by far the most popular technique for generating high concept stories. Take a look at the all-time box-office hits and notice how many fish-out-of-water stories have been successful worldwide: *The Wizard of Oz, Jurassic Park, The Matrix, Some Like It Hot, One Flew Over the Cuckoo's Nest, Beverly Hills Cop, City Slickers, Splash, Crocodile Dundee, Private Benjamin*... You get the idea.

5. ADD A SECOND IDEA TO THE MIX

Imagine you dreamed up a powerful story about an FBI trainee on the trail of a serial killer. Nothing unusual there. But add to it the idea of another dangerous psychopath in custody who becomes her mentor and helps her achieve her goal, and you have *The Silence of the Lambs*. Take another cop on the trail of a serial killer story, and add the idea that the killer kills victims guilty of the seven sins, and that both the cop and the killer represent two of those sins, and you have *Se7en* (sorry for the spoiler—you still won't guess the twist ending if you still haven't seen it). As a fun exercise, flip through a video guide, and combine a movie idea with another's. This is how the clichéd pitching shorthand "X meets Y" to describe a concept came about, as in *"Tootsie* meets *Kramer vs. Kramer"* to describe *Mrs. Doubtfire.*

6. CHANGE TRADITIONAL STORY ELEMENTS

Start with any produced idea and change its genre, for example. *West Side Story* is basically the musical version of *Romeo and Juliet; Outland* is the sci-fi version of *High Noon;* and Hitchcock's thriller *Strangers on a Train* became the comedy *Throw Momma from the Train.*

Genre is not the only element you could play with, of course. How about changing the main character's sex (male to female or vice versa), or changing the setting, as in *Broadcast News,* which was basically *All About Eve* in the world of television news. You could change time periods, the main character's age, sexual orientation, or even change the point of view from main character to minor. For example, *Rosencrantz and Guildenstern Are Dead* is Hamlet's story told from the point of view of two minor characters from the original play. The bottom line is that if you change any element of a story, it automatically changes the whole concept. Let your imagination run wild.

7. REVERSE PREDICTABLE PLOTS

Kidnappers nab the wife of a rich man and threaten to kill her if he doesn't pay a ransom. But he's *delighted,* and urges them to go ahead! This is, of course, the concept for *Ruthless People.* Here the writer reversed the predictability of a husband in despair calling the police, and created a unique and exciting comedy. Take any idea and immediately discard the first thought that comes to mind. See if the opposite works.

8. CREATE AN INTERESTING INCITING EVENT

Often you'll find the hook in the inciting event, the key point in the story that creates the main conflict, changes the protagonist's world forever and forces him to solve a problem. Often, the inciting event is the answer to the question most writers ask to start things off—"What if?" What if something weird happened to a character? What if a man met the woman of his dreams, and she turned out to be a mermaid? (*Splash*); what if the president were kidnapped on Air Force One? (*Air Force One*); or what if a smooth-talking lawyer had to tell the truth for 24 hrs? (*Liar, Liar*)

The inciting event is the cause of the problem. It's the reason action has to be taken immediately, and it's essential in all stories. Not only is thinking about the inciting event a way to come to terms with the problem of your story, but if it's interesting enough, it'll make your concept that much more appealing.

9. TAKE IT TO THE EXTREME—THE ULTIMATE (BLANK) FROM HELL

A good way to make something interesting is to make it the best, the most, the biggest, the worst, the quintessential, the ultimate whatever. Think of the ultimate shark (*Jaws*), spy (*James Bond*), or superhero (up for debate, but all of them have been made into great movies, *Superman*, *Batman*, and *Spiderman*). Think of the worst something, also known as "The (blank) from Hell:" the dog from hell (*Cujo*), the roommate from hell (*Single White Female*), the nanny from hell (*Hand that Rocks the Cradle*), or the husband from hell (*Sleeping with the Enemy*). By magnifying a situation, taking it to the extreme, you can create an interesting idea.

10. EMPHASIZE OR ADD A TIME LIMIT

One often-used technique to inject suspense into a plot is to add a time limit or a deadline of any kind. This is known as a "ticking clock" or "time lock" because its clichéd use is in stories where a bomb must be defused before the clock reaches zero. Obviously, a time limit doesn't have to be a ticking clock. Creative writers are always developing new and interesting time pressures (in bold), such as planes running out of **fuel** (*Die Hard 2*); a bomb set to go off if a bus goes under **50 miles per hour** (*Speed*); a cop must stop a serial killer before he kills his **next victim** (*Se7en*); or an innocent man must prove his innocence before **being caught again** (*The Fugitive*). Any time you add a deadline to a concept, it adds excitement because it intensifies the conflict—time is now an extra factor. There's a difference between "He'll be executed unless he's proven innocent," and "He'll be executed by ten o'clock tonight unless he's proven innocent."

11. EMPHASIZE A SETTING, ARENA, WORLD (BEHIND THE SCENES)

An in-depth look behind the scenes of a unique arena is always appealing, although it's becoming more and more difficult to explore a setting that hasn't been written about. But if you have an interesting setting in your story, emphasizing it in your concept will make it more appealing. A good example of this is the primal story of a woman fighting to be treated as equal in a man's world. The writer could choose to set this story in the corporate world, which would make it average. But by setting it in a unique world, like the Navy SEALS, for instance, the writer of *G.I. Jane* turned an average concept into an appealing one.

12. MAKE THE CONCEPT AN INTERESTING DILEMMA

If you have a complex or impossible dilemma in your story, you could highlight it in your concept for extra appeal. We then look forward to exploring the character's emotional tug-of-war between two equal choices—a "Sophie's Choice," named after the movie where a mother during World War II must choose which of her two children to save and which one to kill. A few years back, a small independent film, *Albino Alligator*, explored the dilemma of a woman having to kill an innocent man in cold blood so that she could survive a hostage situation. The more difficult the decision your character has to make, the more you'll engage the reader in thinking about it, and therefore compel him to read on to find out how the script turns out.

CREATING AN APPEALING TITLE

Another way to increase your story's appeal is to create an intriguing title, an important element most neophyte writers tend to ignore. Producers get their first impression from your title. It's the first thing a reader sees, and it shapes perception. If your script has a distinctive title it will receive attention. After all, the main function of a title is to arouse the reader's curiosity and lure him into your story. It's your script's identity. Choose it wisely.

A great title may convey a **genre**, such as *Mission Impossible* (Action Thriller), *Love Story* (Romance), *Star Wars* (Sci-fi), or *Psycho* (Horror).

It can communicate a **unique subject**, thereby becoming intriguing by provoking the question, "Why is this subject so important that a whole movie is devoted to it?" Titles that fit the bill include *Schindler's List*, *Ghostbusters*, *Men in Black*, *Indecent Proposal*, *The Maltese Falcon*, or *Rosemary's Baby*, among others.

You gain bonus points if your title emphasizes **the star's role** because you want actors to think the movie is all about them. In this category, we have *All About Eve*, *Tootsie*, *Forrest Gump*, *Rocky*, *Lawrence of Arabia*, and *Bonnie and Clyde*.

How about conveying the **central conflict**, or the **hero's problem**? Think about the effective titles of most Hitchcock films—*Blackmail*, *The Lady Vanishes*, *The Man Who Knew Too Much*, *To Catch a Thief*, *Vertigo, etc.* Other films include, *Honey, I Shrunk the Kids*, *Mutiny on the Bounty*, *Unforgiven*, *Dangerous Liaisons*, *Home Alone*, *In the Line of Fire*, and *Rebel Without a Cause*. Notice how you immediately know what the movie's about from the title alone.

You could communicate the **hero's main goal**, like in *Saving Private Ryan*, *Finding Nemo*, *Back to the Future*, *Catch Me if You Can*, and *The Hunt for Red October*.

One of my favorite types of titles, especially for thrillers, is the intriguing, **question-provoking** title, like *The Silence of the Lambs*, *Three Days of the Condor*, *The Manchurian Candidate*, *Night of the Hunter*, *The Ox-Bow Incident*, and even *Dead Poets Society*. You wonder what the unique title means, and you want to find out.

Another popular technique is capitalizing on a **cultural reference**, a **popular phrase**, **song**, or **familiar slang**, such as *You've Got Mail*, *A Few Good Men*, *Some Like It Hot*, *To Be or Not to Be*, *Entrapment*, *Presumed Innocent*, *Blue Velvet*, and *Body Heat*.

If your story takes place in an **exotic or unique setting** that resonates on several levels, it helps to emphasize it in your title. Think of *Titanic*, *Sunset Boulevard*, *Casablanca*, *Chinatown*, *42ⁿᵈ Street*, *Air Force One*, *Breakfast at Tiffany's*, and *An American in Paris*.

You may appeal to a reader through a title that evokes a **mood or emotion**, like *Saturday Night Fever*, *Something Wild*, *Mean Streets*, *Yankee Doodle Dandy*, *All That Jazz*, *In Cold Blood*, *In the Heat of the Night*, and *Love Story*.

Similarly, you could make your title a **metaphor**, especially if it's something poetic or literary, such as *The Grapes of Wrath*, *Raging Bull*, *To Kill a Mockingbird*, *From Here to Eternity*, *Reservoir Dogs*, *Gone with the Wind*, *Stranger Than Paradise*, and *A Raisin in the Sun*.

A **contrast**, as you'll see in later chapters on character, story and scenes, is always interesting and appealing. Contrast two words in your title, and you may make it intriguing, like *Back to the Future*, *The Crying Game*, *Bad Santa*, *Magnificent Obsession*, *The Lady and the Tramp*, and *A Hard Day's Night*.

Finally, you can take a common phrase and make it a **play on words**, such as *Back to the Future*, *Who's Afraid of Virginia Woolf*, *Angels with Dirty Faces*, *Natural Born Killers*, and *G.I. Jane*.

Note how *Back to the Future* is mentioned several times. This is because a title doesn't have to convey only one meaning. It can be a combination of two or more of the techniques above, the more the better. Take, for instance, the title *Midnight Cowboy*: it's a metaphor, which also evokes a mood; it provokes the questions, "What does it mean?" and "Who is this guy?"—we want to find out; it highlights the star's role; and it focuses on a unique subject.

CHOOSING A POPULAR GENRE

Choosing the genre of your story is probably the most important decision you'll make before writing your script. In fact, it's so significant that the latest trend in screenwriting seminars and books is to focus entirely on one particular genre, especially the most popular ones, like comedy and thrillers. From the French for "kind," genre is the universally accepted labeling system for filmed storytelling. This is how we classify and choose our entertainment, the same way we classify restaurants by geography—French, Italian, Mexican, or Thai. This is also the reason video stores arrange their title by genres rather than alphabetically, which would make them easier to find. Each genre tells the potential viewer what to expect emotionally from the movie.

The reason choosing your genre is essential is that each genre is inherently "prepackaged" with recognizable emotions. Your genre tells the reader up front what to expect from the script they're about to read. So if you write a comedy, the reader expects many laughs. If you label your script a "thriller," the reader automatically looks forward to visceral thrills from a tense, gripping plot with shocks, twists, and surprises. How well your script communicates these emotions is the way a reader will judge your work. If your words don't deliver these promised thrills, the reader will be disappointed, if not frustrated, and your script will be rejected.

Because genres have been affixed on commercial films telling familiar stories with familiar characters in familiar situations that evoke familiar emotions, they're often thought of as formulaic. But genre doesn't have to mean formula.

Formula is using the same clichéd situations to evoke a particular emotion. Genre is the promised emotional effect on the reader. How you evoke it is up to your talent and craft. Therefore, you should understand the emotional expectations of each genre by studying the best and worst examples of each. Then, as you build your story, you should figure out what emotions you want the reader to feel. Do you want them to laugh? Cry? Make their hearts pound? The key is to create something unique within the familiar expectations of a particular genre. This is why beginners are advised to write the kind of movies they love and see regularly. If you're writing the kind of movies you pay to see, you already have a basic idea of what the genre is all about. Then, the challenge is to transcend that genre.

An effective approach to avoid clichés is to combine genres. In an industry which demands originality, mixed-genres have been popular in Hollywood for many years. For example, *Ghost* is a love story, a supernatural thriller, a mystery, and a comedy; *Beverly Hills Cop* is an action-comedy; and *Alien* is a sci-fi and horror story. Be careful, though, not to end up with an unfocused script. Decide what the dominant genre will be, which is critical because of the desired tone of your story. Many films have failed because their tone was unspecific, and they confused audiences. Picking the dominant genre, such as action, comedy, or thriller, will give you the main "flavor" of your story, while the other genres you combine to it will be the various "spices" that make your script unique.

Originally, I planned to discuss genre and its emotional expectations with more depth, emotion being the focus of this book, but I discovered that someone beat me to the punch. In their excellent book, *Screenplay: Writing the Picture*, professors Robin Russin and William Missouri Downs discuss genre in great detail and offer a classification by emotional expectation. For instance, they break down genres according to *courage* (action, adventure, epic, and heroic sci-fi), *fear & loathing* (horror, dark sci-fi), *the need to know* (detective, thriller), *laughter* (comedy, romantic comedy, farce), and *love & longing* (romance, melodrama, platonic love). If you want to know more about genres, I recommend their book.

ON THE PAGE: CONCEPT IN ACTION

When it comes to good versus average concepts, the bottom line is that most Hollywood producers, agents, and readers know a good idea when they hear it, despite William Goldman's often quoted, "Nobody knows anything." They know it when they see it, read it, eat it, or touch it. And they also know from experience when they don't have it, when their eyes glaze over, and they think, "So what?"

As you've read so far, any idea that fits the two requirements of being uniquely familiar and promising conflict, and fits one or more of the twelve ways to make it appealing, should get a producer's attention. Aspiring writers are always advised to read the trades, such as *Daily Variety* and *The Hollywood Reporter*, to keep up with the concepts that sell. Don't use today's movies at your local multiplex to learn what sells. The movie you see today sold two to five years ago, depending on its development period. Read what sells now. You can also keep up with concept sales online at the *Done Deal* website (www.scriptsales.com).

A great concept by itself is not enough to sell a script, of course. Many aspiring writers bet all their marbles on the high concept without bothering to master the essential elements that make up great storytelling. They know, and they've been told by certain producers, that a great idea sells itself, but they're partially right. A high concept script by a first-timer may sell, but it will often be rewritten by a seasoned professional, as Steven DeSouza (*Die Hard, 48 Hrs.*) says in *101 Habits*, "Nine times out of ten, if a studio buys a script solely for its concept, they'll get rid of you and hire a more established writer to rewrite the script. They don't want to waste time on an untried writer, and have to wait 12 weeks to know something they already know, which is that they'll get rid of you anyway. I can't tell you how many times I've been hired to rewrite a script from a first-time writer. They hire me because they know I can deliver an acceptable script in 12 weeks."

In other words, take the extra time to master your craft and write a great script that delivers on all levels. Let's take a look at another essential element of the screenwriting craft—theme…

4
THEME
Universal Meaning

"Art is a microscope which the artist fixes on the secrets of his soul and shows to people these secrets which are common to all."
-Leo Tolstoy

To appreciate the magnitude of theme in a screenplay, you should understand the power storytelling has in our lives. Because life is often frustrating, illogical, and chaotic, we turn to stories for meaning and structure. We look for answers and for universal values because we want to know how to lead our lives—how to treat one another, how to love, how to triumph over obstacles. We also turn to stories because they explain the world emotionally rather than analytically. One can say, then, that stories are our metaphors for life, our blueprints for living, and theme in particular is the specific truth about the human experience the writer wishes to convey to an audience. It's the message, the moral, the meaning of your story, the reason for its existence besides making money. Theme is therefore what makes your story universal, and thus emotionally significant. Often, the difference between a great script and a mediocre one is the depth of its theme. A script may be entertaining without a strong theme, but it will never be considered great. Without theme, a story has little significance. It's superficial entertainment that leaves the viewer feeling empty.

THE BASICS: WHAT YOU NEED TO KNOW

WHY THEME MATTERS
If you ask yourself why your story matters, or what you want to communicate through your story and characters, you'll head toward theme. In *101 Habits*, Gerald

DiPego (*Phenomenon*, *Angel* Eyes, *The Forgotten*) says, "Sometimes you can have something you might call "pure entertainment," and theme is not very important. But if you want to do more than just entertain, if you want to entertain and enrich, inspire, or say something about the world and the human condition, then you have to think about what you want to say in order to subtly weave it through the story." Writer Dorothy Bryant puts it this way: "We are the voices for the deeper, unspoken dramas in other people's hearts." When you think what life is about— learning, exploring, experiencing, growing, helping and loving others, you realize that these are the same things stories are about thematically.

Another reason theme is so important in a screenplay is that it's the foundation upon which a story is built. Theme is the core of your script, its heart and soul. This means that most scenes, characters, dialogue, and images should ideally be a reflection of your theme. Your story is simply a tool to create circumstances that will showcase your theme. This is why many writers start solidifying their theme before writing the script—once they're clear about what they want to say, they know what belongs in the story and what doesn't.

Although it's generally accepted that theme becomes clear after writing several drafts, the reality is that knowing your theme up-front is a huge time-saver in the rewriting process. As Paddy Chayefsky (*Network, Marty, Altered States*) once said, "The best thing that can happen to a writer is for the theme to be nice and clear from the beginning." Don't panic, however, if you have no idea what your theme is. There are just as many writers who write several drafts to discover what they want to say. Theme is by far the most complex aspect to grasp in any story. Finding it before writing is ideal, but other times you may have to write the script to discover the theme. Once you realize what it is, you can rewrite the script to explore it through characters, dialogue and symbols. The key is being careful not to make it so obvious that it becomes preachy. As Darryl Zanuck once said, "If I want a message, I'll call Western Union!" Theme is not a sermon, and it shouldn't be preached.

PERSUADING AND ENTERTAINING, NOT PREACHING

Preaching is frowned upon in dramatic writing because it's telling. Most writers know that they should "show, not tell." Show your theme in action, and make the reader feel it instead of telling him. You do this by dramatizing your deepest beliefs about human beings and the best way to live their lives. But don't be heavy-handed, and have your characters scream, "Hey, this is my message!" It's more like sweetening a glass of ice tea. Mix in regular sugar and it will sink to the bottom, making it bitter, except at the bottom, which will be too sweet. But try it with Sweet N' Low and the tea will be sweet throughout. Sweetness is your message, and it must be completely diluted to disappear into the beverage of storytelling.

Theme should be the subtext of your story, what's beneath the story. For instance, *E.T.* is more than just a boy helping a stranded alien return home. It's about believing and friendship. *The Terminator* is more than just a woman trying to escape a killing robot. It's a cautionary tale about technology gone horribly wrong. *Thelma and Louise* is more than just two women on the run. It's about freedom. On the surface, story; beneath the story, theme. Story brings an audience into the theater; theme makes it worthwhile. It's what the audience takes with them when they go home, what sticks to their brain long after the lights have gone up. Billy Wilder once said, "You try to make it about something. I don't think I'm writing anything that's going to change the world, but if you make the audience talk about it for fifteen minutes after the picture, then you have done something. If you can get people to repeat that talk in the office or with people that you have dinner with, then this is the root of the success of a film."

Again, it's crucial that your theme remain invisible throughout and resonate beneath the story. As you'll soon see, the best way to do this is through emotion. We learn best when we're emotionally involved, not when we're lectured. Great movies teach us about life while moving us emotionally. The more meaningful the theme, the deeper the emotions. Plato once argued that all storytellers should be banned because they're a threat to society. They deal with ideas, but not in the open, rational manner of philosophers. Instead, they conceal their ideas inside the seductive emotions of art. Whether we write novels, sitcoms, comic books or screenplays, we are artists. Aristotle believed that all art serves two purposes: to delight and to teach. As screenwriters, we delight through story and we teach through theme.

THE CRAFT: REVEALING THEME WITH SUBTLETY

Fiction is the lie through which we tell the truth. -ALBERT CAMUS

UNIVERSAL THEMES

Because theme is a reflection of life and the human condition, it's often concerned with universal emotions and issues, such as love, family, revenge, honor, or the triumph of good over evil—all experienced around the world. To help the novice writer, it may be useful to classify themes that have been successful since the beginning of storytelling because they've resonated emotionally across generations. I've grouped these universal themes into three categories, "*Separation-Reunion*," "*Humanity in Jeopardy*," and "*Relationships*."

"SEPARATION-REUNION" THEMES

These themes are quite common in successful films. They resonate deep within our primal attachment needs—our needs for intimacy, proximity, and dependency to our parent figures, our need for safety, warmth, and acceptance. Most love stories that focus on separating lovers in order to reunite them at the end fit this category. Themes include:

- The underdog triumphs (*Rocky, The Karate Kid*)
- Alienation and Loneliness (*Citizen Kane, Taxi Driver*)
- Returning home (*The Wizard of Oz, After Hours, Cold Mountain*)
- Mistaken identity (*North by Northwest, Dave*)
- Death (*Ordinary People, Old Yeller, Truly Madly Deeply*)
- Mental Illness/Madness (*A Beautiful Mind, Shine, Sybil*)
- Rejection and Rebellion (*One Flew Over the Cuckoo's Nest, Braveheart*)
- Redemption (*In the Line of Fire, The Verdict, Unforgiven*)
- Coming-of-age (*Stand by Me, Risky Business, The Breakfast Club*)
- Midlife crisis (*The Accidental Tourist, The Big Chill, Death of a Salesman*)

"HUMANITY IN JEOPARDY" THEMES

Some tales enlighten us on the right way to live by contrasting it with the darker side of human nature, which jeopardizes our humanity, thus the name. This includes stories of good being seduced by evil, but most often good and justice prevail in the end. Film noirs where a femme fatale mesmerizes a main character to do evil are also a good example. Other themes in this category include:

- Prejudice (*Chocolat, Philadelphia, The Color Purple*)
- The dehumanization of modern society (*Modern Times*)
- War is hell (*Platoon, All Quiet on the Western Front*)
- The innocent man wrongly accused (*North by Northwest, The Fugitive*)
- Conspiracies (*Three Days of the Condor, The Manchurian Candidate*)
- Hope over despair (*The Shawshank Redemption*)
- Good versus evil (*Star Wars, Raiders of the Lost Ark*)
- Revenge (*Death Wish, Cape Fear*)
- The corruption of ambition (*Amadeus, Citizen Kane, Scarface*)
- The dark side of a vice (*Se7en, Wall Street, Raging Bull*)
- Obsession (*American Beauty, Fatal Attraction*)

"RELATIONSHIPS" THEMES

Because love is the most powerful bond between people, the longing to experience it is something all of us can identify with. It's no surprise then that most stories films explore this powerful theme, if not as a primary subject, then as a romantic subplot. The various explorations of this complex topic remain endless, but the most common include:

- Love gained (*The Apartment, When Harry Met Sally, Beauty and the Beast*)
- Love lost (*Annie Hall, Love Story, Casablanca*)
- Selfless love (*City Lights, Forrest Gump*)
- Tragic selfish love (*The English Patient, Gone with the Wind, Othello*)
- Passion (*The Piano*)

- Dangerous attraction (*Body Heat, Basic Instinct, most film noirs*)
- Friendship (*Midnight Cowboy, Lethal Weapon, Thelma and Louise, E.T.*)
- Parental love (*Kramer vs. Kramer, Little Man Tate, Lorenzo's Oil*)
- Animal love (*Black Stallion, Free Willy, Old Yeller*)

FINDING YOUR VISION

The common advice is to write what you know, but it's more effective to write what makes you *feel* because ultimately, the only things you really know are your emotions. After all, doesn't everyone feel in the same language? Emotion, which translates to great writing, transcends genres, ages, economic classes and political boundaries. Emotion is universal. William Faulkner once said, "If you are going to write, write about human nature. It's the only thing that doesn't date."

LOOK DEEP WITHIN YOURSELF

Most professional writers I've spoken with recommend that you feel passionate about your theme before writing about it. One way to find out what you're passionate about is to look deep within yourself. As writers, we all have issues we believe in—justice, freedom, violence, war, love etc. What are you passionate about? What intrigues you? Fascinates you? What are you obsessed about? What do you love, hate, and fear the most? What do you believe in? What do you value? Don't go for the obvious ones everybody writes about. Challenge yourself. Look deep within yourself and discover what you believe is important in life. If you have trouble finding a theme, ask yourself, "If I could change people's minds about something, what would it be?"

"EMOTIONAL INDIGNATION"

A writer once told me, "Theme starts with emotional indignation." Ask yourself, what's unfair in the world? In your life? What gnaws at your bones? What makes your blood boil? Whatever you're incensed about can become a strong, underlying theme in your story.

MAKE UP A VALUES LIST

Values are what's important to you in your life—love, justice, caring, truth, etc. You can make a list from various sources—philosophy books, psychology texts, or a thesaurus.

BUILD A WISDOM LIBRARY

Terry Rossio (*Shrek, Pirates of the Caribbean*) suggests you collect various quotations books for your library, aphorisms, proverbs from different countries, maxims, poetry collections, plays, and sayings. Read them and let your mind wander.

NINE THEME TECHNIQUES TO SHOW, NOT TELL

1. TURN THEME INTO A QUESTION, NOT A PREMISE

The easiest way to reveal theme is to put it in the form of a question rather than a statement or premise, as most have done since reading Lajos Egri's classic book, *The Art of Dramatic Writing*. For instance, rather than state the premise for *Romeo and Juliet* as "Great love defies even death," you could ask, "What does great love defy?" or "Can love survive even death?" and let the story reach a natural conclusion, thus making it less predictable. Ask a question, and let your story provide us with the answer by experiencing it emotionally.

2. WRAP IT AROUND AN EMOTION AND DEVELOP ITS RELATED IDEA

It's been said that emotions unite people and ideas divide. This is why the writer is advised to make the reader feel the theme instead of making him think up-front. An idea expressed only intellectually is just an essay. But when it's wrapped inside an emotion, it's more powerful and more memorable. Great storytelling is the creative, *emotional* demonstration of the truth you want to express. Never explain intellectually. Dramatize emotionally. A useful technique is to pick an emotion and develop its corresponding idea. For instance, if you pick the emotion *anger,* you could develop the ideas of injustice or abuse. Or pick *curiosity* and combine it with loss of innocence or coming-of-age. Out of this combination, characters and scenes should materialize. An example of a great movie that capitalized on this technique is *Chinatown,* whose theme according to Robert Towne was actually an emotion—the feeling of knowing what's going on, while not really knowing it. The related ideas include mystery, deception, corruption, and secrets—all masterfully woven in this classic script. Not only is detective Jack Gittes in the dark as he tries to solve the mystery, thinking he knows what's really going on, but so are the other characters. Lieutenant Escobar is clueless, of course, but Evelyn, with her dark secret, is unaware of her father's water-diverting scheme. Even Noah Cross, the mastermind holding the strings, doesn't know that Evelyn is planning to escape Los Angeles with her daughter.

3. MAKE IT ABOUT THE PROTAGONIST'S INNER NEED AND JOURNEY TO CHANGE

What is the major emotional decision your protagonist must make in order to resolve the story problem? That's where you'll find the theme. Because stories try to convey a truth about the human condition, and stories are about people, it's a common technique for the main character's inner change to represent the theme. If the theme is redemption, the hero will achieve it at the end, or not, depending on what story you're telling. If it's the triumph of the human spirit, clearly the protagonist's inner journey will go from failure to triumph. A great example of this technique is the underrated romantic comedy, *Groundhog Day,* which is about a self-absorbed, arrogant, and cynical TV weatherman who's cursed (or blessed) to relive the same day until he learns how to live it right. He suffers throughout, but then gains courage to transform into an authentic, self-actualized human being. In telling this story, the movie hits on the essential truth that when we go beyond resentment over the conditions of life and death and accept our situation, we can become authentic and compassionate. But the writer keeps this message in the background by focusing on the hero's growth, as he goes through bewilderment and despair to generosity and deep compassion for life. By keeping the protagonist's inner journey at the forefront, the film's message resonates emotionally instead of intellectually.

4. CONVEY POSITIVE THROUGH PROTAGONIST AND NEGATIVE THROUGH ANTAGONIST

Another useful technique to subtly reveal your theme is to shape the antagonist to illustrate the dark side of whatever positive theme the protagonist's journey reveals. In other words, contrast the hero and villain thematically. Show the positive aspect of your theme through the protagonist's journey, while you reveal the negative side through the antagonist. The classic *One Flew Over the Cuckoo's Nest* makes the best use of this technique by having the hero, McMurphy, represent freedom, while Nurse Ratched represents the repression of the human spirit. We also see this technique in scenes where the two characters square off, in conflict or over drinks or coffee, and compare each other. "You and I are very alike," would be a typical dialogue line in these scenes, as in *Raiders of the Lost Ark* when Belloq tells Jones over drinks, "You and I are very much alike. Archaeology is our religion. Yet we have both fallen from the pure faith. Our methods have not differed as much as you pretend. I am a shadowy reflection of you. It would take only a nudge to make you like me, to push you out of the light." The film's climax when Belloq opens the Ark solidifies the theme. Jones tells Marion, "Don't look at it. Shut your eyes, Marion, and don't look at it, no matter what happens," while an obsessed Belloq believes the blinding light is beautiful. The villain is consumed by flames, and the rest of the Nazis are fatally punished for messing around with divine powers. Only Indiana Jones and Marion survive the ordeal because of their humility and reverence for the awesome forces.

5. CONVEY THEME THROUGH A SUBPLOT

Often, the subplot represents the protagonist's character arc, his inner journey to change. But if you have another subplot better suited to convey your theme, this is a good way to reveal it. For instance, *Tootsie*, which comments on gender roles in American society, is about a man who discovers that being a woman makes him a better man. Disguised as Dorothy, the hero, Michael, discovers the everyday humiliations women suffer at the hands of men. What separates this romantic comedy from all the others, besides its universal theme, is its number of subplots, five in all, each representing a different character and the different way they treat women. We have the subplot of how Michael treats his girlfriend Sandy, one about his relationship with Julie, his central romantic interest, another about the male chauvinist director, one about Julie's widowed father who wants to marry Dorothy, and finally a subplot of the show's leading man who tries to seduce Dorothy. Each subplot represents an aspect of the overall theme.

6. HAVE EACH CHARACTER REVEAL A FACET OF THE OVERALL THEME

Tootsie would also be an excellent example of this technique, since each of its sub-plots is represented by a character. However, you can also use this technique if your story does not have a subplot, or if the subplot is not suited to convey your theme. Here, each supporting character in your story illustrates a different facet of your theme. The more characters, the more angles explored, the deeper the theme. This works in *The Godfather*, which is about power: Vito Corleone wants to keep it, despite modern changes in the drug trade, Michael doesn't want anything to do with it at first, but then he's forced or seduced to embrace it, and Sonny can't control it.

7. PRESENT THE OPPOSITE ARGUMENT AS POWERFULLY AS YOUR TRUTH

Sometimes novice writers are so passionate about their message that they mistakenly present a one-sided, biased argument that often turns their story into a sermon. To remedy it, and make your truth stand out, you could present the opposite argument as powerfully and passionately as your truth. This makes the story more impartial. To do this, you'd create scenes that illustrate the positive, negative, and different points of view of your theme, all in an equally compelling way. Spike Lee did this in *Do the Right Thing*, which examined racism in all its complexity, avoiding simple answers and conveying instead a mosaic of different views. Any time you can convey a theme where both sides are right, you have drama, like in *Kramer vs. Kramer*. Although audiences sided with the father, since he was the main character who spent the most time with his son, they also related to the mother. Both had equally compelling arguments.

8. WEAVE IT INTO THE DIALOGUE

Alluding to theme through dialogue is a common technique. However, as discussed in the overview, it's not recommended to state the theme too directly. But it can be stated if it comes naturally out of a situation, and more importantly, if it's implied through subtext rather than explicit dialogue. This is done brilliantly in *Casablanca*, where Rick repeats the line, "I stick my neck out for nobody" at various points throughout the film, reinforcing the theme of isolationism versus altruism through dialogue. Another film with great thematic dialogue is *Sunset Boulevard*, whose themes of self-deceit, narcissism, fame, greed, and spiritual emptiness, are summed up in one classic exchange between Joe Gillis and Norma Desmond: "You're Norma Desmond. You used to be in silent pictures. You used to be big." "I am big. It's the pictures that got small." As long as your dialogue is fresh and "off the nose" (more on this in Chapter 10), you can state your theme through it.

9. COMMUNICATE IT THROUGH IMAGES, LEITMOTIFS, AND COLORS

Because film is a visual medium, screenwriters are fond of using symbolism—objects, images, and colors to subtly reveal their theme. If communicating it directly becomes too obvious through dialogue, try expressing your theme through images, like Lawrence Kasdan does in *Body Heat* by writing about fire and heat to evoke passion out of control. Thematic images are traditionally the first thing viewers experience in the opening sequence. Think of the glass ball in *Citizen Kane*, the "deceptive" booze-carrying hearse in *Some Like It Hot*, the obstacle course in *The Silence of the Lambs*, moving clouds in *Groundhog Day*, or swinging and punching fists in *Raging Bull*. To reinforce a theme, you could repeat related images throughout your script, a technique called "leitmotif," which is a musical term meaning, "a melodic phrase that accompanies the reappearance of a person or situation." In a script, then, a leitmotif is a recurring image associated not only with a theme, but also a person, situation, or idea. A great example of the use of leitmotifs is *Chinatown*, which involves a water scheme. Water is a constant symbol throughout the film, through visuals (water torrents, the ocean, a fish pond), plot (characters drowning, corrupt villains controlling the water supply) and dialogue ("He's got water on his brain.") It is also interesting that in Asian circles, the element Water can represent women, fertility, love, or an obstacle, which are also prominent subjects in this great film. It goes to show how parallel the two storylines, the political (water-scheme) and the personal (incest) actually are.

Another tool at your disposal is the use of color. For instance, red tends to symbolize passion, excitement, desire; blue—serenity, trust, depression, while black is associated with death, power, and mystery, and white is believed to signify life, innocence and simplicity. It's no accident, for instance, that the color red is constantly visible in *American Beauty*, which explores the repressed desires and gnawing insecurities lurking behind the manicured appearances of suburbia.

ON THE PAGE: THEME IN ACTION

In this section, we look at how one film in particular successfully revealed theme. I've chosen *The Silence of the Lambs* because it's thematically rich, tackling not one but at least three major themes, brilliantly interwoven within a standard suspense thriller. First, as the **title** suggests, it's about what it takes to silence the "screaming lambs," how to quiet the demons within each of us and overcome the traumas of our past. This is revealed by the external **storyline** of Clarice trusting Hannibal Lecter to help her catch Buffalo Bill, the **flashback** scenes about her dead father, and her quid pro quo scene, letting Lecter feed on her soul by exploring her past. Lecter's **dialogue** reinforces this theme when he says, "You still wake up sometimes, don't you, wake up in the dark, and hear the screaming of the lambs... and you think if you save poor Catherine you could make them stop, don't you? You think if Catherine lives you won't wake up in the dark ever again to that awful screaming of the lambs."

The story is also about transformation, as **symbolized** by the Death's-Head moths Buffalo Bill collects, and by his desire to become a woman. To escape his self-loathing character, he wants to change his physical appearance by making a new body from the skins of his victims. Change is also revealed through Clarice's struggle to rise above her roots and prove her worth in the male-dominated FBI. Lecter's struggle to escape Dr. Chilton's tortures and become a free man also hints at transformation.

Finally, the film explores the subtle sexual pressures men place upon women. Notice how many **details** in scenes hint at this issue, starting with the opening sequence as Clarice is pulled off the obstacle course to meet Crawford. There's a shot of her standing in an elevator, dwarfed by a group of burly men a foot taller than her. She stands out even further as her bluish-grey sweatshirt contrasts with the men's red shirts. This contrast is no accident. In fact, the visual is repeated when at the town of one of the victims, Clarice is surrounded by staring male deputies. Her isolation within the male-dominated arena is accentuated by the glass wall in Lecter's cell, his cage in Memphis, and the climactic scene in the dark dungeon. Other details include her FBI training scenes such as when holding a punching bag and withstanding the blows of her male co-workers, or when jogging with her roommate, a group of men jogging the other way turn around to ogle the women's behinds. Clarice must also endure lascivious stares, condescension, and harassment from nearly every male in the movie—Dr. Chilton tries to pick her up initially, but when she explains she has a job to do, he becomes angry, insisting she was sent to bait Lecter with her looks; Lecter wonders whether Crawford fantasizes about her sexually; as Clarice exits the prison, Miggs throws his semen at her, after objectifying her when she first arrived; a nerdy etymologist asks her out when she researches the Death's Head moth. Finally, look at the climactic scene when Clarice is in total darkness while Buffalo Bill looks at her through the greenish tint of the night-vision goggles, almost stroking her hair and face. The **color** green, which traditionally symbolizes not only renewal and fertility, but also jealousy and envy (the green-eyed monster), is appropriate here as Buffalo Bill is envious of the female he's about to kill. In the end, it's Clarice who kills him without any male helpers. The tense sequence ends on a close-up of a revolving, paper mobile with a butterfly design, followed by the FBI graduation scene, both symbolizing transformation. The film ends with a transformed Lecter (caged to free) about to change the smarmy Dr. Chilton (from living human to dead meal).

All these details didn't have to be included in this tale of an FBI trainee searching for a serial killer. But they do add depth to its powerful story and a universal resonance that catapults it from a run-of-the-mill thriller to a classic Oscar winner.

So you have a unique concept and a meaningful theme you wish to express through your story. Now, you need to create your characters so that the reader identifies and connects with them. Let's look at character...

5
CHARACTER
Captivating Empathy

"The whole thing is you've got to make them care about somebody."
-FRANK CAPRA

There shouldn't be any doubt that characters are the most important element in storytelling. Without characters, there's no story. What we care about is not what is happening, but to whom it is happening. We go to movies to see characters solve problems and fulfill needs. Characters make us laugh and cry, not plots. Yet many writers obsess so much on plot points and structure that they often forget the people who inhabit the story. Who they are, what they experience, and how they change is what brings a script to life no matter what the genre or subject matter. Characters are all there is to it because the moment you stop caring for the characters, you're no longer involved in the story.

Crafting great characters is also crucial from a marketing point of view. They attach talent to your project and consequently increase the odds of green-lighting the script into production. Great characters also sell scripts because studios want roles for stars.

THE BASICS: WHAT YOU NEED TO KNOW
One of the leading models for character development is what we could call "The Frankenstein Method," which relies on stitching together various answers from character charts. Under this method, you sit down with a chart and fill in the blanks in the physical, sociological, and psychological sections. How old is the

character? How tall? What's his occupation? What are his likes and dislikes? Name, *check*. Birthplace, *check*. Hobbies, *check*.

Although there's nothing wrong with this method, it often doesn't translate well onto the page where it counts. Sure, it may help to create characters from scratch and get to know them well enough to develop scenes. But it doesn't necessarily make us care about or create empathy for them, which is the key factor in holding the reader's attention from beginning to end.

Connecting with a character emotionally is what writers should focus on. How to go about doing this without resorting to character sketches is what we'll explore in the craft section of this chapter. But first, I'll offer an easier method for building a character from scratch. Clearly, before we can reveal a character on the page for the reader to connect with, we need to build one. The Frankenstein method is helpful but takes too long. Most professional screenwriters with deadlines concentrate on the essentials of character, which come from five simple questions. They're all you need to create a solid character.

THE FIVE KEY QUESTIONS FOR BUILDING A CHARACTER

Answer these five questions, and you'll have the seeds to grow a great story. Let's explore each question in depth:

1. WHO IS MY MAIN CHARACTER? (TYPE, TRAITS, VALUES, FLAWS)

The first step is figuring out who your protagonist is. If you don't know whose story you're writing, think of the character whose life is made difficult in your story, the one who feels or suffers the most, the one who'll be forced to learn the most from the story, and hopefully change as a result, or the one through whose eyes we experience the story.

FOUR TYPES OF PROTAGONISTS AND THEIR CORRESPONDING EMOTIONS

Once you discover your protagonist, think about which of the four character types he will be—*Hero, Average Joe, Underdog,* or *Lost Soul*. Each will automatically produce an empathetic emotion, so choose carefully.

The **Hero** is superior to the reader, and produces admiration. Although they're not perfect, they're confident about their skills and take action without hesitation. They have no ambivalence, no self-doubts. We don't identify with them, we fantasize about being them. They give us a taste of who we could really be. Examples include superheroes, such as Superman and Spiderman (whose alter-egos are Average Joes), Indiana Jones, James Bond, and Sherlock Holmes.

The **Average Joe** is equal to the reader. This results in sympathy because we recognize ourselves in them, and thus identify with them, their desires, and their needs. These characters struggle to rise above their doubts, limitations, and obstacles. Alfred Hitchcock made a career out of these protagonists—ordinary people in extraordinary circumstances. Other examples include McClane in *Die Hard*, Racine in *Body Heat*, Joe and Jerry in *Some Like It Hot*, and Elliott in *E.T.* If you make your protagonist an Average Joe, make sure there's a uniqueness and complexity to him.

The **Underdog** character is inferior to the reader. They're the unlikely hero. The odds are against them. They're outmatched by antagonistic forces and overwhelmed by them. So we're inclined to protect, help, or console them as the story progresses. The Underdog is an appealing protagonist because he makes us feel three emotions—compassion for their lack of self-esteem or resources to be successful, including any physical, emotional, social, or mental handicaps; admiration for their determination to triumph over obstacles and take control over their lives; and suspense for the implausibility that they'll succeed, the odds being so stacked up against them—Will this person pull it off? And if so, how? Examples include *Rocky, Forrest Gump, The Karate Kid, Raising Arizona, The Elephant Man, My Left Foot,* and Sarah Connor in *The Terminator.*

The **Lost Soul**, also known as the "Anti-Hero," is a character who's the opposite of the reader—the character who takes the wrong turn, who goes down the wrong path. He's morally defective and represents the darker side of human nature. This character evokes fascination since we're intrigued by glimpses of the dark side. Maybe we feel a hint of guilty admiration for their courage to be bad and challenge established morals. This is why actors often admit enjoying playing flawed characters, especially villains. They're not likable, so to form the crucial bond with them, the reader must understand them and admire something about them—their intelligence, their motives, their lack of options, or even a rare positive value, such as loyalty to family (*The Godfather*), caring for another human being (*Midnight Cowboy*), or passion (*Amadeus*). Other examples of Lost Soul characters include *Bonnie and Clyde, Raging Bull, Citizen Kane,* and *Taxi Driver.*

TRAITS

Once you establish your protagonist's type, it's time to give him traits. How many is up to you, but definitely more than one. It's impossible to feel for someone who's one-dimensional. Real people have many layers—emotional, psychological, and intellectual. Characters with just one or two traits are little more than stick figures. Most protagonists possess a number of attributes, preferably a mixture of positive, neutral, and negative traits. A character that is all good or all bad would not be credible or interesting.

VALUES

A common problem in amateur scripts is that all the characters sound and act the same. Individuality is the key to solving this. You give each character individual points of view, beliefs, attitudes, and values, which will be revealed through their behaviors and dialogue. For example, in *Wall Street*, Gordon

Gekko's attitudes toward money, "Greed is good," is what drives him and the story.

FLAWS

Although most books and seminars advise that your protagonist be likable, it doesn't mean he must be perfect. Human beings aren't perfect. So readers don't believe and certainly don't identify with perfect characters. Think of the way you feel about a relative, lover, or friend. Sure, they're brilliant, and you love all the good things about them. But they're certainly not perfect. Sometimes they drive you crazy, but you love them. If you can love a flawed relative, a reader can surely love a less-than-perfect character. Flaws, which can include negative traits, fears, a lack of objectivity, resentments, psychological wounds, or other emotional troubles, add color and dimensionality to characters by making them more human. They also add tension and appeal to a plot by making the reader wonder how the character will triumph despite his flaws. These struggles produce some of the most compelling emotional moments in stories.

2. WHAT DOES HE WANT? (DESIRE, GOALS)

Desire is the power that drives your script. It's the spine of the story, and any obstacle to that desire is conflict, which in turn produces emotion. All stories are about people who want or need something. Without a goal, there's no story. Ray Bradbury (*Fahrenheit 451*) suggests, "First, find out what your hero wants, then just follow him!" A character who doesn't want something isn't interesting. He wanders aimlessly and the bored reader has no choice but to toss the script in the recycling bin.

Goals can be anything important to the character—resolve a conflict, make a decision, meet a challenge, solve a mystery, or overcome an obstacle. But because film is a visual medium, the goal should be tangible and specific—something we can see accomplished and urgent enough to drive the character through all the plot's complications. If you can't see the protagonist's goals, or if the protagonist has so many objectives that the reader isn't sure which is the most important one, it'll weaken the appeal of your script.

3. WHY DOES HE WANT IT? (NEED, MOTIVATION)

The reader wants to understand not only what the character wants but why. All behavior is motivated. Motivation is the mental force that makes us act, the why of every behavior. When the reader understands why a character behaves a certain way, whether immediately and at the end, it makes for a more satisfying experience.

Motivation begins with what's meaningful to the character. It could be anything, based on their attitudes, beliefs, feelings, or needs, a hero rescuing a loved one (*Die Hard*), fighting against the system (*Silkwood*), or struggling to redeem himself (*The Verdict* or *Unforgiven*). The important thing is that motivations must be compelling and worthy of empathy. In other words, if a character robs a bank because of greed, we don't empathize with that character. But if he robs a bank to pay for a loved one's operation, as in *Dog Day Afternoon*, we identify with that character and understand his situation, even if we don't agree with it.

Clearly, we're delving here into the psychology of character, which is why being an avid student of human behavior is a requirement for the aspiring writer. If you're looking for a shortcut when it comes to understanding need and motivation, study Maslow's Hierarchy of Needs. According to psychologist Abraham Maslow, they are what drive us, what we need, and if ignored, what prevents us from being happy. They include **survival and safety** (the motivation in most thrillers and summer blockbusters about saving the world), **love** (romantic comedies and love stories), **belonging, acceptance, and self-respect** (coming of age or underdog stories), and **the need to know and understand** (mysteries) among others.

It's important to understand that, with few exceptions, desire is not always the same as need. Sometimes what we *think* we need is not what we *really* need. For example, a character may think he needs revenge. But in reality, his need may be for healing, letting go of the pain from the past. In *The Silence of the Lambs*, Clarice's desire is to save the woman from Buffalo Bill, but her need is to silence the lambs of her past.

In fact, stories become more interesting when a need clashes with the goal, like when a character is torn between what he feels and what he wants to do. For instance, in *Some Like It Hot*, Sugar's goal of marrying for money blocks her need for love. In *As Good As It Gets*, Melvin's need for love contrasts with his desire to be left alone. These conflicts between goal and need provide compelling moments where difficult choices must be made, often resulting in personal growth for the protagonist. Traditionally, when the character chooses goal over need, we have an unhappy ending, like in all tragedies. When the character chooses need over goal, this results in a happy ending.

4. WHAT HAPPENS IF HE FAILS? (HIGH STAKES)

The reader understands the character's desire and motivation, and now needs to know what's at stake. Stakes are what your character has to gain or lose. What happens if he fails? What happens if he succeeds? A stake is also known as the "Dreadful Alternative," meaning there should be dire consequences if the hero fails to achieve his goal. These would be negative stakes. This leads to related questions when it comes to stakes: How badly does your character want the goal? What is he prepared to do to get it? What's he willing to risk to get what he wants? Your character should be passionate enough to achieve his goal. If he isn't moved enough by the stakes to overcome all the obstacles in the story, how can you expect a reader to care? Screenwriter Gerald DiPego (*Phenomenon*, *Angel Eyes*, *The*

Forgotten) says in *101 Habits*: "Whenever someone asks me to read a script, or I'm developing my own, I always ask myself, 'What's at stake here?' If you lose sight of that, you'll eventually lose your audience. And not only do you need to know what's at stake, but it has to rise, things have to get worse during the course of your story. If you're in the middle in the story and everyone is having a great time with no conflict anywhere, how can you expect an audience to be involved?"

Stakes can be global, meaning the story problem affects the world or a community, or they can be personal, in that they affect the protagonist. For example, in *Raiders of the Lost Ark*, the global stakes are the Nazi takeover of the world, but for Indiana Jones the personal stakes are his life and that of his love, Marion. In fact, stakes are more compelling when relationships are involved. Think how many great films involve another character's fate in the climax, either directly or indirectly— *Casablanca*, *North by Northwest*, or *Chinatown*.

If a character has no stake in the outcome, the reader won't care if your protagonist solves the problem or not. The reader just reads intellectually instead of participating emotionally. The more emotional the stakes, the more the reader will care about the character, and the more he'll want them to achieve their goal. If a character won't lose everything if they don't resolve the problem, you haven't found the right story. This is why Stanley Elkin says, "I would never write about someone who was not at the end of his rope."

This brings up an important point regarding a character's behavior. Protagonists must be active rather than passive. Readers tend to dislike passive characters who only react to events. Think of an amateur version of *The Fugitive* where Dr. Kimble would only react to Gerard by trying to escape capture but didn't try to prove his innocence by finding the one-arm man. It would be only a simple chase film—not as compelling. Readers prefer active characters, people who do things, who push the action forward instead of reacting to other characters or events. Look at Hannibal Lecter in *The Silence of the Lambs*, who, despite being inside a cell most of the film, is incredibly active: he probes, manipulates, and provokes Clarice to confront her past, while helping her find Buffalo Bill. Your character doesn't have to be active all the time, but should solve the story's problem, like Roger Thornhill in *North by Northwest*, who at first reacts to being mistaken for a spy, but then takes matters into his own hands by investigating the mystery and saving Eve at the end.

5. How does he change? (character arc)

The last piece of the puzzle is the character's arc, how he changes emotionally from beginning to end. Although it's not an absolute requirement (characters in detective and spy thrillers seldom change), it's recommended that your main character go through some sort of transformation, which is often about fulfilling an inner need or conquering a self-defeating flaw that works against achieving a goal. This change can be physical, behavioral, mental, or emotional. Traditionally, it involves healing a psychological wound, realizing that some wrongful thinking or behavior has hurt others, fulfilling one's potential, or learning an important life lesson that improves the character's life. These struggles to change can add power, significance, and an uplifting emotional experience to your script, which is why executives in development meetings always talk about character arcs—How does the character arc through the story? Is the arc too soft and narrow? Too exaggerated? Too subtle? Does it happen too quickly and unbelievably, or should it be more gradual and realistic?

Why are we fascinated with characters who change or grow? Change is more interesting than constancy, which is dull. It creates variety in the story, and stimulates reader curiosity and anticipation by making him wonder whether the character will change, and if so, how? Because change is difficult and stressful, it adds conflict. It also gives the story a sense of significance and importance that it was worth reading or watching, by telling us that the events were important enough to lead to character change. And finally, since most of us have flaws we'd like to improve but don't know how, the fictional characters who change provide us with a model, giving us insights on how to grow as a human being. Their stories give us hope that we too can change.

THE CRAFT: CONNECTING WITH CHARACTERS

Answering the above five questions when creating a main character is a giant leap forward in the development of your script. But it doesn't automatically make a three-dimensional character the reader will care about. This is where many beginners stop with character because that's where most books on character stop. When we think about it, a character is just words on a page, a name, a description, actions, and dialogue. Making him jump off the page and connect with a reader is the challenge. To have any emotional reaction from the reader, your character's traits, flaws, desires, motivations, stakes, and arcs must be revealed on the page. To have the *desired* emotional reaction—empathy for the protagonist and enmity for the antagonist—the reader must connect with the characters. In this section, we'll explore these two essential points—how the writer reveals character on the page and how the reader connects emotionally with that character.

REVEALING CHARACTER AND TRANSFORMATION

Revealing character is what the art of screenwriting is all about. "Characters that leap off the page," is the answer most actors, agents and producers give when questioned about the types of scripts they look for.

CHARACTER EXPOSITION (SHOW, DON'T TELL)

How to reveal character in an exciting way is one of our biggest writing challenges. This is why the ultimate rule of writing, especially screenwriting, is "Show, don't tell." Defining a character through the five questions is helpful, but the answers don't mean anything if the reader doesn't see them dramatized through actions and dialogue.

Your job as a writer is to create events so that the reader can *experience* emotions through the character's actions and dialogue, instead of *telling* the reader how he feels. You create choices that show a character's thought process rather than have a character tell you what he's thinking, which would be "on-the-nose" dialogue (more on this in Chapter 10). For example, in *Taxi Driver*, rather than telling us Travis Bickle is an alienated, psychotic character, writer Paul Schrader shows us in the mirror/"You talkin' to me" scene.

The trick, then, is to show what you know about your character that's important to the story. Many professional screenwriters use "The Two-Column Trick." On a sheet of paper, they draw two columns. One column is labeled "What I know about my character," where they list all the character's main traits. The second column is "How I'll show it in a scene," where they dramatize these traits. This is where the creative process takes over, as the writers come up with original character showcases. For instance, in column one they may write, "Frugal," and in column two, "He washes paper plates and re-folds used paper napkins." Here, his actions reveal his frugality. Actions are the most common way writers show character, but it's not the only one.

SIX WAYS TO REVEAL CHARACTER ON THE PAGE

1. DESCRIPTION AND NAME

Novice writers tend to ignore these two simple tools, preferring to reveal names along with age and general appearance, like "John Smith, 30, attractive." But this is too neutral, bland, and cliché to evoke a unique character in the reader's mind. The reader wants to grasp the character's inner-life, and a description like "attractive" doesn't say anything about the character's personality. With a little effort, writers could do better. Look at how Alan Ball describes a character in *American Beauty*: "This is RICKY FITTS. He's eighteen, but his eyes are much older. Underneath his Zen-like tranquility lurks something wounded... and dangerous." A couple of short but meaningful sentences, and we get a clear image of Ricky's appearance, personality, and inner-conflict.

Names shouldn't be taken lightly either. They have more evocative powers than most would think. For instance, imagine you were fixed up on a blind date. If you're a man, which date would you look more forward to—the one with *Heather* or *Gertrude*? If you're a woman, would you rather spend the evening with *Herbert* or *Richard*? These are silly examples, but you get the idea. Choose names carefully. In addition to phone books, there are plenty of baby-naming books and web sites devoted to names and their meanings. We'll explore character descriptions in Chapter 9.

2. CONTRAST

Another powerful way to reveal character is through contrast, which means comparing two things to show differences. For example, in a painting, if you want to showcase the color blue, you juxtapose it with the color orange or other contrasting colors. Similarly, the way to show how someone feels is to surround them with people who feel the opposite. If you want to reveal that a character is sad or lonely, surround him with happy, social people, and readers will see the difference by comparison. Contrast is such a powerful tool you'll see it mentioned often in this book. Because it usually means the opposite of something, contrast is another form of conflict, which always brings character to the surface and creates clarity. When something is contrasted you see it better. You get it. This is why most drama involves contrasting values, such as good and evil, morality and self-interest, or wealth and poverty. Contrast sheds light on both for a clear argument, but this is thematic contrast. Here, we're talking about revealing character. There are three ways you can contrast character: within himself, with others, and with his environment.

Contrast within himself—This is where you can reveal a character's inner conflict—contrasting traits, flaws, desires, needs, and feelings, which create contradictions and thereby increased interest from the reader. William Faulkner once said, "The only subjects worth writing about are the problems of the human heart in conflict with itself." In *Casablanca*, Rick's inner struggle is revealed by contrasting his decision to get involved or stay out of it.

Contrast with other characters—This is the most popular device in buddy or "odd couple" films, such as *48 Hrs.*, *Lethal Weapon*, *Rush Hour*, and even classics, such as *The Odd Couple*, *Thelma and Louise* and *The African Queen*. Contrasting a character with another distinguishes and reveals their personalities. It can also spice up a story when other elements are contrasted, such as different ambitions, motivations, backgrounds, goals, attitudes, and values. You create even more appeal when two contrasting characters are forced into a relationship, like in *Lethal Weapon*, *48 Hrs.*, and *The Odd Couple*.

Contrast with environment—As you've seen in the chapter on concept, the "fish out of water" device—contrasting a character with his environment is a powerful way to create a compelling story because of the resulting conflict. This also works to reveal character. Think how facets of a coward, for example, could be revealed if he were placed on a dangerous battlefield, a timid woman at a fraternity party, or an ignorant man at a MENSA gathering. Most of Raymond Babbitt's character in *Rain Man* is revealed when he experiences the outside world after leaving the institution. Contrast is a great technique to reveal character.

3. OTHER CHARACTERS

Because films with only one character are extremely rare, your protagonist can't help but interact with other characters, or at least be known by them if he happens to be a recluse. There are two ways you can reveal a character through others—how they talk about him or how they're affected by him through casual and meaningful relationships.

How others talk about him (Gossip)—A perfect example is the opening sequence of *The Silence of the Lambs*, where Crawford establishes who Hannibal Lecter is by warning Clarice before she meets him in person. Revelations continue as Dr. Chilton goes over the necessary safety procedures, which further set up Lecter as the dangerous psychopath he is, and all this is expertly done before we even meet Lecter. Similarly, in *Casablanca*, Renault discusses Laszlo and his mysterious lady before we meet them. He also reveals bits of Rick's backstory when he says, "My dear Ricky, I suspect that under that cynical shell, you're at heart a sentimentalist... Oh, laugh if you will, but I happen to be familiar with your record. Let me point out just two items. In 1935, you ran guns to Ethiopia. In 1936, you fought in Spain on the Loyalists' side." If this exposition came from Rick's mouth, it would have been awkward. Using another character to reveal information works better. This technique may also enhance the reader's fascination with an **absent character**. The less we see a character everyone talks about or is affected by, the more we'll be fascinated by him, and the more attention we'll give him when we finally meet him. This works especially well with villains, whose impact on the reader builds through tension of their absence and anticipation of eventually meeting them, as well as secondary characters who shape the main character. Think of Niles Crane ex-wife, Maris, in the television show *Frasier*—often talked about, interacted with over phone conversation, and being reacted to, but never met in person.

How others are affected by him (Relationships)—Other characters are also useful in conveying indirect information about your protagonist by the way they're affected by him. For example, in the first shot of *As Good As It Gets*, Melvin is instantly established through the old lady going from happiness to disgust when she sees Melvin in the hallway. And note how much we learn about Don Corleone in *The Godfather* without his doing or saying anything simply by how the surrounding characters treat him—their nervousness, fears, reverence, and respect say it all. In fact, the most fascinating aspect of revealing a character is to explore his relationships with others. Here's what Scott Rosenberg (*Con Air, Gone in 60 Seconds, Beautiful Girls*) says in *101 Habits*: "I have to be invested in the characters. To me, the greatest action movie ever made is *Die Hard*, not because of all the shit exploding, but because every time they cut back to Bonnie Bedelia's face, she knows it's her crazy husband who's doing everything he can to save her. It was this connection between the two characters that made me care. Another film where you care about the relationship is *48 Hrs.* With all the other ones, who cares? I despised movies like *Independence Day* and *Godzilla* and *Volcano.* I don't care what you do technically. If I don't care about the characters, I just don't care, period." Relationships are crucial in a script. How does your character relate to others in his life? His wife, friends, relatives, children, even enemies? Each character is an opportunity to reveal something about your protagonist.

4. DIALOGUE

The fourth way you can reveal character is, of course, through dialogue—probably the most effective means to do so, and yet the most under-utilized among novice screenwriters, which is not surprising. Great dialogue is the trickiest script element to master. It's hard enough to avoid common problems, such as stilted, expository, and on-the-nose dialogue without also having to worry about defining character. Dialogue is the most effective method to reveal character indirectly because it shows rather than tells through description or gossip. For instance, through a few lines of dialogue, you may reveal a character's background, education, occupation, personality, attitude, mood, and emotions. But more important, dialogue allows you to individualize a character with his specific voice. One of the best examples is *Rocky*, who is clearly defined through his dialogue. His working-class background, lack of formal education, and occupation are conveyed by how he contracts his sentences ("Wha'd'ya mean?") and how he ends them ("Ya know what I mean?") Choose any of your favorite characters, and chances are they're individualized through their dialogue. We'll explore dialogue in depth in Chapter 10.

5. ACTIONS, REACTIONS, AND DECISIONS

Just as characters may be revealed by what they say or don't say, they may also be revealed by how they act and react to events—what they do or don't do, what they feel or don't feel, what they disclose or hide. Two different characters will react differently to the same circumstance. Imagine you discover someone wants you dead. If you're Joe or Jerry in *Some Like It Hot*, you're terrified and decide to hide in an all-girl band by disguising yourself as a woman. If you're Michael Corleone in *The Godfather*, you nip the problem in the bud by plotting to kill your enemies first. And if you're Roger Thornhill in *North by Northwest*, you're confused and decide to resolve the mistaken identity. As Robert McKee says, "Deep character is shown by how the individual reacts under pressure." Putting your character in emotionally-charged conflicts and seeing how he'll react to them is one of the most effective methods to reveal character. This way you show, rather than tell, who the character is, and more importantly, how they feel. In an interview, actor Ben Kingsley once said that what fascinates him most about a character is their *inevitability*—"everyone has their limits. It's inevitable for a character to act a certain way when pushed to the limit. You don't know anyone until you back them into a corner, until they're pushed and they can be pushed no further. That's where the drama is." Therefore, it's important to know what your characters would do when pushed to their limits, when their lives are in jeopardy, when their jobs are on the line, or even when they're locked out of their houses with only a towel on. This works for villains too. Push them to the limit by depriving them of the thing they want most, thereby heightening their rage, tapping into their fury, and driving them ever closer to the breaking point.

We've all heard that **actions** speak louder than words, that they give insight to character and their states of mind. For instance, an angry character throws a chair or breaks a mirror, while a loving character holds a dear one tenderly. In *Chinatown*, we get a peek at Jack Gittes' snobbery when he pours cheap liquor for Curly, saving his more expensive stuff for his richer clients. These little moments always come from within and are driven by the character's motivations, attitudes, and emotions. Because they illuminate character, they're one of the most effective ways to show their essence rather than tell us about it through description or dialogue.

You can also reveal character by what a character **doesn't do** under pressure. For example, in the classic epic western, *Once Upon a Time in the West*, we learn that the Harmonica Man wants to kill the villain, Frank, but won't tell him why, just that he'll reveal his motives when Frank is about to die. Although he has plenty of opportunities to kill Frank in several scenes between them, Harmonica Man's self-control tells us as much about him as any lines of dialogue. He knows what he wants and how he wants it done, and we know this by his inactions throughout the film, much to Frank's frustration.

Dilemmas are also effective when revealing characters through their decisions. You set up a situation where they have to choose between two equally attractive choices, or the lesser of two evils—two conflicting, life-altering goals, a fork in the road. In *The Matrix*, Agent Smith comes to arrest Neo, who's afraid and chooses not to trust Morpheus' advice to jump off the building. Later, he meets Morpheus, who again gives him a choice of the blue or red pill—forget everything or go on an adventure for the truth. When Neo takes the red pill, his choice reveals more about his character and budding courage.

A **secret** can also define a character by the choices they make in either trying to hide it from others or having the courage to reveal it. One of the most powerful examples of this is Evelyn in *Chinatown*, whose every choice and reaction throughout the movie is influenced by her dark secret.

6. MANNERISMS, SYMBOLS, AND PROPS

Like character moments, this is where adding little details can reveal a lot about a character. These include **mannerisms**, **quirks**, or **habits**, like Don Corleone's stroking his cat in the opening scene of *The Godfather*; Jack Walsh's constant watch-checking in *Midnight Run*, or Kramer's wild entrances into *Seinfeld's* apartment;

hobbies and interests, like Sam Malone's womanizing in *Cheers*, Neo's computer hacking in *The Matrix*, or Hannibal Lecter's cannibalism in *The Silence of the Lambs*; and props, like Columbo's raincoat, Kojak's lollypop, Indiana Jones's whip, or Groucho Marx's cigar. These objects not only have meaning to these characters, but also set them apart from others in the story. Mannerisms may also reveal character emotions, like Inspector Dreyfuss' eye twitch in the *Pink Panther* series every time he thinks of his nemesis, Inspector Clouseau, or Jane Craig's crying in *Broadcast News*. Symbols or images are also powerful in revealing character, like colors (the clichéd white and black hats in westerns for heroes and villains, but used effectively in *Star Wars*—Luke in white, Darth Vader in black), photos, trophies and diplomas, which give the reader additional insight your character.

CONNECTING WITH CHARACTER

You've created your characters and managed to reveal their uniqueness effectively on the page, but the key factor in holding the reader's attention from beginning to end lies in whether the reader likes or dislikes, cares about, identifies, connects, bonds, or empathizes with your main characters. Emotional neutrality is not an option, especially when it comes to your protagonist and antagonist. But this is where most advice on character development often ends—at the building and sometimes revealing stage, forcing aspiring writers to learn by trial and error how to make the reader care about your main character. You'll learn how to do this in the following sections.

HOLDING THE READER'S ATTENTION

When readers describe their emotional reactions to scripts, they often say things like, "I could really identify with that character," or "The script was awful, there wasn't a single character I could identify with." When they say there was no one they could identify with, it simply means they didn't care about what happened to the characters. How can you expect, then, to hold the reader's attention from beginning to end if they don't care about the character, what they do and what happens to them, which is the plot? If you didn't care about something, would you pay attention to it? Identifying with a character not only creates an emotional bond with the reader, but also glues his eyes to the page, forcing him to keep turning pages until the end. The character's journey becomes his journey, so his enthusiasm to follow it creates a forward movement in the story, and therefore interest.

THREE WAYS TO CONNECT WITH CHARACTER

For a clearer understanding of all the dramatic techniques available to the writer, I've organized them into three methods by which the reader may connect with a character, with the corresponding emotional responses in parentheses. They are:

- Recognition (Understanding and empathy)
- Fascination (Interest)
- Mystery (Curiosity, anticipation, and tension)

RECOGNITION (UNDERSTANDING AND EMPATHY)

Remember the five key questions you answered to develop your main character? All his traits, attitudes, flaws, desires, motivations, and needs are elements the reader recognizes and understands, which leads to identification with that character. It's our nature to like what's like us and fear or distrust what's not. So we can identify with a character who shares our values, opinions, and attitudes. When we see our hopes and struggles, the qualities we have or wish to have, we recognize their humanity with our own, and thus experience their emotions vicariously. This instantly forms the symbiotic bond between reader and character called *empathy*.

Empathy means to feel with a character, share and understand their situation, feelings, and motives. We feel for their problem, we want them to succeed, and we'll follow their journey until they do. This is why the reader can even empathize with a flawed character who does bad things but has a clear motive to do so. The reader unconsciously thinks, "I understand this character. I would act the same way if I were in this situation."

Many writers confuse empathy, which is a must in order to identify with a character, with sympathy, which means liking and supporting a character. Looking at some of the greatest characters in movie history, and as we've already seen when creating flawed characters, it's clear that sympathy is not a requirement. We don't have to like a character to care about his goals, but we have to be fascinated enough to connect with them on the page. Melvin Udall in *As Good As It Gets*, William Munny in *Unforgiven*, and Hannibal Lecter in *The Silence of the Lambs* come to mind as unlikable, flawed, and yet highly fascinating. To stress the point even further that connecting with a character happens when we recognize their actions, desires, and emotions, take a look at the success of animated films, such as *Finding Nemo*, *Toy Story*, *The Lion King*, *Bambi*, and features where the main characters are animals (*Lassie, Babe*). We identify with them because we recognize in them our traits, hopes, attitudes, actions, and motivations.

Deep connection to characters also happens when we recognize their emotions. For instance, when we see someone in pain, we feel sorry for them. When they're happy, we feel happy. Emotions are universal, connecting people despite their differences. The key to connection, then, is to create events and experiences that cause familiar emotions in the characters. Don't tell us what the characters are feeling. Show us through dramatization, and we'll experience their journey vicariously. In a nutshell, we see a character on the page, we recognize the experience and the emotions expressed, we support these emotions because we understand their cause, and we experience the emotions the character feels. This process connects us with the character.

FASCINATION (INTEREST)

Because it's our nature to be attracted to what's different, to the unique, anything that raises our curiosity and makes a character fascinating is an effective way to maintain the reader's interest. There are several ways to accomplish this on the page.

Uniqueness—Since we're fascinated by what's different—the unusual, the unique, always ask yourself, "How can I make this character distinctive, unlike anyone else we've seen before in movies and print?" This goes beyond a unique combination of traits. Focus as well on **values**, which are what the character considers important in his life, such as freedom, security, family, adventure, etc; **attitudes**, which are their opinions and point of view about the world around them; a **ruling passion**, which can be an issue, a compulsion, or an intense dedication that drives your character, like Racine's passion in *Body Heat*, or Wallace's dedication to freedom in *Braveheart*; and **details**, the little things that make someone unique and bring him to life, like Baxter using a tennis racket to strain pasta in *The Apartment*, or Harry reading the last page of a mystery novel before the first in *When Harry Met Sally*. By constantly adding fresh touches to a character, you'll maintain curiosity, surprise, and interest in the reader.

Paradoxes—Another technique for crafting complex and fascinating characters is to create paradoxes—contradictions within themselves. You do this by giving your character **conflicting traits**, multiple faces within same body, preferably opposite. Joe Eszterhas (*Basic Instinct, Jagged Edge, The Music Box*) says: "I like to see the grays in characters. I like characters who have one front and many, many layers underneath. I like complexity. I like to surprise people with different facets of personality. I like the surprises within characters, the contradictions." So turn expectations around and contrast elements within the same character, like an evil character who loves birds, or a charity teeming with corruption—clichés, I know, but your job is to rise above them and create unique contrasts. Don't limit yourself to just traits or values. You could **contrast needs with desires**, like in *As Good As It Gets*, where Melvin needs to love but hates other people; or **contrast ambitions**, like in *The Apartment*, where Baxter must choose between his ambition to rise on the corporate ladder and his love for Fran. The more contrast within one character, the more paradox, the more doubts and indecisions, the more fascinating the character will be. The conflict within your characters will also increase the emotional power of a script and further involve the reader in the story.

Flaws and problems—You've already learned why your main character shouldn't be perfect, and that flaws enhance credibility and interest in the reader. In fact, a character's flaws are always more interesting than his strengths because of the conflicts they generate. Put an expert sailor on a rickety boat and you have no conflict, no excitement, and no emotions. Make him afraid of water, like Sheriff Brody in *Jaws*, and we're interested. Intrepid adventurer Indiana Jones is afraid of snakes in *Raiders of the Lost Ark*. **Fears** are one of the most compelling flaws you can give a character, especially emotional fears, like a fear of commitment, fear of success, fear that he's not good enough or that nobody loves him. These fears often relate to the character's transformation, and thus we follow their journey until they change or fail to do so. Robert Towne (*Chinatown*, *The Last Detail*) says, "The single most important question a writer must ask about a character is what are they really afraid of? It's probably the single best way of getting into a character. That's where stories are told... with a character that's real. Jack Gittes, in *Chinatown*, was afraid of being a fool... and he would overreact: 'I won't let anybody put this one over me.' And that would become a self-fulfilling prophecy, and it did. He ended up in the very place he didn't want to be. He was so afraid of being a fool that he brought it on himself. He wasn't going to let anybody push him around." So character flaws, especially emotional fears that hold a character back and make it difficult for him to achieve his goal, are another way to make a character fascinating.

When your lead is unlikable—As I mentioned earlier, this method is particularly useful when writers create unlikable characters or when they reverse traditional roles—the criminal is the protagonist and the policeman the antagonist, like in *Dog Day Afternoon* or *Falling Down*. In these types of stories, the main character is an anti-hero in the reader's mind. He may not be the nicest guy in the block, but he has to be the most interesting one in the script.

When you're dealing with criminal heroes, you need to balance the "criminal" with the "hero." Think of characters such as Travis Bickle in *Taxi Driver*, Tony Montana in Oliver Stone's *Scarface*, Hannibal Lecter in *Hannibal*, or Tony Soprano in *The Sopranos*—not exactly likable or admirable characters you'd want as your best friends. But they're fascinating and involving enough for us to feel compelled to watch them at a safe distance and see what they'll do or say next. The reason we accept these anti-heroes as protagonists is that their flaws and immoral traits are balanced with positive, humanistic attractors. For example, the reason we "care" about Hannibal Lecter, in additional to being fascinated by him, is that he's made to feel like a victim when he's tormented by Dr. Chilton, which makes us feel sorry for him. Though he's a psychopath with a taste for human flesh, he's unjustly mistreated. He also exhibits "positive" humanistic qualities, such as being helpful, highly intelligent, charming, witty, clever, and learned. So the way to solve the "unlikable" hero is to create heroes who seem virtuous to the reader, and villains who are more vicious and repulsive than the hero—virtues like strength, ingenuity, bravery, competence, generosity, loyalty, etc. These are qualities we all admire in a human being. When we perceive these characters are virtuous, we judge their actions as morally correct within the ethical system of the story. That's why we like Hannibal Lecter, even after he still commits crimes. Give a villain attractive and appealing human qualities, and you automatically create complexity and fascination through this balance of virtues and vices.

Backstory & The Ghost—Finally, another element which can fascinate the reader and add texture and emotional substance to your script, provided of course it's not clichéd, is the character's past, known as the *backstory*. This is his history up to where the story begins. Backstory can include where he comes from, how he grew up, and how his past affects his current personality. For instance, in *Casablanca*, Rick Blaine's past as a gun runner in Ethiopia and a loyalist during the Spanish Civil War is his backstory. It affects his attitudes, values, and personality in his current life as a café owner in World War II Casablanca.

Now, for those who jumped ahead and are wondering why I didn't mention his doomed Paris romance with Ilsa, it's because that event is actually a *traumatic* incident known as "The Ghost." This is a part of the backstory, but it has a more pronounced effect in the character's present life. The Ghost is a specific trauma from his past that *still haunts* the character in the present story, often contributing to the inner need and the character's arc. In Rick's case, Ilsa's betrayal in Paris (from Rick's point of view) is a deep emotional wound which causes Rick's bitterness and isolation in his daily affairs. Most often, the Ghost involves traumas such as abandonment, betrayal, or a tragic accident which leaves the character permanently injured or disfigured, or causes guilt if the character feels he has caused another's death (*Cliffhanger* and *Vertigo*). It can also be the death of a loved one. Basically, any traumatic incident that created a sense of loss, or a psychological emotional wound. In *Ordinary People*, Conrad's Ghost is the loss of his brother during a boating accident and his guilt of having survived it. In *Citizen Kane*, it's young Kane's sense of abandonment and loss of familial love when he's taken away from his family. The difference between Backstory and Ghost is that the first molds the character's personality, whereas the latter is still an open wound which haunts the character in your story and affects his inner need. Both, if interesting, can add emotional complexity and fascination to your character.

MYSTERY (CURIOSITY AND ANTICIPATION)

Another effective device that will connect the reader to your character is mystery. Nicholas Kazan (*Reversal of Fortune*, *Fallen*) once said, "What makes a great character is mystery." What he means is mystery in the *emotional* sense, as in "What will this character do next?" Not in the *genre* sense, as in a detective story. Mystery always attracts the reader's attention by evoking curiosity and anticipation, two major storytelling emotions. As it relates to character, I divide mystery into three parts: *Mysterious Past* —the character's mysterious past, abilities, and secrets; *Mysterious*

Present—why does the character react or behave in a particular way? And *Mysterious Future*—how will the character react in future situations, what will be revealed about the character and when, and how will he surprise the reader?

Mysterious past (abilities and secrets)—The difference between a character's mysterious past and his backstory or Ghost discussed in the prior section is, of course, how much of it is actually revealed to the reader. As the story's creator, you choose what to reveal and what to keep hidden, hence the mystery, which creates a strong interest in the reader to want to know more. One of the reasons Rick Blaine is such an effective character in *Casablanca* is that we're given hints at a past suffering but not informed about it until the Paris flashback. We're also intrigued by his past because he keeps dodging and evading questions about it from other characters such as Ugarte and Renault. This leads them, and the audience, to speculate about it, which keeps us fascinated. Exposing a character's **abilities** and gradually revealing their mysterious origin, parceling out clues like a time-release pill, also adds interest to the character. Examples include Samantha in *The Long Kiss Goodnight* and Jason Bourne in *The Bourne Identity*, where these characters, and the reader, are intrigued by their mysterious abilities, not remembering their past as secret agents. Character **secrets** are also a great way to add mystery and fascination, especially when they're too embarrassing, hurtful, or dangerous to be revealed, and when the character is willing to do anything to protect them. Think of Evelyn Mulwray's dark secret in *Chinatown*.

Mysterious present—This is about creating curiosity about a character's behavior and reactions in a present situation. For instance, a character may behave in an unusual manner, maybe overreact to something, or avoid a subject, prompting the reader to wonder why, or what he's hiding. Similarly, other characters may react mysteriously to the character, making the reader curious about what they know about the character that the reader doesn't.

Mysterious future—Wondering how a character will behave and react to a future situation, knowing the character's personality and attitudes, will create additional curiosity in the reader, as well as anticipation and uncertainty. This unpredictability keeps the reader connected, wondering how and when the character will surprise him next. **Surprises** can be anything—lines of dialogue, behaviors, or reactions, as long as they're unpredictable but consistent with the character's attitudes and desires. The more complex and fascinating the character, the more opportunities to surprise the reader. One way to do so is to present the character with a strong **dilemma**. Aristotle observes in *Poetics* that the dramas that grip an audience tend to have a powerful dilemma, building to a crisis, and forcing a decision, action, and resolution. In other words, a reader will connect emotionally to a character caught between two excruciating choices, a character who must have or do something for powerful reasons, and yet can't have or do it for equally powerful reasons. Both sides are right, or wrong. When you present a character with a fork in the road and force him to take a path, like having to choose between love and duty, marriage and career, or ambition and sacrifice, it creates curiosity, anticipation, and uncertainty in the reader, who waits at the edge of his seat for the character to make that difficult choice. In *Sophie's Choice*, Sophie's dilemma of having to choose which of her two children to save and which to kill is such a powerful predicament that many writers label an impossible dilemma as a "Sophie's choice."

TECHNIQUES FOR INSTANT CHARACTER APPEAL AND EMPATHY

Reading a script is a dance of emotions, as you'll see in the next chapter, but when it comes to characters, it's a dance along an empathy line (I care, I like) and an enmity one (I don't care, I dislike). It happens fast. We're a critical and opinionated lot. The second a character shows up on screen, we start building an opinion about that character. Everything that character says and does counts. This is why you want empathy as soon as possible. If the reader doesn't care about your characters, he won't care what happens to them throughout your script, and he won't care about the story.

There are a number of strategies writers use to instantly enhance the reader's identification with the main character. Because there are so many, I've divided them into three categories of appeal:

- We care about victims—characters we feel sorry for
- We care about characters with humanistic virtues
- We like characters with desirable qualities

WE CARE ABOUT VICTIMS—CHARACTERS WE FEEL SORRY FOR

As human beings, we can't help but feel compassion and pity for victims. Thus, victimizing a character creates immediate empathy in the reader and identification through recognizing a situation and its emotional consequences. A writer can create numerous events to victimize a character, but the following cover the most effective ones. As always, it's up to you to go beyond the clichés and present these techniques in fresh, original ways.

UNDESERVED MISTREATMENT, INJUSTICE, AND CONTEMPT

Show others unjustly mistreating your character. This includes being **teased** unjustly (The Tramp in *City Lights*, *Dumbo*), **humiliated**, **being laughed at**, **embarrassed** (*American Beauty*, where wife and daughter make fun of Lester), **snubbed**, **passed over** on a deserved promotion (*Lost in America*, *Working Girl*), any type of unjust **prejudice**, like the social injustices of racism or sexism (Tibbs in *In the Heat of the Night*, Beckett in *Philadelphia*, Guido in *Life Is Beautiful*). The injustice of being **falsely accused** is also affecting (*North by Northwest*, *The Fugitive*, *The Shawshank Redemption*). If you add **brutality**, you double the empathy—

enhancing sympathy for the protagonist and loathing for the abuser. Think of a character **being raped** (*The Accused*) or **viciously beaten** (Simon in *As Good As It Gets*). The emotion is even more poignant when a **defenseless** character is **abused, exploited,** or **made to suffer** (John Merrick in *The Elephant Man*, Celie in *The Color Purple*, Oliver and the rest of the orphans in *Oliver Twist*).

UNDESERVED MISFORTUNE (SAD CIRCUMSTANCES, BAD LUCK)

Misfortune is another word for bad luck. When it's undeserved, it creates empathy, like when a character goes through terribly sad circumstances, such as the **death of a loved one** (Munny's wife in *Unforgiven*), **losing something or someone important** ($8000 missing in *It's a Wonderful Life*, losing a son in *Finding Nemo*) or someone who's **down on his luck** (Buck and Rizzo in *Midnight Cowboy*, most of the characters in *The Full Monty* and *The Grapes of Wrath*, Billy Ray Valentine in *Trading Places*), experiencing an **accident** (*Erin Brockovich*), or just plain **bad luck** (Bernie Lootz in *The Cooler*).

PHYSICAL, MENTAL, HEALTH, OR FINANCIAL HANDICAPS

Extra empathy is gained with a character who was born **deformed** (John Merrick in *The Elephant Man*, Quasimodo in *The Hunchback of Notre Dame*), **handicapped** (Christy Brown in *My Left Foot*, Edward in *Edward Scissorhands*), or **mentally challenged** (Chance in *Being There*, Raymond Babbitt in *Rain Man*, *Forrest Gump*); **trapped by their situation** (L.B. Jeffries trapped by a **cast** and forced to become a voyeur in *Rear Window*, Scottie Ferguson trapped by his **fear of heights** in *Vertigo*, Marty Pilletti in *Marty* and Seymour in *Ghost World* by **being ugly and shy**, C. D. Bates by his **huge nose** in *Roxanne*, Ron Kovic by a **wheelchair** in *Born on the 4th of July*); burdened by any **addiction** or **terrible disease**, such as alcoholism, major depression, cancer, or Alzheimer's (Frank Galvin's alcoholism in *The Verdict*, Emma's cancer in *Terms of Endearment*); situations of **extreme poverty** or any **financial hardship**, like being hungry and not having enough money to buy a loaf of bread. All the above may qualify under one heading—**The Underdog**, which has proven to be a compelling sympathy producer. Think of Rocky, Erin Brockovich, and even Maximus in *Gladiator*, who struggle against overwhelming odds to ultimately get what they want.

HAUNTED BY THE PAST, WOUNDED, AND REPRESSING PAIN

Previously, we explored backstory and the Ghost to create fascination with a character. When the ghost creates a painful wound, it generates empathy. Look at Conrad feeling guilty for his brother's drowning accident in *Ordinary People*, Salieri's guilt over killing Mozart in *Amadeus*, and Rick Blaine's numbness in *Casablanca* due to the pain over his ill-fated affair with Ilsa.

ANY MOMENT OF WEAKNESS AND VULNERABILITY

Empathy is also established when you depict a character in a moment of weakness, like when all hope is gone, he's reached rock bottom, he's at his most vulnerable, and you show his suffering. This includes a character displaying pain, grief, self-doubt, insecurities, and fears, like most Woody Allen films and Indiana Jones' snake phobia in *Raiders of the Lost Ark*.

BETRAYAL AND DECEPTION

Another proven device that makes us feel sorry for a worthy character (this creates the opposite effect when it happens to a villain) is to have a character deceive or betray the main character. Think of Frank Galvin's love interest, who's really a spy for the opposition, in *The Verdict*, and Eve in *North by Northwest*.

NOT BELIEVED WHEN TELLING THE TRUTH

There's an element of dramatic irony when a character we know is telling the truth is not believed. It also makes us feel the character's frustration. Examples include Elliot in *E.T.*, Molly in *Ghost*, Roger Thornhill in *North by Northwest*, and Axel Foley in *Beverly Hills Cop*.

ABANDONMENT

Being abandoned or deserted by a loved one is another primal device that creates pity. Think of Oliver left on the doorstep of an orphanage by his unwed mother in *Oliver Twist*, Ted Kramer and his son abandoned by his wife/mother in the opening scene of *Kramer vs. Kramer*, and Kevin forgotten by his vacationing parents in *Home Alone*.

EXCLUSION AND REJECTION

Because wanting to belong to a group or family and craving love are such universal needs, to be excluded or rejected is an effective way to create instant appeal. This includes **unrequited love**, like when Tom Ripley is rejected when professing love to Dickie Greenleaf in *The Talented Mr. Ripley*, or when Forrest Gump is rejected by Jenny in *Forrest Gump*. Also, any involuntary outcasts, loners, or misfits who aren't in the mainstream of life, and as long as other techniques are applied, will be engaging because they're excluded from normal groups—Chance in *Being There* and Edward in *Edward Scissorhands*.

LONELINESS/NEGLECT

When a character feels lonely or is neglected by another, we root for the melancholic character. Examples include Kane when he dies alone in his mansion in *Citizen Kane* and Melvin Udall, who's lonely because of his medical condition and abrasive personality in *As Good As It Gets*. This technique is often used with teenage characters, like in *Rebel Without a Cause*, where the tormented teenagers portrayed by James Dean, Natalie Wood, and Sal Mineo can't help but get into trouble in a desperate bid for attention from their neglectful parents.

MAKING MISTAKES AND REGRETTING THEM

Someone who makes mistakes is human. This is why when your hero makes a mistake we might make, we don't dislike him. Instead, we sympathize. This gives us a point of identification with the protagonist—he's human, and he makes mistakes just like we do. When a character **regrets** making that mistake, we connect with him even more. In *Finding Nemo*, Marlin feels responsible for the loss of his son due to his over-protection. In *Spiderman*, Peter Parker ignores an armed robber who later kills his uncle. Rather than disliking him for the error in judgment, we feel sorry for him because he regrets the error and he loses a dear family member. He feels guilty, and tries to redeem himself by fighting crime as a superhero.

SUFFERING INJURY

Any time a character gets injured and needs medical care, either from a doctor or a romantic interest, we feel empathy. Examples include most characters in action-adventure films and thrillers. Think of Indiana Jones, James Bond, and John McClane in *Die Hard*. How about the ultimate high concept—trying to solve your own murder in *D.O.A.*, where Frank Bigelow discovers he's been poisoned and has only a few hours to live. We can't feel any sorrier for him than that.

JEOPARDY

Audiences love it when the characters they care about are put in jeopardy. The deeper the trouble, the more we love it. When a character risks losing something dear, like his life, a lover, or the respect of others, we worry about the character's well-being. Any threat is an effective device—the threat of being captured, exposed, injured or killed. Think of the constant jeopardy in *Ferris Bueller's Day Off*, *No Way Out*, and *Raiders of the Lost Ark*. *Tootsie* is an interesting example because there's no central antagonist to battle Michael. The primary conflict is whether he can maintain his deception—he's in constant jeopardy every time he's disguised. This keeps the reader involved in the story.

WE CARE ABOUT CHARACTERS WITH HUMANISTIC VIRTUES

Humanistic virtues are the qualities that make up our humanity, the individual forces that affect others in a positive way. Virtues are a way of being and acting toward others. They include love, politeness, justice, generosity, compassion, and tolerance. When we recognize them in others, we can't help but care about them. Giving virtues to your characters, therefore, is another effective method to connect them with the reader. Humanistic virtues include:

HELPING OTHERS, ESPECIALLY THE LESS FORTUNATE

This is another primal empathy device because lending a hand is such a universally recognized action. Human beings are supposed to help each other in troubled times. When they do, we like them. Think of Mother Theresa, or one of the most beloved characters in film history, George Bailey in *It's a Wonderful Life*, and the multitude of selfless acts he performs—he rescues his younger brother from drowning, losing the hearing in his left ear in the process; he endures a beating rather than allow a grieving druggist to deliver poison by mistake to an ailing child; he foregoes college and a long-planned trip to Europe to keep the Bailey Building and Loan from letting its customers down. Is any wonder we like him so much? Helping others comes naturally when you give a character a service profession, like a doctor, psychologist, teacher, nurse, priest, police officer, or firefighter. Any character who cares about someone or something other than himself will generate appeal.

RELATING TO CHILDREN OR CHILDREN LIKING HIM

Because children represent innocence, any character who likes children, relates to them, can play with them, and who's liked by them will become appealing by default. Think of *Mary Poppins*, Maria in *The Sound of Music*, child psychologist Dr. Malcolm Crowe in *The Sixth Sense*, and *Jerry Maguire*, who's instantly liked by Dorothy's little boy.

"PATTING THE DOG" (LIKING ANIMALS OR ANIMALS LIKING HIM)

Similar to the above, a character who likes animals or is liked by them is also appealing. "Patting the dog" is a screenwriting term for scenes where a character is nurturing toward an animal, such as patting them on the head, caressing them, or feeding them. This shows their nurturing side, which showcases their altruism and selflessness. Examples include Martin Riggs' introduction in *Lethal Weapon* where he saves the abused dog, Macon Leary in *The Accidental Tourist*, and the fish-loving stutterer in *A Fish Called Wanda*. Also, when an animal warms up to a character, no matter how repellent he is, we like him too because we trust that the animal can sense his true nature underneath the social mask. A perfect example of this is *As Good As It Gets*, where the dog warms up to Melvin, even after he threw him down a garbage chute.

HAVING A CHANGE OF HEART OR FORGIVING

Audiences are pleased when a character forgives others or has a change of heart, such as accepting someone who was disliked earlier or agreeing with him when he didn't before. Rocky is supposed to break a man's thumb for defaulting on a mob loan, but changes his mind and lectures him instead in *Rocky*, while in *Armageddon*, oil driller Harry Stamper is furious at A.J. Frost for dating his daughter and tries to kill him. Later in the film, he sacrifices his life on the asteroid and gives his future son-in-law his blessing for the relationship.

Risking Life or Dying for the Sake of Others

Willing to sacrifice yourself for the sake of others, especially a loved one, generates a fair amount of empathy. In *Beauty and the Beast*, Belle offers her life to save her father's; and in *Casablanca*, Rick risks everything to help Ilsa with the transit letters.

Fighting or Dying for a Just Cause

The same goes for any character who cares about something important outside of himself. Fighting for a just cause is often a courageous and selfless act. Think again of Harry Stamper's sacrifice for humanity in *Armageddon*, Rick sacrificing his happiness with Ilsa for the sake of the resistance against the Nazis, Wallace fighting and dying for freedom in *Braveheart*, and Terry Malloy standing up against corruption in *On the Waterfront*.

Being Ethical, Moral, Dependable, Loyal, and Responsible

These are the most appealing humane virtues. Any character who applies these qualities, especially when there's no self-interest involved, will be viewed in a positive light. For example, in *Mrs. Doubtfire*, Daniel quits his job after taking a moral stand against his company who refuses to run an anti-smoking public service announcement. Others include George Bailey in *It's a Wonderful Life*, Atticus Finch in *To Kill a Mockingbird*, and *Forrest Gump*.

Loving Other People (Family/Friends/Neighbors)

Any character who loves something or someone deeply will be appealing, especially if it's his family and friends. In fact, this is one of the ways writers can create empathy with "criminal" or anti-heroes who operate outside the law, such as mobsters Vito Corleone and Tony Soprano. After all, they couldn't be that bad if they have a loving family and friends.

Being Important to Others

Clearly, a character will be appealing if others in the story like him too. If he's surrounded by people at work or at home who adore him, admire him, respect his skills, if he's someone who's an expert at something or holds a position of vital importance, this will make him likable. Think again of Atticus Finch, George Bailey, and Forrest Gump, and you'll understand their deep appeal.

Showing Humanity in Private Moments

When a character lets down his defenses and shows his humanity in private moments, when he thinks no one is looking, we sympathize. Combine it with underserved mistreatment as a result of being vulnerable, like ridicule and humiliation, and you generate more sympathy for the hero and stronger enmity for the abuser who invades his privacy.

ACTING IN ANY NURTURING WAY

Any act of kindness, caring, and generosity—tucking in the blanket, healing the wounded, especially if it's a child, or giving a dollar to a homeless person, creates instant connection with the character.

WE LIKE CHARACTERS WITH DESIRABLE QUALITIES

Whereas humanistic values affect others directly in the generous actions of the character, the following qualities involve more personal traits and actions that don't affect others as much, other than they're highly attractive and desired by most of us. A character who exhibits these qualities will be appealing to the reader.

Power, charisma, leadership—Has power over other people (*The Godfather, Citizen Kane, Patton*); does what needs to be done (*Rambo, Braveheart*); expresses his feelings and opinions regardless of other's opinions (*Beverly Hills Cop, One Flew Over the Cuckoo's Nest*).

A glamorous profession—Any job that has allure—artist, advertising executive, architect, author, photographer, adventurer, airline pilot, race car driver, spy, high-class thief, professional athlete, chef, etc.

Courage (physical or mental)—We admire people who have the courage to solve their problems. It doesn't mean the character is courageous in general but that he courageously solves his problem at the end. In *As Good As It Gets*, Melvin sends the dog down the garbage chute instead of dealing with his peeing—this is not what we may do, of course, but we secretly admire his courage to take action, just as we admire a character's courage to redeem himself (*The Verdict, Tender Mercies, Schindler's List*), to fight the system (*Norma Rae, I Am Sam, Whale Rider*), and physical courage (*Saving Private Ryan, The Right Stuff*).

Passion—In the sense of emotional intensity, passion fills your characters with deep emotional feelings of love or passion for some activity. This is easily demonstrated in *Braveheart* and *Shakespeare in Love*. Increasing the passion of your characters puts the audience in touch with similar feelings hidden within themselves.

Skills/Expertise—Make your character the best at his job, a sought-after expert in a particular field (Indiana Jones, James Bond).

Attractiveness—No surprise here. Beautiful people are appealing.

Wisdom, wit, and cleverness—These traits are often reserved for the mentor (Obi-Wan Kenobi in *Star Wars*, Gandalf in *Lord of the Rings*) and the trickster (Phil in *Groundhog Day*, Axel Foley in *Beverly Hills Cop*). Readers love characters who cleverly solve their problems; anyone who gets out of trouble by using their intelligence, matching their wits against the world.

Sense of humor and playfulness—You can have the most unlikable character in the world, but if they're funny we'll hang around them for a couple of hours, like the Joker in *Batman*. Other playful characters include Axel Foley,

Austin Powers, Arthur, Holly Golightly in *Breakfast at Tiffany's*, and Jeff Spicoli in *Fast Times at Ridgemont High*.

Childlike innocence or enthusiasm—Chance in *Being There*, *Forrest Gump*, *Amelie*, Dorothy Gale in *The Wizard of Oz*.

Physicality and athleticism—A dancer, a warrior, or an athlete.

Persistence (making an effort, actively struggling despite vulnerabilities)—A reader rewards his sympathy to characters who make heroic efforts to solve their problems, especially if they're underdogs who try hard to become a better person (*Rocky*, *Forrest Gump*). Audiences admire a character who shows persistence, who keeps going despite obstacles, setbacks, and poor odds. They respect someone who refuses to give up. Readers prefer active characters who take action to solve their problems rather than passive characters who only react to events, especially if they persist despite vulnerabilities or handicaps. In *Finding Nemo*, if Marlin felt sorry for the loss of his son, but then didn't do anything about it, we would have stopped feeling sorry for him.

Misfit, rebel, or eccentric—A character who follows no one, flouts authority, who has a unique way of living in the world and is happy with himself regardless of what the world thinks of him, is appealing because he's an outsider, a misfit who doesn't belong, which is technically a fish out of water. Think of *Harold and Maude*, *Dirty Harry*, and *One Flew Over the Cuckoo's Nest*.

ON THE PAGE: CHARACTER IN ACTION

Here, we look at one of the most colorful and complex characters ever written for the screen, Melvin Udall in *As Good As It Gets*, who's like a fairy tale creature simultaneously too evil and too fascinating to be true. Following the script page by page, let's take an in-depth look at all the techniques the writers, Mark Andrus and James L. Brooks, used to make us care about this flawed character. They did a masterful job of pointing out his abrasive, obnoxious, and misanthropic attitudes—hated by his neighbors, throwing his neighbor's dog, Verdell, down the garbage chute, and insulting everyone around him. They also balanced Melvin's negative traits with several of the character appeals presented above. I'll only point out the positive techniques.

The first one comes after his confrontation with his neighbor, Simon. He slams his apartment door, locks it five times and washes his hands in near-boiling water with two freshly opened soaps, which he then discards. This is okay because he has a medicine cabinet full of them. These bizarre routines clue us in that Melvin suffers from obsessive-compulsive disorder (Mental handicap).

We see he's a romance novel writer, and by the looks of his fancy New York apartment, we assume we assume he's successful at it—we learn later on he's working on his 62nd book (Skills/Expertise and Glamorous profession). When Simon confronts him about his dog, Melvin takes charge and completely dismisses him by insisting never to be disturbed when he works at home (Power, courage, cleverness). But when Simon's art dealer, Frank, threatens Melvin, we feel for his OCD condition when he says, clearly panicked, "No touch, no touch, no touch." (Vulnerability, a moment of weakness).

We get more on his medical condition when we see Melvin walk on the street, as he avoids walking on lines in the sidewalk. At his favorite restaurant, where he sits at the same table and orders the same breakfast, we meet Carol, the only waitress in New York City who is somehow fascinated by Melvin's eccentricities and even seems to sense a spark of decency lurking deep behind his scathing put-downs. We get our first glimpse of Melvin's humanity when he asks Carol about her sick son (the second time he's at the restaurant; the first time he mentions that her sick son will probably die soon, and Carol set him straight).

When Simon is brutally attacked and robbed, Frank orders Melvin to take care of Verdell while Simon is hospitalized—a nice piece of irony after what he did to the dog (bad luck for Melvin who's stuck with him), and a brilliant touch of self-disclosure when he says, "Nobody's ever been here before." (Vulnerability and Loneliness) The funny thing is that Verdell actually warms up to Melvin (Animal likes character), and Melvin's heart of stone begins to soften, though he still keeps everyone around him at a safe distance through a barrage of blunt insults. At the restaurant, he shows he cares about Verdell by keeping an eye on him and saving leftover bacon for him (Patting the dog).

When Carol doesn't show up at the restaurant to serve him, which disrupts Melvin's routine, he goes to her apartment to tell her he's hungry, and he demands she return to work. To expedite things, he sets up unsolicited medical care for her son (Helping a friend and Important to others). He also brings Chinese soup to the convalescing Simon (Act of kindness).

Eventually, Melvin is cornered into driving Simon and Carol to Baltimore, and during a hotel stopover, in one of the movie's best scenes, Carol forces Melvin to give her a compliment, or she walks. He tells her with some difficulty, "You make me want to be a better man." After a long pause, Carol answers, "That's maybe the best compliment of my life." (A change of heart from taking medication to have an acceptable relationship with Carol). Then, he inadvertently insults her again (Feeling guilty for making a mistake that hurts another), and she doesn't speak to him until they return to New York. In fact, she doesn't want to see him again, even after his considerable financial help to her son (Rejection). When Melvin learns Simon's apartment has been sublet, he offers to let him stay at his (Helping a friend).

Melvin realizes he can't live without Carol and wins her back by saying how important she is to him, that he's the only one on Earth who truly appreciates her, and he reaches out to give her a kiss (Vulnerability and Courage).

You can now see how these techniques enhanced Melvin's appeal. Some readers may argue that fascination with Melvin's utter abrasiveness alone kept them glued to the page in anticipation of how he would behave or what he'd say next. This is true. It would have been sufficient were he not the protagonist through whose eyes we experienced the story, but because he's the hero we had to care about, and because he's so unappealing at the beginning, Andrus and Brooks used these character appeal techniques.

It's easy to repel the reader by making a character unappealing. Making the reader identify with and care enough about a character to follow his adventures until the end of the script is where craft comes in. You've seen how professional writers do it. Now it's time to apply these techniques to your own characters. When they become three-dimensional, when you have found ways to reveal them on the page and have the reader connect with them emotionally, bits and pieces of a plot will emerge. However, this is not enough to craft a complete story that engages the reader. For this, we need to explore the essential emotions of all great stories...

STORY

Rising Tension

"No tears in the writer, no tears in the reader. No surprise for the writer, no surprise for the reader."

-ROBERT FROST

I f you developed your premise and main characters, you should already have the broad strokes of a story, especially when a character's goal, his emotional arc, and what's at stake are what a story is about. All that's missing is conflict—the obstacles that prevent the character from reaching the goal.

Beginners often assume that writing a story is easy because it's basically a sequence of events—people doing things, or things happening to people. Obviously, there's more to this, and it's useful for aspiring writers to get a solid understanding of what a story is in order to avoid countless rewrites down the line.

THE BASICS: WHAT YOU NEED TO KNOW

WHAT'S A DRAMATIC STORY

So what's a story? Most screenwriting books offer a definition, and most of them are helpful, depending on their depth. For instance, you learn that at its core, a story is simply about a character with a problem, or that something happens to someone, and something must be done. According to former UCLA professor William Froug, a story is a "series of events that have vivid, emotional, conflicting, striking interest or results." Author James N. Frey labels a dramatic story as "a narrative of consequential events involving worthy human characters who struggle and change as a result of those events." Script consultant Michael Hauge defines story as "a sympathetic character who overcomes a series of increasingly difficult, seemingly insurmountable obstacles, and achieves a compelling desire."

There are, of course, many more, but you get the idea. They all say the same thing because that's what a story is in its purest form—a "character who wants something, and is having difficulty getting it," the simplest definition I've come across, formulated by Frank Daniel, co-director of the Columbia University Film Division. You should write it down in bold letters and post it on your bulletin board where you can see it at all times as you develop your story— "Somebody wants something and is having difficulty getting it." (Or any other definition, if it works better for you.)

Bottom line, if your story doesn't fit these criteria, it can't be called a dramatic story. This is where drama comes from—conflict, struggle against difficult obstacles. Every story is about a character trying to deal with some sort of difficulty. This is why the focus in all storytelling is always on conflict.

Thus, all stories have three elements—conflict, struggle, and resolution. Something happens to someone, which causes a problem (conflict); they must take action and face obstacles to solve this problem (struggle); and they either win or lose (resolution). If this sounds familiar, it's because this is the classical structure of most tales—beginning (setup—conflict), middle (complications—struggle), and end (resolution). We'll explore structure in the next chapter, but for now, I want to make sure you have a solid grasp on what a story is.

STORY VS. PLOT

Another area where I see a lot of confusion is the difference between story and plot. Many writers believe the two mean the same thing, but this could be detrimental to their craft. Because many aspiring writers are constantly searching for magic keys, formulas, and story templates, there's been a lot of focus on plot construction, which unfortunately has not translated into great stories. What it's done, though, is produce too many predictable, cookie-cutter, and formulaic storylines. I'm not saying plot is not as important as story, just that you should know the difference, and that your focus should be on story. Lillian Hellman once said, "Story is what the characters want to do. Plot is what the writer wants the characters to do."

Story is your creation, your art. Plot is the vehicle for telling your story in an entertaining way, your craft. Story is the deeper understanding about the human condition your reader will gain as a result of experiencing a sequence of events. Plot is the progression of these events, the way you chose to structure the story. A great example of this distinction is the classic *Citizen Kane*. The story of Charles Foster Kane is his lifelong attempt to get love without being able to love back.

The plot is the reporter's search for the meaning of "Rosebud," and the way the writer arranges the scenes to reveal Kane's story.

Plot answers the basic questions—who, what, where, when, how, and why, to make sense of the story's deep meaning. It's just a series of dramatic situations connected logically—this happens because that happened earlier, etc.

Now, the key element to plotting your story, in other words the arrangement of events, is its intended effect upon the reader. Plot is designed to make your story emotionally satisfying to the reader, not create the story. Story creation comes from concept, theme, premise, and character development. Then comes how you want to present that story through plot. This is what this chapter will explore—the craft of plot arrangement to evoke the major emotional responses such as anticipation, tension, curiosity, surprise, etc. As Irwin Blacker once said, "Plot is more than a pattern of events; it is the ordering of emotions."

THE CRAFT: ENGAGING THE READER FROM BEGINNING TO END

Now that you know your story—what the character wants, what's keeping him from getting it, and how he changes, it's time to create a dramatic journey that will engage the reader through roughly 100 to 110 pages to a satisfying and fulfilling resolution. Creating the story is the easy part, in my opinion; choosing how to tell that story on the page in a way that will captivate, mesmerize, and fascinate the reader is where the challenge comes in—that's what craft is all about.

So how do we do it? How do we maintain consistent emotional appeal from beginning to end?

IT'S ALL ABOUT BEING INTERESTED

At its core, the reader's emotional engagement comes from interest, or attention. This is where it all starts. Interest is simply about keeping the reader's attention from beginning to end.

What's opposite of interest and attention? Boredom and indifference—the Hollywood writer's biggest sin, the only inviolable rule in writing, and unfortunately, the most common flaw in amateur works. No reader recommends a boring script, no executive green-lights a boring movie (unless, of course, a major star wants to make it), and no audience pays $10 to be bored for two hours. Best-selling author Elmore Leonard once shared an anecdote about a fan letter he once received. The letter said, "My husband is getting tired of me spending more time in the sack with a Leonard book than with him; so I told him, 'Get my attention.'"

It's all about getting the reader's attention and keeping him interested through emotional engagement. Good writing is good writing because you feel something. This is why a movie can be three hours long and you don't even notice. To paraphrase playwright William Gibson, "The first business of the screenwriter is to keep the reader from throwing your script in the reject pile." Every time you sit down to write, you should be afraid of losing the reader at any moment of any page.

The only way to maintain the reader's interest from beginning to end is for him to experience the key visceral emotions he wants to feel. Think about the most desirable emotions we all like to experience during a story, not just the pleasure of seeing problems being solved, but the concentrated experience of emotions that are not often triggered in our daily lives—amusement, anticipation, curiosity, empathy, excitement, fascination, fear, hope, intrigue, tension, etc. These are the emotions we pay money for, and what readers look for in a great script. These emotional responses are the core of entertainment, and what we'll explore in depth in this chapter, starting with the most essential of feelings—interest.

INTEREST/FASCINATION/INSIGHT/AWE

The reason I say interest is the most essential reader emotion is that it encompasses all the other storytelling emotions. When you read a script or watch a film, and something in the scene arouses your curiosity, you're technically "interested." When a character states his goal, and you anticipate his success or failure, you're interested. When you're gripped by intense suspense in a thriller, you're interested. As I've said before, interest is the opposite of boredom, and boredom is the most frowned-upon sin in Hollywood. This means that the critical requirement of every page, ideally, is to capture and hold the reader's interest.

Obviously, whether a story is interesting or boring is a subjective opinion, but if you look at the most successful and critically acclaimed films of all time, you'll notice similarities when it comes to craft and the emotional responses of audiences around the world. If a film can move different audiences—different in age, ethnicity, and geographical location, generation after generation, surely there must be techniques that influence a reader's emotional response to a script. As Wayne C. Booth said in *The Rhetoric of Fiction*, "Every literary work of any power—whether or not its author wrote it with his audience in mind—is in fact an elaborate system of controls over the reader's involvement and detachment along various lines of interest." In a screenplay, your opening scene ideally captures the reader's interest, the development of the first act holds that interest, the obstacles and complications increase it, the climax exalts it, and the resolution satisfies that interest.

Although we'll explore dramatic techniques that arouse curiosity, anticipation, tension, and surprise, here are some ways to generate simple interest on the page, including its related feelings—fascination, insight, and awe.

CAUSE AND EFFECT

As human beings, we are logical animals who thrive on our reasoning abilities. Because stories are metaphoric models for our lives, we have an innate desire for logical plotlines that follow a clear cause and effect progression to a climax and resolution. Stimulus and response are the building blocks of any story because this is how we make sense of our lives—by understanding how things respond to others, how they're caused by others. We have an inner emotional need to make sense out of things, the world, and the universe. We know that everything has a cause, and when we know the cause, we understand the effect. E.M. Forster once gave this example: "The king died and then the queen died." This is just a chronicle of events. But if you say, "The king died, and then the queen died of grief," it's a more satisfying sentence because you added a cause. The cause links the two events, which gives us emotional satisfaction and interest. Thus, a clear plot where we understand how each event causes the next will hold more interest than one whose events are episodic and random. I'm not saying that episodic, non-linear plots are to be avoided, or that they're not interesting scene by scene. Just that they won't hold the reader's interest as tightly as a plotline that has linear causation—one action causing another, adding up to some meaningful point that touches the thoughts and emotions of the reader.

CHARACTER

As you've read in Chapter 5, a unique character can be fascinating, and thereby hold the reader's interest. In fact, all the essential elements of character development— goals, motivations, stakes, traits, flaws, and relationships are essential because they generate interest on the page. Every time you reveal an additional layer from a character, you arouse interest. If you haven't done so already, refer back to Chapter 5 for more details.

CONFLICT

Most books and seminars emphasize conflict in stories for its dramatic effect, and for good reason: Without conflict, there is no drama, and without drama, there is no interest in the reader. Conflict is crucial in maintaining the reader's interest in the story and in the characters. Because conflict is discussed the world over, I'll try not to repeat what others have said. Instead, I'll focus on some critical points as they relate to reader's interest. If you're familiar with them, consider them a basic review. If you're not, pay close attention because conflict is the essence of storytelling, the fuel that drives a story, and the glue that keeps the reader's attention on the page.

This doesn't mean you must create conflict on every page to generate interest, since it's one of several techniques to hold the reader's attention. However, you should be aware that it's one of the *best* ways to do so, and you should always think about it. The impact of conflict in storytelling presents an interesting paradox for human beings: While most of us abhor conflict in our lives, it actually creates interest in dramatic stories. The more we hate to experience something in real life, the more interest is created on the page when fictional characters experience the conflict.

So what exactly is conflict? "Two dogs, one bone" is how someone once described it. Conflict comes from **the intention of a character (goal, need, want)** meeting some form of **resistance (obstacle).** Two committed forces in conflict will always create interest and heighten tension. By itself, this principle of goal versus obstacle creates drama and initial interest, but there's a third element which makes the conflict more dramatic—the **unwillingness to compromise.** If the stakes are high, and both sides are unyielding, you have intense drama. Think how ineffective the opposite would be. Imagine a character needs money for his mother's operation. He asks his best friend who's a millionaire, but the friend says no. The character reacts by saying, "Oh, okay. Never mind." That's a compromise and a letdown for the reader. An unwillingness to compromise would have the begging character insist, threaten his friend, pull out a gun, wound him if there were still no agreement, or even kill him in desperation, the tension rising with every beat in the scene. So think of conflict as a triangle—goal, obstacle, and unwillingness to compromise.

The writer must also think of **the outcome of a conflict.** There are three possible ways a conflict can proceed: A character wins or loses, but tension disappears; the characters compromise, and as you just read, it's not an option if you want to maintain interest; or the conflict is aggravated. The latter is what keeps readers glued to the page, wondering how it will all turn out in the end.

Be careful **not to repeat the same conflicts.** You must have a constant flow of new information, new conflicts, and new twists and turns. You want your script to move, each conflict leading to another without repetition, forcing the character to take new actions and overcome more difficult challenges.

Make your conflicts compelling. If the obstacles are too easy, the reader won't care. If Bill Gates loses a hundred dollars, it's not a significant problem. But if a poor deliveryman loses his bicycle, and then his job and his ability to care for his family, that's compelling. The bigger the conflicts, the more things are uncomfortable and difficult for your characters, the more the reader will want to see how they will get out of the situation you've put them in. That's interest. Here's what Michael Schiffer says in *101 Habits*: "Good drama requires obstacles along the way, and if a section is very flat, one of the things a writer can ask is, 'This is too easy for them, what could happen to make it absolutely difficult, painful, agonizing, impossible?' If you have a good story that goes from A to B, ask yourself what obstacles would make the journey from A to B more exciting and interesting to watch. The more legitimate and difficult the hindrance, and the more the characters care about reaching their goal, the more exciting the story."

Take note that **conflict doesn't mean arguing**, or fighting, as in "Yes... no, yes... no, is too ... is not, it's red... no, it's burgundy!" Many beginners make the mistake of thinking two characters arguing in a scene is conflict. But arguments or disagreements are *hollow* conflicts, unless there are emotional stakes for the main character. Then, the argument is an obstacle to the character's want or need. Remember, conflict is **desire against obstacle**.

CHANGE

Life is about change, and all stories are about change—external change, internal change, change in the status quo. **Every story, every scene, and every beat is about a change**—a change in knowledge caused by discoveries, and change in actions caused by character decisions. A character starts at point A, in a state of unfulfilled longing and ends at point Z, satisfied and fulfilled, or if it's a tragedy, destroyed. Either way this journey implies a change, meaning the end is different from the beginning, or else what's the point of telling that story? When anything changes in a story, a scene, or a beat, it generates interest.

Alfred Hitchcock once said that an audience can only stand about an hour of storytelling. After that, it starts to get tired, so it needs the injection of action, movement, and excitement, which is all about keeping the audience occupied mentally. Fast action, quick cutting, and people running around is not the answer. What keeps the audience engaged is the **changing of one situation to another**. This is the reason why writers are told to escalate the action and the stakes in the story. If the conflict is the same on page 90 as it is on page 30, what's the point of the middle 60 pages? The same goes for inner conflicts and character arcs, which produce the emotional changes in the character at the end of the story.

The two most powerful categories of change in stories, and in our lives, are **discoveries,** which are changes in knowledge, and **decisions,** which are changes in actions. In a story, these moments are plot points. In a scene, they are beats. Regardless, these discoveries and decisions create emotions in your character and in the reader.

ORIGINALITY AND FRESHNESS

It shouldn't be a revelation that another way to generate interest in the reader is to write about new and original subjects. Since they say, "There's nothing new under the sun," freshness must come from your vision, the original way you write about common things. Readers always hope to find something unusual that will spark their interest, whether it's a creative approach to structure, plot, characters, theme, or dialogue. Most professional writers focus on originality of concept, since it drives a whole story and is the main factor in interesting potential buyers.

This is where the term "High Concept" comes from—the greater the concept's freshness, the higher its appeal.

SUBTEXT

Although we'll explore subtext in depth in Chapter 10, you may use it in scenes to evoke additional interest in the reader. As the name implies, subtext is the meaning beneath the text. It's what the scene is really about, though the actual words are about something else. When a scene tells the reader directly what it's about, it's often dull and emotionally unsatisfying. Through subtext, you hint at the conflicts in the scene without actually identifying them. The reason why readers welcome subtext is that it challenges them, engages them, and makes them active in the reading experience. When the reader's mind is engaged, it's automatically interested by what's on the page.

INSIGHTFUL EXPOSITION

Another way to evoke interest is to create thoughtfulness through interesting exposition, either through an **insightful voice-over**, like in the opening of *American Beauty*, or through **fascinating information** that sets up the story, like the scrolling exposition that opens *Star Wars*, or the opening graphics in *Casablanca*. The key, of course, and clearly this is a subjective issue, is that the exposition must be fresh, fascinating, insightful, and interesting.

BACKSTORY

There are two types of backstories—**character and situation**. You should already be familiar with character backstory, as it was discussed in the previous chapter as it relates to character fascination. Obviously, if you're fascinated by a character's past, you're interested by that character's actions on the page. But you can also create an interesting situation backstory, which is about what happened before the story starts. By the very nature of stories, which begin at a particular point in time, everything before that point is technically backstory. Another word for situation backstory would be the **context** of the story. For instance, before *Jurassic Park* begins, the backstory is that John Hammond has successfully cloned dinosaurs. Before *The Matrix* begins, most humans have been disconnected from reality and used for energy without their knowledge, and in *The Silence of the Lambs*, serial killer Buffalo Bill has already murdered several women when the movie starts. Again, the backstory must be compelling and unique enough to be included and to evoke interest in the reader.

CURIOSITY/WONDER/INTRIGUE

Curiosity is the emotional state of wanting to learn more about something, the intellectual **need to answer questions** and **make sense of things**. We love stories because we long to know **what happens next**. Without curiosity throughout, a story would grind to a halt. Any writer who can evoke this essential emotion is guaranteed an audience.

THE POWER OF QUESTIONS

Because curiosity comes from our desire to answer questions, the best way to evoke it in the reader, and thereby heighten interest, is to **set up story questions**. A question demands an answer. Therefore, setting up a question automatically creates an emotional itch that needs to be scratched. Each turning point in the plot creates a curiosity that makes the reader ask what will happen next. The writer can accomplish this by withholding bits of information, not telling the reader everything all at once, foreshadowing, or hinting at an outcome, all of which force the reader to play a more active role—filling in the blanks, making guesses, and assuming things. When the reader is active, he is involved, and therefore interested.

As you read earlier, a plot is a sequence of events, but a well-constructed plot will raise dramatic questions in the reader who will follow each event to its conclusion to get answers, and satisfy his curiosity. As you'll see in a moment, every act within a story has its own question to answer. Within each act, every sequence sets up a sub-question, as does every scene within each sequence, and every beat within each scene. You basically create a trail of questions for the reader to follow, as he develops an increasing need to know the answers to each question, which provide a sense of satisfaction when they're revealed at each step of the journey.

Although the writer should set up and answer questions throughout the script, the ideal place to do so is in the opening sequence. This is because curiosity is almost automatic from your first words. Open with an arresting image, like fire in *Body Heat*, or a grainy photograph in *Chinatown*, and the immediate question are, "What is this... where are we... where are going... what does it mean?" Introduce a character, and we want to know who this person is, and whether we care. Or start in the middle of a scene, with dialogue, like the opening of *Blood Simple*, and you set up intrigue, as the reader wonders what is going on. From the opening page on, you move the reader through the story by evoking a series of questions. The key, however, is not having too many at once, or keeping them unanswered for too long, as this could backfire and produce confusion and irritation in the reader. I'll discuss additional opening techniques in the next chapter.

For the rest of your script, you can arouse curiosity in the reader through the following techniques:

SET UP ONE CENTRAL QUESTION

Every story is about one central dramatic question that takes the whole script to answer. In fact, what makes a compelling plot is the kind of questions a reader will follow a story to the end to get answers for. For example, in Ernest Lehman's classic *North by Northwest*, advertising executive Roger Thornhill is mistaken for a spy named George Kaplan, and must then run for his life as he tries to identify the real Kaplan. The central dramatic question, then, is "Will Thornhill survive after being mistaken for a spy?" It isn't answered until the last page of the script.

SET UP A QUESTION FOR EACH ACT

Each act answers a different question. In *North by Northwest*, the first act sets up the question, "Will Thornhill prove he's not Kaplan?" The act ends at the United Nations building where he's framed for the diplomat's murder. This propels us into the second act, which sets up the question, "Will Thornhill clear his name?" The first act question remains unanswered, though we get an exposition scene where we find out Kaplan is a fictional character designed to draw attention away from a real undercover spy. The second act ends when Thornhill, betrayed by Eve, confronts her at the auction and lets himself be captured by police in order to escape the bad guys again. This takes us into the third act where the Professor reveals the truth about Kaplan and Eve being the real undercover spy. This answers the second act's question, and sets up another for act three—"Will Thornhill be able to save Eve?" which is unanswered until the climax on top of Mt. Rushmore.

Since your ultimate goal is constant reader engagement, asking a central question for each act is a good start, but it's not enough. Boredom can creep into any act, especially the second, which is always a challenge for writers. So you have to think about the sequences in each act.

SET UP A QUESTION FOR EACH SEQUENCE

I won't go into each sequence of the entire script, but I'll illustrate how Ernest Lehman maintained interest throughout the second act, which begins after Thornhill is on the run, wanted by the police for murder. The first sequence of scenes is the train sequence, which sets up the question, "Will Thornhill escape police capture, and get to Chicago?" The second sequence is Eve's betrayal, which sets up the question, "How will Thornhill be killed?" The crop duster scene answers that question. The third and final sequence of act two is Thornhill's payback, when he confronts Eve and Vandamm at the auction. The question for this sequence is, "Will he get the truth about Eve?"

Having a different question for each sequence already increases reader interest every ten pages or so, but you can go even deeper and focus on individual scenes.

SET UP A QUESTION FOR EACH SCENE

Let's look at the individual scenes that make up the train sequence. I include the questions for each. The first scene is at the train station—will Thornhill get on the train? Then, on the train, he must elude police officers—will he escape them? He meets Eve, who helps him hide—will Eve turn him in? A bit later, the steward sits him at Eve's table—why? Eve and Thornhill are clearly attracted to each other, and Thornhill gladly plays along in Eve's seduction game—will they sleep together? The train stops to let in detectives looking for Thornhill—will he be discovered? Eve hides him in her bunk bed while the detectives question her—will she lie for Thornhill? They resume their seduction, and while Thornhill is in the bathroom, Eve gives a note to the porter—what's in the note? We discover Eve works for Vandamm when the note is revealed to say, "What do you want me to do with him in the morning?" This sets up the obvious question—what will happen to Thornhill in the morning?" which hooks us into the next sequence.

Set up a question each beat in a scene

You can go even deeper and set up a question for each beat in a scene, but due to space constraints, I won't analyze a scene in depth. You may refer to Chapter 8, however, for more on scene beats. For now, you can learn that a scene is like a mini-story composed of individual beats, which are the smallest unit of storytelling. A beat usually changes when there's a shift in a character's emotion or strategy to get what he wants in the scene. A beat is to a scene the same way a scene is to a plot, so setting up a question for each beat in a scene will arouse the curiosity of the reader throughout that scene.

Establish mystery by withholding information

Because a good story is carried by the questions set up by the writer, all stories are technically mysteries, not in the criminal "whodunit" sense, but in not knowing how the question will be answered at the end. Think of these questions as little hooks to pull the reader along from beginning to end. The motion of story is from question to answer, from doubt to certainty. Without questions, there's no script, and without answers, there is no emotional satisfaction.

One way to establish mystery is to withhold information the reader is itching to know. For example, you can set up a character with unclear motives, which will keep us wondering until the end, provided everything else in the story is interesting. In Sergio Leone's *Once Upon a Time in the West*, Harmonica Man's motives for the final showdown with Frank are withheld until the end.

Create intrigue by emphasizing illicit activity and secrecy

Another way to arouse curiosity is through character secrets, which create intrigue, like Evelyn's big secret in *Chinatown*. Any time you establish secrets—a secret scheme, a covert operation, a cover-up of information, or an assassination attempt (*JFK* had it all), it creates intrigue, especially if the scheme is illegal. I'll discuss secrets in depth in the section on surprise later in this chapter.

ANTICIPATION/HOPE/WORRY/FEAR

Anticipation is the feeling of looking forward to something that will happen in the future, whether it's positive, like winning a big prize, or negative, like a big showdown against a superior opponent. Once you've set up a piece of information, anticipation propels the reader into the future of the story, makes him wonder what will happen next, and thus forces him to turn the pages of your script to find out. Alfred Hitchcock, the undisputed master of suspense, once said, "There is no terror in a bang, only in the anticipation of it." Without anticipation, a story will drag and fail to hold the reader's interest. In fact, a plot is a series of events designed to create anticipation in the form of **curiosity** (what will happen), **suspense** (will it happen or not), **tension** (when will it happen), **hope** (looking forward to it happening), or **worry** (not looking forward to it happening). And when the anticipation is fulfilled, there's another array of potent visceral emotions, depending on the payoff: **surprise** (unexpected anticipation), **disappointment** (not getting what was hoped), or **relief** (not experiencing what was feared). This is an important point: Anticipation should always be fulfilled or else you risk creating dissatisfaction in the reader. I'm sure many of you have experienced the feeling of waiting for a promised phone call that never happened. So if you've established anticipation, make sure it's always paid off.

There are several techniques you can apply to your story to create this forward momentum known as anticipation:

ESTABLISH CHARACTER TRAITS

As you learned in the previous chapter, establishing character traits is a key requirement for building major characters. Once these traits are established, the reader will anticipate character behavior. For example, in *The Silence of the Lambs*, Hannibal Lecter is established as a vicious cannibalistic serial killer. This arouses our anticipation that if Lecter escapes, he will be a dangerous predator. In fact, this anticipation is fulfilled in the escape sequence where he viciously attacks the guards, and alluded to in the last scene, when Lecter says he's having an "old friend for dinner."

SET UP CHARACTER GOALS

Similarly, you can set up a goal for a character to create anticipation. Kurt Vonnegut once said, "Always have a character want something, even if it's a glass of water." And not just your protagonist and antagonist. Every single character in your story should want something at any point because desire will always create anticipation. It doesn't mean you have to create a whole subplot around that desire, but you can build a moment around it. Let's say we cared about a character in the story—we'll call her Tess. We learn in a scene that the villain plans to murder her because she witnessed him committing another crime. Once you set up this fact, we fear for Tess, and hope the villain will fail to murder her. We feel worry and hope simultaneously because we're looking ahead to the moment the villain will murder Tess. It's the anticipation of an established goal that causes forward movement in a story, not the dialogue or the action. Imagine that the villain visits Tess, but we're unaware of his intentions. The dialogue is hip, fresh, edgy, and witty, and the scene ends before the reader becomes bored. The scene lacks forward movement because there's no anticipation of any goal or intention. Now imagine we know he intends to kill Tess before this scene. When he meets up with Tess, he talks about the weather. No matter how dull the dialogue, the scene has forward movement because the intention has been established. Now you have suspense (will he accomplish his goal or be frustrated?) and tension (when will he strike?). You can make the scene even more fascinating by adding curiosity to the mix. Instead of letting the reader know he intends to kill the woman, how about he learns she betrayed him? When he visits her, and they talk about the weather, we are curious to know what he will do to her, and how. This compelling mix of suspense, tension, and curiosity is evident in *North by Northwest*, where Thornhill confronts Eve following the crop duster scene.

OVERLAP PROBLEMS AND SOLUTIONS/QUESTIONS AND ANSWERS

This technique is based on the principle that a problem attracts our attention until it is solved. Once a character accomplishes his goal, for example, we lose interest. Therefore, to sustain continuous interest not only do you want to delay the payoff, but also create a whole bunch of mini-problems and mini-goals throughout the story. More important, make sure that a problem is not resolved before another starts. In other words, try to sequence the problem-solution tracks so that there is no point in the entire story that has a hole of disinterest. As long as there's always an unanswered question, the reader will remain emotionally involved and keep turning the pages.

TALKING ABOUT THE FUTURE

Any time a character refers to a future event, we anticipate it, as it takes us forward to that event. For example, in the opening of *Sunset Boulevard*, Joe Gillis' voice-over tells us, "The body of a young man was found floating in the pool of a mansion, with two shots in his back and one in his stomach. Nobody important, really. Just a movie writer with a couple of "B" pictures to his credit. The poor dope. He always wanted a pool. Well, in the end he got himself a pool, only the price turned out to be a little high... Let's go back about six months and find the day when it all started." This is an interesting effect, as we technically go back to the past, and yet look forward to the future on the movie, anticipating Gillis' murder. The same technique opens *American Beauty*, when we meet Lester through his voice-over: "This is my neighborhood. This is my street. This... is my life. I'm forty-two years old. In less than a year, I'll be dead." This foreshadows his death, hooking the reader into wondering who will kill him.

It doesn't always have to be a voice-over. Any character talking about the future does the trick. In the opening scene of *Casablanca*, the European Man explains how things work in Casablanca: "As usual, the refugees and the liberals will be released in a few hours... the girl will be released later." This pulls us into the future, as we visualize the scene and understand what he means. Later, at Rick's Café, we eavesdrop on a conversation, as a man says, "Waiting, waiting, I'll never get out of here. I'll die in Casablanca." And when Renault says, "Rick, there is going to be some excitement here tonight, we are going to make an arrest in your café." All these are great examples of characters talking about the future.

PLANS AND DAYDREAMS

When a character sets up an intention to do something, going over a plan to accomplish a goal, they automatically create anticipation in the reader. Using *Casablanca* as an example again, when Renault says to Strasser that they know who murdered the couriers, he adds, "There is no hurry. Tonight he will come to Rick's. Everybody comes to Rick's." By mentioning his plan, we anticipate the arrest later that evening. Similarly, when Ugarte says to Rick, "After tonight, I'm through with the whole business. Rick, I'm leaving Casablanca." And later, "I will sell these for more money than even I ever dreamed of. Then... farewell to Casablanca." Plans and daydreams are an effective tool to engage the reader through anticipation.

But they don't necessarily have to be revealed. They are even more effective when they're secret because they add curiosity to the mix. **The secret plan** is when a character says, for example, "I know exactly what to do," then whispers it in someone's ear, and we cut away. It can also be the villain's secret plan to accomplish his goals, like in *Die Hard*, where we think his goal is the ransom for the hostages, but in fact, it's to have the FBI cut off electrical power to the building to open a vault. And remember all the *Mission Impossible* TV shows? The opening scenes often included the team talking about a plan that was never entirely revealed, but through the gadgets presented, we assumed a plan had been formulated and we looked forward to the mission.

APPOINTMENTS AND DEADLINES

We could argue that an appointment to meet or be somewhere is a goal, and thus creates anticipation. The same goes for a deadline. When someone is forced to accomplish something by a certain date and time, it's a goal too, albeit a more intense goal. This is why limiting time has been used often to create the more intense form of anticipation—suspense. I'll discuss time limits, or "ticking clocks," in the next section, but for now, look at this technique as another way to create anticipation in the reader. Any time a character tells another something like, "Meet me in the park at 3 P.M." or "You'd better finish your homework before your TV show starts," we automatically anticipate this future event. There are, of course, many film examples you could think of. For instance, in *North by Northwest*, when Thornhill escapes from the hotel into a cab and says, "Take me to the United Nations," that's technically an appointment with a location, and it takes us there mentally.

WORRIES AND PREMONITIONS

Worrying about something is feeling anxious about a future event. Therefore, having a character worry or feel uneasy about something, like having a premonition, will create anticipation. This becomes a more powerful effect when you make the reader worry as well, like when he cares about a character who may be in danger. In *North by Northwest*, in the exposition scene where the agency discusses Thornhill's predicament of being mistaken for an agent who doesn't exist, the housewife worries Thornhill won't survive much longer, while the stockbroker adds that they can't just wait to see who kills him first, Vandamm or the police. This small scene makes the reader look forward to the dangers ahead, but also worry about Thornhill.

WARNINGS

Warnings, which also include **predictions** and **omens**, are usually promises of unpleasant events to come, and thus set up the anticipation of conflict. Anytime a character warns another, it takes us into the future. You may be familiar with the term "foreshadowing," which is about setting up hints of future conflict. When you foreshadow, the reader anticipates. In *E.T.*, when Elliott's mom says they can call somebody to take the alien away, Elliott responds, "They'll give it a lobotomy or do experiments on it or something." And in *North by Northwest*, when Eve sees the detectives board the train, she warns, "Incidentally, I wouldn't order any dessert if I were you." Later in her drawing room, she says, "I've been thinking, it's not safe for you to roam around Chicago looking for this George Kaplan you've been telling me about. You'll be picked up by the police the moment you show your face."

THE MACGUFFIN

The MacGuffin is a term coined by Alfred Hitchcock, who made extensive use of this plot device in his thrillers. Its only purpose is to motivate the characters and advance the story. It's often a priceless, elusive object that almost everybody in the story is after, and some would even kill for it. Examples abound: The MacGuffin in *The Maltese Falcon* is the falcon statuette; in *Notorious*, it's the uranium hidden in wine bottles; in *Citizen Kane*, it's the unsolvable mystery of "Rosebud;" and in *North by Northwest*, the MacGuffin is the fictitious character "George Kaplan" who's being chased by enemy spies and by Thornhill, who tries to figure out who

Kaplan is. Again, this device works to create forward momentum because it is technically a goal to go after it, which arouses the reader's anticipation.

Moods

Setting the right mood can create a predisposition in the reader toward particular emotions in the future of the story. You can look at mood as the emotional climate of your story or scene, whether your intent is a humorous climate or suspenseful climate. The reason it works to create anticipation is that it promises the reader future emotions. For example, the opening sequence of *The Silence of the Lambs*, and most thrillers, sets up a tense suspenseful mood, which subconsciously tells the reader, "Stick around and you'll experience a lot more of these emotions." Setting up the right mood according to the genre of your story is an effective way to create anticipation in the reader because it's often subliminal, rather than the overt effect of the previous techniques. How to create specific moods will be discussed in depth in Chapter 9.

Dramatic Irony (Reader Superior Position)

I saved the most powerful tool for last, as it's the most effective way to create forward momentum in a story or scene. Dramatic irony is about putting the reader in a "superior position" to the characters by revealing information not known to the characters. It's like being let in on a secret. Based on this information, the reader knows what might happen (or not happen) to the oblivious characters, and he can only hope they make the right choices. This hope and fear takes the reader to the future and thus creates anticipation and active involvement. Alfred Hitchcock, to illustrate suspense, used the example of two people sitting at a table in a restaurant with a bomb ticking away underneath, and two versions of the same scene. In one version, like the two characters, we don't know there's a bomb. When it goes off, we're surprised and that's it. The other more potent version tilts the camera underneath the table so that we know there's a bomb, and we feel a whole gamut of emotions as the bomb is ticking down. The information doesn't have to be a bomb, of course. The reader can be made aware of another character eavesdropping on a damaging secret, a killer waiting in an apartment, an ally who is secretly the enemy, or a couple falling in love on the doomed Titanic. Using *North by Northwest*, note how often Ernest Lehman uses dramatic irony to keep us engaged: When we find out "George Kaplan" is a fictional character, while Thornhill and Vandamm are unaware; when Eve writes the note "What do I do with him in the morning;" when she arranges a meeting with Kaplan that turns out to be a lethal crop duster; when Eve turns out to be the real Number One; when Thornhill is "shot" in front of Vandamm; when Vandamm realizes Eve is a spy and plans to throw her off the plane; and when Thornhill tries to rescue Eve.

Dramatic irony also works when the character knows something we don't. This would be "Reader inferior position," where we know less than the characters. This creates curiosity. We want to know why the characters behave in a mysterious way, and anticipate the moment the secret will be revealed, like Evelyn's dark secret in *Chinatown*.

Dramatic irony can come from a **misunderstanding** between two characters, a device often used in comedies. When we realize one character has misunderstood another, we anticipate the moment when the error will be revealed. Think of the wonderful comedies driven by misunderstandings: *Bringing Up Baby*, *Dr. Strangelove*, *Some Like It Hot*, and *Tootsie*. The TV show *Three's Company* was driven by misunderstandings and misinterpretations, one character talking about one thing, and the other understanding another. In tragedies, misunderstandings often lead to death, like in *Romeo and Juliet* and *Othello*, where our superior position leads to compassion for the victim and helplessness for our inability to do anything about it. This is an effective device in horror films, where we know the killer is in the house, and the victim is unaware.

Deception is another plot device based on this concept of superior position, where in addition to creating anticipation, it also creates suspense, by setting up the questions, "Will the characters we care about be harmed by the deception," and "Will they discover it before it's too late?" Because anticipation to unpleasant events creates uncertainty in the mind of the reader, which is suspense, I will expand on this technique in the next section.

SUSPENSE/TENSION/ANXIETY/CONCERN/DOUBT

As the heading states, this essential visceral response is all about tension, anxiety, and doubt, which arise out of an uncertain, undecided, or mysterious situation. This offers an interesting paradox: In real life, we don't like to feel this stress, but we gladly spend our money to experience it in theaters. It's probably the most important element in dramatic storytelling because it holds the reader's attention from beginning to end. Since every story must be maintained by a level of uncertainty (what will happen next), and keep us guessing to avoid predictability, suspense is an absolute requirement in all stories, not just thrillers or action-adventures. Every story should create this feeling of eagerly wanting to know what will happen next.

One of the main reasons scripts are turned down is lack of suspense and uncertainty. In other words, they're predictable. Suspense should be everywhere in the script: At the story level—Will the hero achieve his goal? At the scene level—Will the hero get what he wants? And at the beat level—How will the hero react emotionally?

Suspense is more than just feeling uncertain about something. I can feel uncertain about how tomorrow will turn out, but I don't feel anxious or tense about it.

There has to be more to it. To complete the equation, let's look at what makes up suspense.

Caring about the character is the first crucial requirement. This is why the chapter on character comes before this one. It all starts with character. Once you have the tools to create connection with a character, you can set up threatening and uncertain situations that cause suspense. If the reader doesn't care about a character, there won't be any suspense when that character faces jeopardy.

The next step is establishing the **likelihood of threat**, meaning that the more likely a threatening event is to happen (a bomb with seven seconds to go, a plane running out of fuel, a diver running out of air, a bridge about to collapse, etc.) the more intense the suspense. We wouldn't feel the same tension if a character had a month to defuse a bomb because it's *unlikely* it will explode soon. This is why it's better to use reader superior position, and let the reader in on the potential danger, than keeping him in the dark, which only creates surprise when the bomb explodes out of nowhere. Knowing the bomb is there increases the likelihood of jeopardy. This is also why one of the most effective ways to create suspense is to limit time, like a ticking bomb or running out of air, because this increases the likelihood of failure. In fact, the more likely the threat, the more suspense we'll feel. For example, in *Speed*, we feel suspense throughout the script because it's unlikely that the speeding bus won't blow up.

The last element is **uncertainty of outcome**. This means the sympathetic character must have equal odds of succeeding and failing, which keeps the reader guessing and doubting, going from anticipating victory (defusing the bomb in time) to dreading defeat (the character being blown to bits). In short, suspense is about the potential of bad things happening to a character we care about. It is this play between knowing what might happen and not knowing what will happen that causes this potent feeling of suspense, and keeps us at the edge of our seat. Thus, the formula for suspense is as follows: Character empathy + Likelihood of threat + Uncertainty of outcome = SUSPENSE.

Although many refer to suspense as tension, you should be aware that tension is a slight offshoot of suspense. Tension is about **prolonging anticipation of outcome**. In fact, anything that causes suspense causes tension when it's unrelieved. Tension comes from the Latin "to stretch." Think of slowly stretching a rubber band, more and more… and more… and… Are you feeling the tension? The competent writer always tries to make the reader anxious over how things will turn out, and then delays the resolution for as long as it's effective. The longer the delay, the more tension. William Goldman once said, "Make 'em laugh. Make 'em cry. But most of all, make 'em wait." It can be overall tension (will protagonist achieve his goal?) or tension within a scene (will a character get what he wants?)

A couple of caveats about confusing suspense with similar sensations, specifically curiosity and surprise. Curiosity is often mistaken for suspense because our reaction is similar—intense involvement through mental doubt. In both cases, we wonder what's going to happen? But curiosity comes from *not knowing what the character wants*, while suspense comes from *not knowing whether his goal will be fulfilled or frustrated*. For example, the TV show *24* constantly plays with these two emotions: First setting up curiosity by showing an assassin prepping a rifle and waiting. We don't know whom he will shoot. This arouses curiosity. When we learn his target is the President of the United States, curiosity is out and immediately replaced by suspense—will he accomplish his mission or not? Curiosity is our desire to find the goal, while suspense can only exist if we know the goal. Once you know the goal, curiosity disappears and suspense takes over.

Another common confusion is with surprise. Remember Hitchcock's example of the two men sitting in a restaurant with a bomb under their table? When the bomb suddenly explodes, we have surprise—a shocking and unexpected event that lasts for a few seconds. If, however, you show us the bomb ticking under the table, then focus on the men calmly enjoying their meal, we would feel suspense. The longer we have to wait until the bomb explodes, the more tension we feel, a sensation that can last for a long as the bomb is ticking down, say fifteen minutes. Hitchcock was right when he said that fifteen minutes of tension was better than ten seconds of surprise.

So how do you achieve these most potent emotional states known as suspense and tension? Look at the following dramatic techniques:

CONTROL THE BALANCE BETWEEN FRUSTRATION AND REWARD

As you've just read, a key element of suspense is the uncertainty of outcome. The way to achieve this doubt is to control the balance between frustration and reward. In other words, play around with how often a character wins and loses. Frustration happens from the prevention or postponement of a desired goal; reward is when the goal is achieved. This is all about making sure your character wins some and loses some to avoid predictability. If character always wins, or always loses, there's no suspense, no uncertainty of outcome. The key is to go back and forth. This technique is often used in bad horror films where the heroine runs away from the monster (reward) but he's rapidly closing in on her (frustration); she reaches her car (reward) but can't find her keys (frustration); she finally finds them (reward) but as she tries to unlock the door, she drops them (frustration); she picks them up, manages to open the door, get in, and close it just as the monster reaches for her (reward); she tries to start the car, but it doesn't ignite (frustration); as the monster pounds on the windshield, the car finally starts and takes off, leaving the monster in the dust (reward).

CREATE IMMEDIACY

Immediacy is when you have to do something now! Quick! Not a second to spare! NOW! As human beings, we're excited by the now because that's when we feel most alive. Thrillers and horror films are particularly good at creating this sense of immediacy, which always happens when you deal with life-or-death situations. The reason comes from the likelihood of threat. As time runs out, the stakes get higher and higher, raising tension and immediacy. There's an effective scene in *Sneakers* when Bishop and his team call the NSA to make a deal and have set up nine relay stations around the world to avoid any traces. As Bishop speaks on the phone, we see a map of the world and a visual of the NSA tracing each relay, one by one. As the last one approaches Bishop's physical location, tension mounts, when Whistler yells out "Hang up, they've almost got us!... Hang up!!" That's immediacy, and a compelling way to excite the reader.

CREATE OPPOSITION/OBSTACLES/COMPLICATIONS

Because there can't possibly be any doubt in achieving a goal if there's no opposition, creating conflict is a prerequisite to suspense. No conflict means no doubt, and no doubt means no suspense. This is why conflict is the essence of all dramatic stories. Since conflict is discussed in every screenwriting class and book, and explored earlier in the tools to generate interest, I don't want to repeat basic information. By now, it should be clear that dramatic conflict establishes doubt that a character will accomplish his goal, and this creates suspense.

CROSS-CUT BETWEEN TWO DIFFERENT EVENTS (PARALLEL ACTION)

The word "suspense" comes from the Latin meaning, "to hang." You literally leave the reader hanging over the edge without rescue for as long as possible. This is part of the long tradition in television season finales when you see the words "to be continued." The technique of cross-cutting, also known as "Parallel Action," also works in scenes where you cut between two cliffhangers at the end of each scene. A perfect example is the cross-cutting in *The Silence of the Lambs* with Crawford and the SWAT team in one location, intercut with Buffalo Bill dealing with his victim holding his dog, and Clarice investigating the first victim as she eventually finds Buffalo Bill.

DELAY OUTCOME FOR TENSION

You already know that tension is prolonged anticipation. The longer you delay the fulfillment of an expectation, the more tension you create. You can prolong any expectation, like the moment before a jury announces a verdict, or a character makes a crucial decision. The best place to delay outcome for tension is usually after a surprising revelation. Think again of Hitchcock's restaurant bomb example. We're initially surprised when the bomb is revealed, and tense when we return to the innocent couple talking. We're also surprised in *North by Northwest* when Eve's note to Vandamm is revealed. We're shocked to discover she works for the enemy, but from this point on, we feel tension until the end of the script. We also see this in the climactic scenes of clichéd action films where the villain can kill the hero any time he wants but delays it with speeches, giving the hero time to think of an escape.

DISPLACE YOUR CHARACTER (FISH OUT OF WATER)

Displacing your character to a contrasting environment, commonly known as "the fish out of water," is another popular tool that creates conflict and doubt as to how the character will react to it. Think of a character's trait or attitude, find its opposite, and place that character in a corresponding setting, like sending an introvert to a party, or an aquaphobic on a cruise. There are plenty of script examples: *Beverly Hills Cop*, *The Wizard of Oz*, *Crocodile Dundee*, *E.T.*, and *One Flew Over the Cuckoo's Nest*.

FOCUS ON AN OBJECT

When an object can cause potential danger to a character we care about, focusing on it is an effective way to create tension. Think of a rope slowly unraveling on a rope bridge, the bomb under the table, a weapon on a table with two characters who hate each both eyeing it, the key in *Notorious* or the trunk in *Rope*. First, make sure you set up the object, then focus on it for tension.

FORCE CHARACTER INTO A DILEMMA

The dilemma is where the character confronts a critical choice between two equally attractive propositions, or the lesser of two evils. This is the fork in the road we usually see in the crisis at the end of Act 2. Remember that a *good* conflict isn't all black and white, right or wrong. A conflict with a clear answer isn't a conflict at all. If you had to choose between killing a pedophile or a kleptomaniac to save your life, the choice would be clear (I hope). This is not a dilemma. But having to choose between killing an innocent police officer or a firefighter, that's not such an easy choice. The longer you make the character agonize over the choice, the greater the tension. Think of *Casablanca*, where Rick must choose between love and politics, *Training Day* (morality and admiration), *The Godfather* (morality and family), or the mother of all dilemmas, *Sophie's Choice*—having to choose which of your two children survives.

FORCE A CHARACTER TO FACE HIS FEARS

In the previous chapter, you saw how adding fears to a character greatly enhances his complexity. When you force a character to face his fears, it also enhances suspense. A great example of this is the final moment of the opening sequence in *Raiders of the Lost Ark*, where Indiana Jones faces a snake in the plane's cockpit and later in the tomb. Any fear that must be confronted in a scene will create tension—how will the character react, and what will happen next?

INCREASE JEOPARDY

Anything that has a high risk of injury or death, any dangerous situation, is jeopardy to a character, which creates doubt that he will survive. Thus, adding jeopardy is always a good way to create suspense. And by increasing the danger, you increase the tension. This, of course, is the way writers engage the reader in thrillers, action-adventures, and horror films.

INCREASE REVELATIONS

Any time a character learns something so important it affects the plot, it can be labeled a revelation. Traditionally, in thrillers and mysteries, an increase in revelations means the protagonist is getting closer to his goal, which gives us a sense of immediacy, and therefore tension. Also, in the earlier section on delaying outcome for tension, you've seen how a surprising revelation can lead to tension by delaying the consequence of that revelation. Think of the moment towards the end of *The Empire Strikes Back* when Darth Vader reveals he's Luke's father—a shocking revelation that creates intense suspense, as we wait to see how Luke will react.

INCREASE UNPREDICTABILITY

You already know that the threat of violence can create suspense, but when you don't know where or when that threat will be paid off, the tension can be unbearable. This is all about unpredictability. You can raise the tension even higher by breaching the reader's expectations for the worse. If the reader thinks it knows what will happen, like when a character has seven days to rescue hostages, and suddenly he learns something worse is in store, like a nuclear strike, you increase tension. You can also make the deadline unpredictable, like suddenly pushing up a due date, or a ticking bomb counting faster after cutting the wrong wire.

READER SUPERIOR POSITION

As promised, we revisit this powerful tool, also known as *dramatic irony*, knowing it can arouse anticipation in the reader by revealing information that's not known to the characters. When this information is threatening to the characters, you also establish suspense. This is a proven way to engage the reader through a myriad of emotions. For example, one of the more tense scenes in *Die Hard* is when hero and villain come face to face. When Gruber pretends to be one of the hostages, we know he's the villain, but McClane doesn't. Suspense is established, tension rises throughout their conversation, and peaks when McClane gives him a gun.

REMIND THE READER OF THE STAKES

Stakes are the consequences of a character reaching, or failing to reach, his objective. Writers always ask themselves what's the worst thing that could happen if a character doesn't get what he wants, which adds a believable and compelling motivation to their actions. You've read about stakes in the previous chapter, so

I won't repeat myself here. I'll just remind you how important they are, the same way your characters can remind the reader of what's at stake in the story. Think of *Casablanca* and how often the importance of the letters of transit is mentioned. Each mention is not only a reminder in case you forgot, but an additional injection of suspense. Obviously, stakes have to be high in order to be effective, which is why most are usually about survival—life or death, physical and emotional.

RAISE THE STAKES

Knowing that the higher the stakes the more intense the suspense, gradually increasing them adds to the tension by increasing the character's desperation. This is where Maslow's *Hierarchy of Needs*, explored in the previous chapter, comes in handy. As they relate to the concept of stakes, the needs are arranged from least crucial (self-actualization) to the most vital (survival). When you reach the top, you can then escalate the threat from individual to global survival. Make things worse and worse for your character until you finally reach the climax. This is no longer just about the hero surviving but about the fate of the entire world.

SET UP A CHARACTER WITH UNCLEAR MOTIVES

By keeping a character's motives hidden, you establish curiosity. As long as they remain unclear, the reader will feel tension until they're revealed. One of the main drives in the classic western *Once Upon a Time in the West* is the Harmonica Man's secret motive for wanting a duel with the villainous Frank. Hints are peppered throughout the film, but the tension remains high until the very end when his motives are finally revealed. Obviously, you don't have to keep a motive unclear for the entire story. Maybe you can do so here and there for just a scene to add extra tension.

SET UP AN "ODD COUPLE" SITUATION

The same way you can create suspense by contrasting a character with the setting in the fish-out-of-water technique, you can have the same effect by pitting contrasting characters, or odd couples, against each other. You already know this is a good way to increase your concept's appeal, which is why "buddy" pictures are always popular. This technique also works in individual scenes with minor characters, any time you want to inject additional suspense in a scene.

SET UP DANGEROUS WORK

We usually associate tension with individuals involved in dangerous work like bomb defusers, deep-sea divers, fire fighters, police officers, soldiers, or spies. So this is about setting up a dangerous task or mission to establish suspense. It can be brain surgery, going out in space, exploring the Amazon Jungle, searching for a serial killer, etc.

SET UP DEADLINES OR LIMIT TIME (THE TICKING CLOCK)

A bomb will go off in *eight hours*. We only have *an hour's* worth of air in the submarine. You must marry before turning *twenty-one*. These are examples of the famous ticking clock technique, one of the most used techniques because it works. Time pressure creates suspense because it increases the likelihood of failure by introducing an additional obstacle—time. The time limit can last the length of the entire movie, as in *High Noon*, or just one scene, as in James Bond defusing a nuclear bomb in *Goldfinger*.

Deadlines don't have to be just about time. They can be a **potential victim**, like in most serial killer movies (*The Silence of the Lambs*, *Se7en*) where the detective tries to stop the killer before he kills again. It can be **what's at stake** for an innocent man wrongly accused, like in *North by Northwest* or *The Fugitive* where the hero tries to clear himself before he's caught by the cops. It can be **the ground** when somebody is falling from a tall building, like Lois Lane falling to her death in *Superman*—can he save her before she hits the ground? It can be the bus's **speed** in *Speed*, or **air** in *Apollo 13*.

SPACE SUSPENSE

Whereas a time limit deals with doubt as to whether something will be accomplished in time, space suspense deals in not knowing where the threat is. This is all about the anxiety of the unknown. Where is the killer? Where is the bomb? Space suspense depends, of course, on a confined area, like when someone stalks an alien in a confined spaceship. We're not waiting for the clock to tick down, but for the alien to strike out of anywhere. The chill comes knowing the threat is hiding somewhere, but we don't know exactly where. Most of the tension in *Alien* comes from this technique.

UNPREDICTABLE CHARACTER RESPONSE

Any kind of unpredictability creates doubt, and thus suspense. This technique is about making a character's response to a situation unpredictable, creating doubt as to how a character will respond to an event. The most memorable scene in *GoodFellas* is Joe Pesci's terrifying "Do I amuse you?" speech. When Ray Liotta innocently calls him "funny," Pesci suddenly turns scary: "Whaddaya mean I'm funny?... Funny how? I mean funny like a clown? I amuse you?" Another tense scene caused by character unpredictability is the Russian roulette game in *Deer Hunter*. Also, the unstable behavior of Mr. Blonde in *Reservoir Dogs* peaks in tension at the cutting of the cop's ear.

THE TRAP OR CRUCIBLE

Remember how conflict involves a goal, an obstacle, but more important an unwillingness to compromise? To be effective, a character must be bonded to his goal, meaning that he can't just quit and walk away, or else there wouldn't be a story to tell. He must accomplish the goal because he doesn't have a choice. This is called "The Trap" or "The Crucible," which is usually a closed environment from which characters cannot run away. Think of *Apollo 13*, *Castaway*, *Phone Booth*, or any "*Die Hard in a (Blank)*" thriller. The characters don't want to be there, but they have no choice. They're stuck. The trap can be anything that causes a character to feel trapped. It can be a marriage, family, prison, a ticking clock, an island, a haunted spaceship, or even a character trait, like in *As Good As It Gets*. The crucible in *The Terminator* is the cyborg himself, because Sarah Connor has no choice but to be involved in the conflict. If she ignores him, she dies. So the trap can be any reason a character must act, where no compromise is possible. There's no turning back.

TENSION RELEASES

Because tension is a physical effect, too much of it can become unpleasant. When film critic Roger Ebert reviewed *Open Water*, he said that after the movie was over, he felt the need to go outside and walk in the sunshine to shake all the tension out of him. This is because the film had constant intense tension from beginning to end, without any tension releases. Regardless of your genre, if you plan to have scenes of concentrated tension, it's always a good idea to have tension releases, like laughter or crying, or any sort of relief. In *The Terminator*, the slow scenes act as tension releasers in order to balance the film. Imagine what it would feel like if it were just intense action sequence after intense action sequence from beginning to end. One of the biggest laughs in *Raiders of the Lost Ark* happens when Indiana Jones shoots the swordsman after such a long buildup with the sword. All this tension, including the prior chase sequence, is released by the quick shooting, which was original and surprising, causing the laughter, and a release of tension. This technique is also evident in Oliver Stone's *Scarface*. When Tony shoots his boss' two bodyguards, there's a long, tense moment as the third bodyguard sweats it out. Tony then says to his buddy, "Offer him a job," and both we and the bodyguard let out a sigh of relief. Tension release can also be established through tears when separated loved ones are finally reunited, like at the end of *The Joy Luck Club*.

SURPRISE/DISMAY/AMUSEMENT

With the four major storytelling emotions I've discussed so far—interest, curiosity, anticipation, and suspense, you should be well on your way to holding the reader's attention. Unfortunately, there always comes a point when a script risks becoming predictable. This is because a reader always tries to figure things out, creating possibilities, and guessing what will happen next. It's part of the fun. The more his guesses turn out to be accurate, the more predictable your script becomes, giving it the kiss of death. There is nothing more discouraging than anticipating correctly the direction of a story, a character's next move, or what he will say. As the writer, you can take advantage of the reader's tendency to look ahead, thereby avoiding predictability through surprise.

When Jean Cocteau was asked, "What can I do to be a better writer?" he replied, "Surprise me." Surprise is the most powerful enrichment of suspense since it often comes before or after suspense. For instance, when we learn a killer waits in the house, we have surprise, followed by tension until the victim enters the house. Then, depending on the writer's creativity, we can have predictability if the killer strikes as expected, or surprise if the victim turns the tables on the killer, thus twisting our expectations.

Surprise is all about the unexpected. William Goldman advises writers to "give the audience what they want, but not in the way they expect." The real question in the reader's mind is not, "Will the hero win in the end," which is the realm of tension, but how. If a man intends to kiss a woman, we anticipate he will. When he does, it's fine. It's the way he finally gets to it that should be surprising and unpredictable.

The way to achieve surprise is, of course, through **unexpected twists and turns**. The sudden shock of the unexpected. The unforeseen revelation or unanticipated reversal. Readers love being thrown off-balance by clever twists. The bigger the better. In fact, huge surprises, the kind that turn a story upside down, are so rare in screenplays that they can often sell a script on the spot. Think of *The Crying Game, The Usual Suspects, The Sixth Sense,* or *Se7en.*

Great scripts are full of surprises. But they don't have to be just about plot. You can create character surprises by revealing unexpected flaws in the hero, or an unexpected virtue in the villain. You can even surprise the reader through dialogue. It doesn't matter how you do it as long as it's unexpected and logical. In other words, a twist can't come out of nowhere. It must always come with a rational explanation.

Because surprise comes from unfulfilled expectations, you first need to establish anticipation, which you can then play with. In fact, comedy is based on the use of surprise to cause laughter. We laugh at a punchline because it twists our expectations. Let's explore the ways you can create surprise in the reader:

UNEXPECTED OBSTACLES AND COMPLICATIONS

You've read about conflict in previous sections. Here, we explore it as it pertains to the unexpected obstacle or complication. Because many writers confuse the two, it's helpful to discuss each one separately, though they're two sides of the same coin. On one side is the obstacle, which is something that stands in the way of achieving a goal. It can be anything—a person, an object, or event that blocks the way. The key is that it causes a character extra thought, effort, and time to overcome it. Once the obstacle is surmounted, the character is back on track.

Imagine a flooded roadway on your way to New York from Los Angeles. You just take a little detour and eventually you're back on track.

Complications, on the other hand, would be losing your car and having to take a plane to New York. Same destination, but a completely different path. Like an obstacle, a complication can be person, object, or situation, except that it alters the course of the action that follows. An obstacle creates a temporary change, while a complication takes you on a completely different track, and things just aren't the same. An elevator not working on your way to an interview is an obstacle. Falling madly in love with the interviewer is a complication. This is why complications are called "plot twists." They deviate a character from a previously expected path. As always, the key to using obstacles and complications in your story is that they must be unexpected to create surprise in the reader.

DISCOVERIES AND REVELATIONS

Whatever piece of information the protagonist learns which advances the story—a clue, a secret, evidence, a weapon, a diary, can be considered a discovery or revelation. For discussion purposes, a discovery is an *active* process, meaning that it's the hero who finds the information, whereas a revelation is *revealed* to the hero—a passive process where the hero learns the information from another source. The hero is given that information. *Chinatown's* biggest secret when Evelyn reveals her daughter is also her sister is a revelation because it is Evelyn who tells Jake, even if he beats it out of her. If it were Jake who discovered this shocking secret through his own investigation, like going over records, it would have been a discovery. This minor distinction is nonetheless important in balancing your story with active discoveries and passive revelations.

A discovery can occur when a significant fact dawns on a character—that moment of realization, the light bulb, Eureka moment when the solution to the puzzle appears, like *In the Line of Fire* when Frank Horrigan finally figures out the killer's plan and rushes to the hotel.

Usually, discoveries and revelations are learned simultaneously by the hero and the reader, creating surprise in both. But only a revelation can be part of the reader superior position technique when a key piece of information is revealed to us, but not the hero. For example, when the George Kaplan mystery is revealed to us by the Professor and his team in *North by Northwest*—a crucial reveal—Thornhill has no idea.

When the discovery or revelation comes at the end of a story, it's often a twist ending that not only startles or shocks, but also changes everything we have seen before, like the endings of *The Sixth Sense* and *The Usual Suspects*.

Obviously, for something to be discovered, first it must be hidden. To be surprised is to discover something previously unknown. Therefore, to have surprising discoveries and revelations, you have to master the art of hiding and revealing information. You have to control when, how often, and how much information you give the reader. The best way to do so is to leave events off-screen, which makes their discovery emotionally satisfying. For instance, in *The Sixth Sense*, leaving out just one crucial scene—Malcolm Crowe's death, funeral, or any mention by other characters that he actually died, changes our perception of the entire story when we discover it at the end.

REVERSALS

Reversals are a more compelling form of discoveries or revelations because they turn the story upside down. This is what the word means—a change from one situation to its opposite, like going from rich to poor, happy to sad, ally to enemy, or vice versa. In *Some Like It Hot*, when Joe and Jerry reappear at the train station in drag, that's a reversal.

The reason reversals are so compelling is that you can't get more unpredictable than that. 180 degrees is the most something can turn. When we expect a kiss and we get a slap instead, like in *Moonstruck*, that's a surprising reversal. When we expect a fight with the swordsman in *Raiders of the Lost Ark* and we get a quick shooting, this reversal generates the biggest laugh. This is the key to surprise: if the reader expects one thing to happen, make sure it doesn't always happen that way.

Like a discovery or revelation, a reversal can be anything—an action, event, or verbal statement, as long as it creates the opposite of what the reader anticipated. In *American Beauty*, we expect Lester to be fired. Instead, he blackmails his boss and walks away richer. In *Finding Nemo*, one of the highlights in the film is the Dory character, who has short-term amnesia problems. Talk about reversals throughout the film: every time we experience hope when she helps Marlin, the feeling reverses to disappointment and frustration when we realize Dory can't remember what she's helping about. In *Casablanca*, one of the classic examples of reversal is when Louis says, "Round up the usual suspects," after Rick has shot Major Strasser. It reverses our expectation that Louis will arrest him. Using reversals to surprise the reader is one of the most powerful tools to keep your story fresh and unpredictable.

SECRETS

Secrets revealed are the essence of surprise. You can't have one without the other. It can be a **story secret** that drives the entire script, and is revealed at the end climax, like in *Chinatown*, *The Usual Suspects*, and *The Sixth Sense*. It can be a **scene secret** that only drives one scene, like keeping a secret from your résumé in a job interview. Or it can be a **character secret**, like a secret character trait or a dark secret from their past. We always enjoy it when a new layer of character is revealed, especially when we thought we knew everything about that character. When the reader knows the secret, we have, of course, superior position, as the reader is held by the tension that the secret may be reveled at any time. Think of *Tootsie* or *Some Like It Hot*. When the secret is both unknown to the hero and the reader, we have surprise, like in *The Usual Suspects*.

READER INFERIOR POSITION

Whereas reader superior position is about the reader knowing more than the hero does, this is the reverse technique—the hero knows more than the reader. This creates curiosity, but more important, it leads to a potential surprise when the information is revealed to the reader. This tool is often used in heist films, like *Ocean's 11* and *12*, where the characters know more about their plans and schemes than the audience. This completes the trilogy of creative choices when it comes to revealing information: **discoveries and revelations**, where both character and reader learn information simultaneously; **reader superior position**, where the reader learns information but the character remains in the dark; and **reader inferior position**, where the character knows information the reader doesn't, and which eventually leads to a surprising revelation.

SHOCK

When a surprise is sudden and intense, or when it knocks your socks off, fills you with disgust or revulsion, or even grips you with horror or terror, it can be said to be shocking. Think of the most shocking moments in films—the gut buster scene in *Alien*, the horse's head in *The Godfather*, or most scenes in *The Exorcist*. It doesn't have to be a bloody moment in a horror film. It can happen in a comedy, like the shock of seeing Michael in drag for the first time in *Tootsie*. In fact, shocking moments in comedies often create the biggest laughs. The key is to make sure the moment is completely unexpected, sudden, and extreme. Killing off your protagonist in the first act would be quite shocking, as Hitchcock proved in *Psycho*. Only do this if it makes sense in your story, otherwise you risk frustrating the reader.

RED HERRINGS AND MISDIRECTIONS

Since surprise is based on unexpected anticipation, one of the best ways to surprise the reader is to make him anticipate something else by misdirecting his attention—the same technique used by magicians, showing you their sleeve while palming a coin. In stories, this is called the "Red Herring," which can be a false lead the detective pursues to solve a mystery, a clue, a suspicious character, or an incident, like in *The Silence of the Lambs* when the FBI raids the wrong house. Remember how surprised you were when Gumb answered the door and it was Clarice standing there? We were intentionally misdirected by the writer. And we can't omit one of the cleverest misdirections of all time in *The Sixth Sense*. When the truth is finally revealed, we revisit each scene and realize we weren't tricked, simply misdirected into believing Crowe survived his shooting.

Although red herrings are a staple of mysteries, they can be used in any genre, like when a character pursues a wrong goal, or trusts the wrong person who will later betray him. It doesn't matter what it is as long as you intentionally lead the reader in the wrong direction, while still following the logic of your story. Just make sure the mislead is always revealed later in order to have the surprising effect on the reader.

SETUPS AND PAYOFFS

Great films are memorable because they have many surprises in them. By now, you should be aware that surprises come from the audience expecting one thing and the writer delivering another. This is done through setups and payoffs. Throughout your script, you should be "planting" the seeds that will come to fruition later in the script—an object, action, place, or a line of dialogue that you can later payoff to create surprise. Think of the matchbook in *North by Northwest*, the pen in *The Silence of the Lambs*, the snake phobia in *Raiders of the Lost Ark*, the "bad for glass" comment in *Chinatown*, or the "I'll be back" line in *The Terminator*. It's important to note that although a setup can be clichéd, its consequence or payoff should be unique enough to be surprising. One of the joys in *Pulp Fiction*, despite its violent content, is the surprising payoffs to the familiar setups, such as a couple intending to rob a diner, or a boxer who fails to throw a fight and must skip town.

THE LIFELINE

In the book *Story Sense*, former USC professor Paul Lucey talks of the *lifeline*, which can be a skill, a tool, a weapon, an ally, a piece of information, a strategy, or whatever the hero uses to solve a story problem. You could look at it as the hero's ace in the hole. Examples of lifelines include the spacesuit in *Alien*, the loading machine in *Aliens*, and the gun taped in McClane's back in *Die Hard*. Obviously, lifelines need to be set up earlier for an emotional payoff or else you risk a "Deus Ex Machina" contrivance, as you'll see next.

COINCIDENCE (DEUS EX MACHINA)

Although most events should follow a logical progression, sometimes you can get away with using coincidences, contrivances, or accidental events in a story, like being at the wrong place at the wrong time and witnessing a crime, or a chance meeting between characters. In fact, you could argue that most inciting events are coincidences that ignite a story to a logical conclusion.

Therefore, it's okay to use a coincidence to make things worse for your character, like an obstacle or complication. What is usually frowned upon, however, is the use of coincidence to solve a problem or make things easier for your main character during a crisis. This is called "Deus Ex Machina," a term that literally means "God from the machine." It comes from the ancient Greek plays, which used gods to resolve difficult story problems. Today, the lazy writer would create a sudden storm to get his hero out of a burning house, or win the lottery to pay off a gambling debt to the mob. As much as possible, you should avoid such easy outs for your characters. They insult the reader and are emotionally unsatisfying. Make sure you set up the logic of what may be construed later on as a coincidence, and that it doesn't solve the main crisis. You want to make the hero work, solve the problem through his own skills or allies, and thus earn his victories.

COMBINE IT WITH TENSION AND RELIEF

Many writers like the emotional impact created by the triple punch of surprise combined with suspense and relief, especially in horror scripts. For example, a teen hears a noise. We know the killer is waiting, but she doesn't—suspense. The teen is scared but we feel even more tension because of our superior position. She checks the nooks and crannies in the dark—tension. She hears the noise again. Her cat jumps off the sofa—surprise, and gradual relief. Then, the killer strikes—shock. Sure, it's a familiar scene, but it works, especially in the hands of great storytellers who have mastered the art of emotional manipulation. This combination technique involves false payoffs to suspenseful setups. We expect tragedy so we brace ourselves for the shock, but when nothing happens, we relax, then tragedy strikes, and we're shocked.

THRILL/JOY/LAUGHTER/SADNESS/TRIUMPH

Here we deal a group of emotions that are both vicarious, meaning characters may feel them because of the events they experience, and visceral—the reader feels them as well. When a character feels joy or sadness, for example, so does the reader, provided he's bonded with that character. But the reader may also feel joy or sadness from learning something the character doesn't know through superior position.

While these emotions are not as essential as the previous five we've explored so far, they're nonetheless important enough to warrant a brief look at how they come about. These are emotions we pay good money to experience at the theatre, especially thrills, triumph, and laughter. So let's look at the tools that create these desired feelings:

SPECTACLE

Most writers rely on spectacle to generate thrills in their reader by describing over-the-top events, death-defying stunts, or special effects that excite the senses and make you go "WOW!" Think of the opening scenes of most James Bond movies, the *Titanic* sinking sequences, the dinosaurs in *Jurassic Park*, the stunts and imagery in *The Matrix*, and most of *Star Wars*. Opening your script with spectacle may also be a good strategy since it's such an intense attention grabber. Just remember not to overdo it at the expense of your story. Rather, make sure it's part of the plot and that your main character is involved in the scene.

SEXUALITY AND VIOLENCE

Another form of spectacle is sexuality and violence. Sigmund Freud said that our simplest impulses are sex and aggression. This is why they can be so viscerally gripping in stories—violence, the most visually gripping form of conflict; sexuality, the most visually gripping form of love. Both produce strong emotional reactions in the reader and should be used with caution. Like spectacle, they can be part of an opening scene, like in *Basic Instinct*, which combines the two to kick-start the story.

HUMOR

Comedies have always been an appealing genre for producers and a proven commodity at the box-office, so generating laughter is clearly a useful tool to engage the reader. Space constraints, however, prevent me from analyzing the dynamics of humor in depth. Note that there are many excellent sources that analyze how laughter is created. I'd highly recommend aspiring writers take the time to study them. For now, understand that humor is usually based on surprise, or unexpected anticipation, so most of the techniques discussed in the previous section on surprise are the first step in producing laughter.

Obviously, humor is the essential element in writing comedies, but it can also be useful in any genre, including dramas. The reason is that it can act as a tension releaser, providing the lulls that balance the dramatic intensity of the story.

ESCAPES

Heroes escaping from dangerous situations, or confinements such as prisons, can provide a sense of relief and exhilaration over their newfound security and freedom. Think of Indiana Jones' close escape from Belloq and the Indians in the opening sequence of *Raiders of the Lost Ark*, or Captain Hilts's in *The Great Escape*. When they involve a character we care about, escape will bring about joy and relief. If it involves a dangerous villain, however, it'll arouse dismay and dread, as exemplified in Hannibal Lecter's brilliant escape in *The Silence of the Lambs*.

SEPARATIONS AND REUNIONS

When you separate or reunite two characters we deeply care about, it puts the reader in touch with the sorrow of separation and the joy of reunion. Think about the sad feelings you experienced at the end of *E.T.* when Elliott and his extraterrestrial friend are separated, or in *Titanic* when Rose lets go of the frozen Jack. And how about the joy of an overdue reunion between parent and child, like in *I Am Sam* or *The Joy Luck Club*?

VICTORIES AND LOSSES

The same goes for victories and losses. When a character wins a difficult contest, for example, we experience a vicarious sense of triumph, especially when the victory, literal or emotional, was highly unlikely (*Rocky, The Karate Kid, Seabiscuit*).

Similarly, we experience sorrow when a character loses a contest or something very important to him (*Titanic, E.T., Ghost*) As you saw in the previous chapter, any loss or misfortune brings about pathos for the character we care about, while winning and good fortune creates happiness. A proven technique to keep the reader's eyes glued to the page is to alternate your main character's victories and losses throughout your story. When the reader asks the central question, "Will the hero accomplish his goal?" you answer it with a "Yes" by providing a small victory, and a "No" by providing a defeat, back and forth—yes, no, yes, no, which makes the reader go through hope and fear, happiness and sorrow, triumph and tragedy.

POETIC JUSTICE

This has more to do with the supernatural belief of karma and heavenly retribution than with legal justice. Poetic justice is the highly satisfying emotional response we feel when the innocent is vindicated and the guilty punished when the law doesn't accomplish it. For example, if you write a story about a man who kills his wife, gets away with it, and buys a boat with the insurance money, but then, the boat sinks and the man drowns, that would be a satisfying poetic justice. This is all about the villain getting his due, or the good guy experiencing good fortune when all else fails, and it works especially well in endings.

EMPATHY/COMPASSION/ADMIRATION/CONTEMPT

I include these feelings here, even though they were discussed in the previous chapter, because they're essential to the positive emotional experience of a story. Without character bonding, we may experience curiosity and surprise from the story's events, but never the more satisfying ones, such as anticipation, dread, suspense, joy, or sorrow. Without empathy and compassion for the main character, and contempt for the antagonist, the reader will never be fully engaged in your story.

MELODRAMA AND SENTIMENTALITY

When it comes to character emotions in dramatic situations, don't overdo it. When a character bursts into tears or explodes in a rage, the reader needs to see the strong circumstances that lead to these extreme emotions. Otherwise, you create melo-drama, or sentimentality, instead of drama. To be credible a dramatic scene depends on the emotional truth of the characters. If the reader doesn't believe the emotions, you have melodrama. In real drama, the emotions expressed are well motivated and honest, whereas in melodrama they're under-motivated, meaning the resulting emotions are over-dramatized. They're often shallow and comedic, like in bad soap operas, and therefore emotionally unsatisfying.

The best way to write emotional truth is to imagine feeling the same emotions as your characters based on the circumstances of the story. Ask yourself, "If I were this character in these circumstances, how would I feel, and what would I do?" As Robert Frost said, "No tears in the writer, no tears in the reader."

ON THE PAGE: STORY IN ACTION

I chose *North by Northwest* because it's an exciting story on many levels. It also has examples of many techniques discussed in this chapter.

Due to space constraints, I can't go through the whole script. Besides, I've already used most of the script's first and second acts as examples so far. This leaves me with the third act to highlight how many of the techniques are evident in the script. I'll go over the act beat by beat, indicating which technique was used to arouse a particular emotion in the reader. This way you can see these techniques in action as they create an exciting act from beginning to end.

The third act begins when Thornhill is captured at the auction by police (victory and defeat) and driven to the Professor (reversal), who explains everything (revelations): Vandamm is trying to take microfilmed government secrets out of the country; George Kaplan never existed—he's only a decoy created to divert attention from a real agent.

The Professor asks Thornhill to be Kaplan for another 24 hours to help save the life of the endangered agent (immediacy-dilemma-high stakes-dangerous work) but he refuses, claiming he's only an average citizen (opposition). The Professor reveals that the endangered double agent is Eve Kendall (revelation-reversal-secret-shock). Thornhill reluctantly agrees to go to Rapid City, follow Vandamm, and pretend to be Kaplan in order to save Eve's life (plan-anticipation).

At the Mount Rushmore cafeteria, Thornhill meets Vandamm, Leonard, and Eve with a proposition: He will let Vandamm leave the country without interference in exchange for Eve (curiosity-tension). Vandamm refuses. Thornhill grabs Eve, but she pulls out a gun and shoots him, then rushes out and drives away (surprise-reversal-shock). Thornhill, helped by the Professor, is carried out on a stretcher (curiosity).

Later, in a forest, an unharmed Thornhill meets with Eve (reversal, deception implied, reunion) where she apologizes for lying to him (empathy). She reveals how she became involved with Vandamm and that now she's in love with Thornhill (revelation). They kiss, but Eve says she must get back to Vandamm to continue spying (loss-opposition). When Thornhill says he'll want to spend more time with her after Vandamm has left the country, he learns from the Professor that Eve's mission is to fly away with him for good (revelation-reversal-stakes raised). Thornhill is furious for being duped and losing Eve (separation).

Amid radio news reports that Kaplan is in critical condition after the shooting scene at Mount Rushmore, Thornhill is locked up in a hospital room (defeat-obstacle). After sending the Professor to fetch a pint of bourbon, he escapes through the window and into another room, surprising its female occupant (reversal-escape-tension). She cries "Stop," but after putting on her glasses, she purrs another more inviting "Stop" (humor-tension release).

Thornhill takes a cab up to Vandamm's house at the edge of Mount Rushmore to prevent Eve from leaving (jeopardy-high stakes). Outside the window, he overhears Vandamm and Leonard (superior position). Leonard distrusts Eve—the shooting was just too neat (complication-jeopardy-immediacy). He shoots Vandamm with Eve's gun to prove his point (unpredictable character response) and Vandamm is shocked and disappointed that Eve betrayed him (discovery-reversal-loss). He plots to throw her off the plane (plans-higher stakes-superior position).

Eve rejoins them in the living room for a drink (delay outcome for tension). Thornhill tries to warn her by scribbling, "They're on to you" on his monogrammed (ROT) matchbook (focus on object-warnings-payoff-revelations) and drops it next to her. Alerted, Eve makes an excuse to go back to her room (reward) and finds Thornhill who tells her her life is in danger (stakes reminder). But her duty to complete her mission wins out, and she joins Vandamm and Leonard as they escort her to the plane (reversal-separation-delay outcome for tension).

The housekeeper discovers Thornhill when she notices his reflection in the television set. She detains him at gunpoint (focus on object-obstacle-reversal). As Eve is about to board the aircraft, two gunshots are heard from the house (unexpected complication-concern-lifeline). In the confusion, Eve takes off with Vandamm's statue/microfilm and joins Thornhill who's escaped with a getaway car (reward-victory). But the estate is surrounded by a locked gate (frustration-obstacle), so they ditch the car and escape by foot through the woods, eventually finding themselves at the top of Mount Rushmore (obstacle-increased jeopardy).

Chased by Leonard and his henchmen, Eve and Thornhill are forced to climb down the monument (spectacle-trap), a tension relieved for a few seconds when Thornhill asks Eve to marry him (humor). One of the henchmen jumps Thornhill with a knife (increased jeopardy-unpredictability-frustration), but he's soon thrown over the edge (reward-hope). Leonard snatches the statue from Eve's hands and throws her down the rock wall, where she clings for life (high stakes-frustration). Thornhill reaches down to pull up her outstretched hand, while clinging for support with his other hand (jeopardy-reward-hope). Leonard appears above him and sadistically grinds and crushes his hand with his foot (frustration-reversal-high stakes-dread). A shot rings out, and Leonard falls to his death (reversal-reward).

As Vandamm is arrested by the Professor, Thornhill struggles to pull Eve to safety from the rock ledge (one last jeopardy-frustration), and abruptly pulls her into an upper train berth, saying, "Come along, Mrs. Thornhill" (reward-victory-joy).

There you have it, dramatic techniques in action in the last act of a classic script. Sure, most of them were designed to evoke anticipation, tension, and surprise since this is, after all, a Hitchcock film, but you must be aware by now that they can be used in the telling of any story, regardless of genre. These techniques enrich any story.

Now that you've developed a compelling story, it's time to put it all together in a form that's universally appreciated. Let's talk about structure...

7
STRUCTURE
Engaging Design

"Screenwriting is like fashion. All clothes have the same structure. A shirt has two sleeves and buttons, but not all shirts look alike."
-AKIVA GOLDSMAN

It's remarkable that the simplest concept in storytelling is the one that has generated the most debate. So much has been written and taught about structure that there isn't much I could add to the discussion. For this reason, this will be the shortest chapter in the book. Just in case you're still confused by the subject, allow me to review the most important basic points.

THE BASICS: WHAT YOU NEED TO KNOW

Structure, at its core, is simply about the form or shape of your story, how the events you've created to make up your story all fit together into a unified whole that arouses maximum emotion. Structure is the architecture, the design of your story. Just as a building can't be built without architecture, a story can't be built without structure. Story is what happens; structure is the way the story is told. Story is the creation; structure is the form into which the creation is poured. Using the skeleton analogy, it would be as if you explored every single bone and its purpose in the human body, and now it was time to put them all together to build the foundation of the human being, upon which you will hang the muscle, nerves, and skin of your story. Remember that *all* stories need structure, the same way all human bodies need a skeleton, for without one, a body would just be a rag doll.

Regardless of which structure theory works for you—the hero's journey, the twenty-two steps, the seven-act structure, etc., it all comes down to the same thing. No matter how you look at it, all stories have three movements—a beginning, middle, and end. You could structure a story as *setup, complications, and resolution*; or even look at it in emotional terms as creating *attraction, tension,* and *satisfaction* in the reader. Any way you look at it, three seems to be the magic number. This is why the three-act structure has been the most taught and adopted paradigm when it comes to universal storytelling.

Keep in mind that this dramatic structure was not invented by someone who sat down and out of the blue imposed these laws of storytelling. They've existed since humans first started telling stories. Aristotle first discovered them over 2400 years ago, the same way scientists discover the laws of nature. All he did was observe that successful, emotionally satisfying, and well-liked plays followed similar dramatic principles, and wrote about them in *Poetics.*

I realize that for some of you the three-act structure may seem formulaic. However, just because it looks the same in most stories, it doesn't mean most stories are identical. Most human beings are unique, and yet their skeletons are relatively similar. So if you decided to build a human being, you'd have to start with the "formulaic" skeleton, otherwise the end result wouldn't look like a human being. The same can be said for storytelling. For instance, the films *American Beauty* and *E.T.* couldn't be more different from each other, and yet they have an identical structure.

So don't confuse structure with formula. The trick is what you *do* with that structure—where you start, where you end, and what you put in-between. You create moments and events, then put them into scenes, scenes into sequences, sequences into acts, and acts into a unified product called a "screenplay." These moments should lead the reader to wonder what will happen next, or else you have boredom—the worst offense you can commit as a writer. The three-act structure prevents boredom by arranging events in such an order that conflict causes change, which in turn causes more conflict, building and building until the story's final confrontation and resolution. Three acts. Beginning, middle, and end. From a plot point of view: Set-up, Conflict, Resolution; from an emotional point of view: Attraction, Tension, Satisfaction; and from a thematic point of view: Subject, Development, Fulfillment.

THE CRAFT: THE EMOTIONAL ELEMENTS OF EACH ACT

Here, we look at structure in terms of emotional response—how to design your acts for maximum emotional impact on the reader. As you just saw, you should divide your story into three parts: *Act I*, the beginning, which should attract or hook the reader into reading on; *Act II*, the middle, which should arouse tension and anticipation as we head towards a climactic showdown; and *Act III*, the end or resolution, which should produce emotional satisfaction—the purpose of all entertainment.

So let's look at the emotional requirements of each act. These elements should not be regarded as formula but as a recommended foundation for great storytelling.

ACT I—ATTRACTION

The first act serves to set up your story and get it moving, but the key is to grab the reader's attention and not let it go until the words "Fade out." You do so by establishing the genre and mood, which create the anticipation of desired feelings, such as laughter for a comedy, or tension in a thriller. First, you introduce the main character with whom the reader will bond; then, you establish the main problem, which captures the reader's interest and creates curiosity and anticipation as to how the protagonist will solve his dilemma. Because you must capture the reader's attention from the very first page, the opening hook is an essential emotional element in this act.

THE OPENING HOOK

Your opening scene must engage the reader's interest and make him forget he's reading a script. You can't be in the room with the reader to tell him, "Don't worry about the first couple of pages; keep reading. It gets better later on." If the reader is not intrigued right off the bat, he immediately judges your script as another boring coverage he has to write, instead of the exciting emotional experience it should have promised. A great opening hook tells the reader he's dealing with a professional writer. There are several types of openings:

Hero in action—You introduce your protagonist in the middle of conflict. Not only is this the most common opening, but also the most effective because it grabs attention on two fronts—character bonding and drama. Think of the opening scenes for *The Aviator* as we first meet young Howard Hughes learning about germs, then as an adult directing his epic *Hell's Angels*; alcoholic Frank Galvin hunting for clients at funeral homes in *The Verdict*; or bounty hunter Jack Walsh apprehending a felon in *Midnight Run*. Opening with a hero in action gives you additional choices to focus on, such as the **character's uniqueness,** as in the opening card game in *Butch Cassidy and the Sundance Kid*; Harold committing a fake suicide in *Harold and Maude;* or getting acquainted with Thelma and Louise's lives in *Thelma and Louise*. You can also focus on **character empathy**, by opening with misfortune or mistreatment (or any of the techniques discussed in Chapter 5), which create instant empathy. Think of Erin Brockovich being turned down for a job, getting a parking ticket, and getting into a car accident in the span of a couple of pages, or Marlin losing his wife and unborn kids in *Finding Nemo*.

Villain in action—Rather than introduce the hero, you can open with an exciting action sequence involving the antagonist. Think of *Star Wars*, *The Usual Suspects*, the burglary in *All the President's Men*, the hearse chased by police in *Some Like It Hot*, or the killer dispatching his first victim in *Scream*.

Backstory/prologue—In Chapter 5, we explored this element as part of the character's life. Here, you can open your screenplay with an exciting event that occurs prior to your main story and creates anticipation of what's to follow. Think of the traumatic prologues that open *Vertigo* and *Cliffhanger*.

Spectacle—We also discussed in the previous chapter how spectacle (stunts, special effects, and over-the-top events) generates thrills in the reader. For this reason, spectacle is an ideal way to open your story as long as it's a part of the story, and not some gratuitous visuals designed to distract the reader. Think of the intense opening of *Saving Private Ryan*, or the aerial acrobatics in *Top Gun*. Opening with spectacle may also include sex and violence, like the opening of *Basic Instinct* and *Betty Blue*, as well as joyous occasions like a wedding (*The Godfather*).

Mystery—Any intriguing event that arouses curiosity in the reader, making him wonder what is going on, is also a great way to open a script. Think of the opening scenes in *Alien*, *The Matrix*, *Blood Simple*, *The Usual Suspects*, *Citizen Kane*, or *E.T.*, all designed to create questions in the reader—Where are we? Who are these characters? What are they talking about? What's going on? The reader is hooked and wants to find out.

Unique world—Introducing the reader to a unique world never before seen captures the reader's interest and makes him want to read on to learn more. Examples include the unique world of aliens on earth in *Men in Black*; small town USA, which is really a giant TV set, in *The Truman Show*; the Amish world in *Witness*; the world of the mafia in *The Godfather*; or the panoramic bird's-eye view of a future Los Angeles in *Blade Runner*.

Exposition—Opening with basic information about the world of your story can be a good strategy, but only as long as the information is interesting and crucial to the understanding of the plot, like the scrolling exposition that opens *Star Wars*, or the maps and radio voice-over in *Casablanca*.

Breaking the fourth wall—A rare but effective way to open a story is with a character speaking directly to the reader, which creates immediacy and connection. You can do so through a **voice-over**, like in *American Beauty* or *Sunset Boulevard*, or by having the character **speak directly into the camera**, thus "breaking the fourth wall," like in *High Fidelity*, *Ferris Bueller's Day Off*, or *Annie Hall*.

Book-ended flashback—Just as fairy tales used to captivate us with the words "Once upon a time," this is a popular device, or structure, to open period pieces or detective stories that involve the investigation of a past event. Your opening and closing scenes are in the present, while the bulk of the story is in the past, recounted to the reader in a long flashback. Think of the book-ended storytelling in *Titanic*, *Amadeus*, *Citizen Kane*, *The Bridges of Madison County*, or *Double Indemnity*. Just make sure the story in the past is more important than the one in the present.

The bottom line when it comes to opening pages is that if they don't captivate, the reader's immediate thought is that you don't have the power to captivate him later on. He becomes biased in his negative judgment of your script until the last page. Not a position you want to be in, especially if your pages are fantastic later on.

THE HERO'S INTRODUCTION

As I just said, a common and effective way to start a script is to involve the hero in the opening scene. But if you've chosen a different opening, you should introduce your main character as soon as possible to establish identification and empathy. The reason is that the reader's subconscious expectation is that the first character to appear in your screenplay is the protagonist. This is why most writers choose to open with the main character in action. Also, when introducing your main character, make sure you get the reader to care about or feel sorry for him using any of the techniques from Chapter 5, before you reveal any of their flaws. It's easier to accept the flaws of a character we already like than to like a flawed character.

THE INCITING EVENT

This is the single most important event in the first act, for without it there wouldn't be a story. It's been referred to by many names—*The Inciting Incident*, *The Catalyst*, and *The Trigger* because it's the event that sets the story in motion. It's also been called *The Disturbance*, since it's such a significant event that it disturbs the hero's everyday life to the degree he must do something about it. Until this event happens, your characters are just muddling through their everyday lives, which is not that compelling. The inciting event sparks the reader's interest by kicking the plot into first gear, and sending the hero from order into chaos, forcing him to search for a new equilibrium. This event can be anything—a coincidence, a meeting, or a discovery. For instance, in *E.T.*, being stranded on an alien world is the inciting event for the alien's story, while meeting the alien is the inciting event for Elliott's story. In *The Godfather*, the trigger in Michael's story is the assassination attempt on his father. In *Some Like It Hot*, the disturbance is when Joe and Jerry witness the St. Valentine's Day Massacre. Remember, to have maximum emotional impact, the inciting event must affect your hero in a major way, and something must be done about it. If it's not compelling enough and it can be ignored, there's no story.

THE CENTRAL QUESTION

If your inciting event is powerful, it should automatically create the question "How will the hero resolve this problem?" which becomes the central dramatic question for your story. To maintain curiosity, anticipation, and tension, this question shouldn't be answered until at least the end of Act II, if not later. Revisiting the examples above, you can see how the inciting events generate the central questions that keep us enthralled until they're answered. When Elliott meets E.T., we wonder how their friendship will evolve. When Michael's father is shot, we wonder whether Michael will get involved in the family's business; when he does, we wonder how far he will go. And when Joe and Jerry go on the run, we wonder they'll escape the mob.

THE POINT OF NO RETURN (ACT ONE CLIMAX)

Once the central question is established, your main character struggles with a dilemma: should he get involved or should he ignore the problem? He's at a crossroads, and must make a major decision that will change his life. This is the *point of no return*, for once the protagonist proceeds further, he can never go back to the way things were before this moment. Look at this climax as a one-way gate. Once he moves through the gate, he has entered a unique situation (Act II), and he'll never be the same. Obviously, if he ignores the problem, you have no story, so the decision should always be to get involved. This decision ends the first act and propels the reader into Act II. In *E.T.*, this turning point is when Elliott decides to "keep" the alien as his friend and hides him in his closet; in *The Godfather*, it's when Michael chooses to hide his father at the hospital, scare off the assassins, and confront McCluskey, the corrupt police captain who beats him; and in *Some Like It Hot*, it's when Joe and Jerry decide to flee Chicago disguised as women.

ACT II—TENSION AND ANTICIPATION

This is where most of the action takes place, as your hero pursues his goal amid obstacles and complications that threaten to defeat him. This is the largest act in terms of size, and where most scripts fall apart, making it the greatest technical challenge for the writer. Special attention is needed to pace this section well, using an assortment of the techniques covered in the previous chapter to arouse the major storytelling emotions. Tension is essential here, as the reader should constantly wonder whether your main character will win or lose. The greater the conflict and urgency in achieving the goal, the greater the reader's interest level. In short, the second act is all about the hero's struggle and the escalation of tension.

Obstacles and Complications

To ensure a struggle, you need conflict—roadblocks in the form of obstacles and complications. Again, refer to the previous chapter for more on the subject. Just make sure the obstacles are different throughout the script, since redundant conflicts eventually diminish emotional impact. Looking at the obstacles and complications in *Some Like It Hot*, they are: having to dress up as women to join the all-girl band; avoiding detection by the band's leader; resisting temptation being among women; falling for Sugar; and having to fend off men's advances at the Florida hotel, especially from Osgood Fielding III, who's interested in Daphne/Jerry.

The Midpoint

Because the second act is so long and attention spans so short, the midpoint is often a highly intense pivotal moment, twist, or reversal that re-energizes the hero on his quest. It's called the midpoint because it usually happens halfway in the act, splitting it in two. The midpoint is often when the hero decides to stop being reactive and becomes a more active hero, or is forced into being one. He becomes fully committed to his goal and takes more desperate actions. In *E.T.*, it's when the alien tells Elliott he must phone home, and Elliott decides to help him; in *The Godfather*, it's when Michael kills Sollozzo and McCluskey at the restaurant and flees to Sicily; and in *Some Like It Hot*, it's when Joe decides to seduce Sugar by disguising himself as Junior, the heir to the Shell fortune.

Progressive Complications and Reversals

From this point on, you want the obstacles and complications to increase in intensity as we head towards the climax of the second act. More reversals and discoveries occur to stir up additional emotions in the reader. In *Some Like It Hot*, the progressive complications following Joe's decision to go after Sugar include: Jerry's jealousy as he tries to sabotage Joe's scheme; having to accept Osgood's dinner date so that Joe can use the yacht to impress Sugar; Sugar believing Joe is a millionaire; Daphne announcing her engagement to Osgood after her great date; and Spats arriving at the hotel for a mob conference.

The Darkest Moment (Act Two Climax)

During the progressive complications stage of the story, the protagonist makes a series of choices that eventually lead him to the boiling point—the second act's climax, known as the *Darkest Moment*, an event that brings a major crisis. The antagonist is winning; the hero is doomed; all seems lost, and he may even give up his quest. This is often the moment of choice, the fork in the road, the dilemma that tests the hero's resolve—when all seems lost, how could he possibly achieve his goal now? In *E.T.*, it's when the alien dies; and in *The Godfather*, it's when Michael's Sicilian wife is murdered, and Don Corleone compromises his ethics in a truce with his enemies in order to guarantee Michael's safe return to America; and in *Some Like It Hot*, it's when Joe and Jerry pack their bags to escape Spats, and Joe breaks up with Sugar. This third turning point drives the reader into the final act.

ACT III—SATISFACTION

The third and final act is the resolution of your story. Act I and II have created and developed problems, and this is where they get resolved, where the hero overcomes all conflicts and reaches his goal, as the dramatic tension is brought to its highest point. If you've done your job at the emotional level, if you've created sufficient conflict, tension, and urgency, if you've resolved all the loose ends, and if you've provided an unpredictable yet inevitable resolution, this final act should produce emotional satisfaction in the reader.

THE HERO'S RECOVERY AND GROWTH

Because the second act often ends on a low point, Act III must start with the hero's recovery, so that he can participate in the final showdown. This is where you must get your protagonist out of the hole you've put him into. Special care must be taken that this recovery is believable in the context of your story. How many times have we seen bad action films where the wounded hero who's probably lost half his blood fights the villain as if he were healthy? Also, don't be tempted to use a "Deus Ex Machina" solution to save your hero. If a secondary character, or a coincidence, saves him, make sure this possibility is set up earlier to avoid breaking the reader-page bond.

The hero's recovery often indicates the end of your character's arc, meaning that this is where your hero grows and resolves his inner-flaws, which gives him the strength and courage to march on towards his quest. The darkest moment has forced him to change for the better (or for the worse if you're writing a tragedy). Once your hero recovers physically and emotionally, he's ready for the final showdown. Note that this emotional change can also happen after the climax, although audiences tend to prefer the former—character growth before the climax.

THE FINAL SHOWDOWN

If you look at the first two acts as the setup, then the final showdown is the payoff. If the previous acts are tension, then this showdown is satisfaction, where the core conflict is resolved. This is the final face-to-face confrontation between protagonist and antagonist, also known as *The Climax*, or *The Obligatory Scene*, so named because it's the scene foreshadowed by the events in the first act. For instance, in *E.T.*, the alien running away and hiding from the scientists demands a scene where they will confront each other. In *The Godfather*, the central tension of whether Michael will become the new Don demands a scene where he will prove himself a worthy successor to Don Corleone. In the climax, he shows who the boss is by having all his enemies gunned down as his godchild is baptized. In *Some Like It Hot*, the final showdown is when Joe and Jerry run away from Spats and the other mobsters in the hotel. Whether the showdown is an epic battle scene, or a small but powerful moment, the key factor is that the climax must be emotionally satisfying.

AN EFFECTIVE ENDING

How you end your story is your last chance to leave a lasting impression on the reader. Choose your ending wisely, since it will be the last thing the reader will remember before writing his coverage. As an audience member, you will probably agree that while a good opening hooks you, a great ending will generate good word-of-mouth and leave you talking about the film long after you've left the theatre. Also known as *The Resolution*, the ending is where you resolve all conflicts and any loose ends in an emotionally satisfying way. This means it has to be surprising and yet feel like it was inevitable, as opposed to "It came out of nowhere." Like a concept being "uniquely familiar," a "surprising yet inevitable" ending may seem like an oxymoron, but it is not. "Inevitable" simply means that it's the most logical resolution for the story you've told, while "surprising" comes from the unexpected way you've resolved the conflict. In other words, unpredictable. Remember from the previous chapter that surprise is an essential visceral emotion. Therefore, all endings should be surprising, even when we know the hero will defeat the villain, or the boy will get the girl.

There are five types of endings to choose from: *Happy*, *Tragic*, *Bittersweet*, *Twist*, and *Open-ended*.

Happy ending—The hero wins, the antagonist is defeated, and everything ends up wonderfully. This is the most popular ending in Hollywood, and therefore the most used. Examples include *Star Wars*, *Die Hard*, *When Harry Met Sally*, *Sneakers*, and *The Shawshank Redemption*.

Tragic ending—The antagonist wins and the hero loses, although the premise must be validated at the hero's expense to be an emotionally satisfying ending. Think of *Chinatown*, *Se7en*, *Butch Cassidy and the Sundance Kid*, *Rosemary's Baby*, *Arlington Road*, and *Taxi Driver.*

Bittersweet ending—Also known as *ironic*, this type of ending is when the hero or antagonist loses but wins, or wins but loses. This is when the hero sacrifices himself for the greater good, or when the hunter becomes the hunted, the sudden reversal of fortune, or being beaten at your own game. Although it's a challenging ending to create, it tends to be highly satisfying since this is the way we see life—people winning and losing at the same time. Examples include *Casablanca*, *E.T.*, *The Godfather*, *The Silence of the Lambs*, *One Flew Over the Cuckoo's Nest*, *Titanic*, *Roman Holiday*, and *Thelma and Louise.*

Twist ending—Also known as *The Surprise Ending*, the surprise is a revelation that changes your perception of what the story was about. If you can pull it off, the twist ending is probably the most emotionally satisfying because it will generate a lot of buzz among executives. It may even sell a script on the spot. Think of *The Sixth Sense, The Usual Suspects, Unbreakable, The Village, The Others, Planet of the Apes, Primal Fear, No Way Out, Fight Club, 12 Monkeys,* and *Identity*.

Open-ended ending—An effective way to end your story, but not as popular as the others, is to leave it up to the reader to decide how the story ends, like the ambiguous ending of Charlie Chaplin's *City Lights*. It's the ending that tells us, "It's not over yet, folks." An example of this type of ending is where the villain appears to have been killed, the hero walks away, and the last image is of the villain's hand moving or the empty space where the body used to be, like in *Halloween*, and every horror film in a series.

The bottom line, regardless of which of these five types of endings you choose to resolve your script is, of course and as always, emotional satisfaction. Without it, your script will never get past its first reader.

ON THE PAGE: STRUCTURE IN ACTION

Again, because this topic is the focus of every screenwriting book and basic seminar, it would be redundant to analyze the structure of a classic film. Most books do a good job in pinpointing the essential elements discussed above, and offer many examples to illustrate them. If you feel you need more on the subject, I invite you to study them for further analysis. But now that you have a story and a structure for it, it's time to go deeper and learn about the individual events that make up your story. It's time to explore the dramatic scene…

8

SCENES
Mesmerizing Moments

*"Screenplays are carefully written and ordered in such a way that
the audience has no choice but to feel exactly what the writers
want them to feel."*

-F. SCOTT FITZGERALD

A scene is the basic unit through which you tell a story, and probably the most important element in a screenplay, since the bulk of the emotional impact on the reader comes from individual scenes. We all remember individual scenes from our favorite movies. In fact, a movie becomes well loved because of the impact of its individual scenes.

THE BASICS: WHAT YOU NEED TO KNOW

THREE TYPES OF SCENES

There are three types of scenes you should be aware of because many books lump them into one kind—the dramatic scene. This leaves the student confused and leads to flawed screenplays. Dramatic scenes are the most important scenes in a screenplay, but this doesn't mean all scenes should be dramatic. Let's take a brief look at each type:

EXPOSITION SCENES

As the name implies, the purpose of these scenes is to provide information and often set the mood and tone of upcoming scenes, like the fiery opening of *Body Heat*. They're also known as *establishing scenes* because they establish location, like the opening scene in *Blade Runner*, or *transition scenes* in that they're often used to show a character moving from one location to another, like the connect-the-dots map scene when Indiana Jones travels by plane to Tibet in *Raiders of the Lost Ark*. Regardless of their label, exposition scenes provide information to the reader so that he can understand the context of an upcoming dramatic scene. Conflict is not required. Exposition scenes can establish an era in a period film, setting, theme, or the passage of time—fluttering calendar pages, changing seasons, a spinning clock, or clouds speeding by as day turns to night. You can also use them to relieve tension, pausing between two intense scenes so that the reader may catch his breath, like a rest stop on a highway.

SPECTACLE SCENES

We covered spectacle in Chapter 6 as a tool to thrill the reader. This is where you'd use it. Again, no conflict is required here because the main purpose of spectacle scenes is to make you go "Wow!" and add flash and pizzazz to the script. Think of *E.T.* and the bicycles flying against the moon, the flight sequences in *Top Gun* and *Superman*, the fresco scene in *The English Patient*, the dinosaurs in *Jurassic Park*, the car chase in *Bullitt*, or the tornadoes in *Twister*. Spectacle scenes can be the song and dance productions, like Gene Kelly dancing in the rain, or Tom Hanks playing the giant piano in *Big*. The bottom line is that spectacle scenes mesmerize us and make us forget we're watching moving images on a screen. They're part of the entertainment drive. No conflict needed. If there's conflict, we have a dramatic scene.

DRAMATIC SCENES

These are the core of storytelling. Story is drama; therefore, conflict is essential in these scenes. These are the scenes that change a character, move the plot in a different direction, and produce the most emotional impact. The length of a dramatic scene is not important as long as you construct it in terms of its impact on the reader. It can be a quarter of a page or eight pages long. Most, however, are two to three pages long. From this point on, everything I'll discuss when it comes to a scene will refer to the dramatic scene.

A SCENE IS A MINI-STORY

The great thing about a scene is that it's basically a mini-story. This means it should be structured like a story, with a clear beginning, middle, and end, a dramatic question, rising tension, and a climax, which should lead the reader into the next scene. It also means that you can use all the techniques covered in Chapter 6 to craft a fascinating scene for emotional impact.

A scene has a triple duty—advance the story forward through conflict, reveal additional character layers, and more important, have an emotional impact on the reader—whether it creates tension, arouses curiosity and anticipation, or even surprises the reader. You should never have a neutral scene. Neutral means tedious. In today's market, you don't have the luxury of a dull scene. Every scene, and every page of that scene, should be fascinating in its own way. Just like a story, the simplest way to think of a scene is that a character wants something badly and is having difficulty getting it. As you've already discovered, a goal against opposition creates anticipation and tension. If page three, for example, creates anticipation, the reader will read page four. If page four creates tension, he'll read page five, and so on. To make your screenplay a page-turner, you need to create emotional impact on each page of your script. No exceptions.

KEY ELEMENTS OF A DRAMATIC SCENE

Because a scene is a mini-story, you should take the time to plan it before writing it. In *101 Habits*, Ron Bass (*Rain Man*, *The Joy Luck Club*, *My Best Friend's Wedding*) describes how he blocks a scene before actually writing it, figuring out all the elements that will go into the scene—what everyone is going to feel, where to start and end the scene, what the exposition, emotional tone, and character changes will be. Let's explore the elements you need to figure out before actually writing a scene, starting with why you should write it in the first place.

PURPOSE

In my consulting work, when I come across a flat scene that doesn't seem to belong in a script, I ask the writer why it's there. Nine times out of ten, the response is "to reveal character." This would be fine if the scene also affected the reader through tension, anticipation, humor, or surprise. Remember that a dramatic scene's primary duty, like the overall story, is to impact the reader. If it also advances the plot, which it should, and reveals character, you get bonus points. But never ignore the emotional impact of the scene. Think of your script as a house of cards, each scene a card. If you can remove a scene, and the house still stands, in other words, if the story still works without it, that scene doesn't belong in your script. No scenes should be just about revealing character or setting up clues to be paid off later. They should also advance the plot through conflict or at the very least, impact the reader.

LOCATION

The next essential element in a scene is where it will play. Location can greatly affect a scene's mood or tone. Think of a scene that takes place in a park versus one in an abandoned warehouse; a large city versus a small country town; a beach versus a jungle; a bar versus a fancy restaurant—different moods that can add to the overall emotional impact of the scene. Location alone can save you the extra description you need to set the mood. Just make sure you choose the right place for the purpose of the scene. Sometimes, changing the location of a scene in the rewrite is a great way to turn it into something unique and unexpected.

TIME

Like location, the time of day a scene takes place is an important factor in its effect. Think of a scene happening in New York's Central Park at lunchtime, and one at midnight. Same location, different emotional associations. In a scene's slugline, your only choices to indicate time are DAY or NIGHT. You could even get away with DUSK or DAWN, but you should embellish them by adding specifics in the scene's description if it affects the tone of the scene.

WEATHER

In *101 Habits*, Eric Roth (*Forrest Gump*, *Ali*, *The Insider*) talks about changing the weather whenever he's stuck in a scene. This is the first trick he thinks of when the scene is not as compelling as he'd like. He changes the weather and nine times out of ten, this solves the problem. Think of the different feelings associated with a particular weather condition—a scene taking place in the rain, a sunny meadow, lightning and thunder, a foggy beach, snow, wind, etc.

SCENE CHARACTERS

WHOSE SCENE IS IT?

A dramatic scene will always include at least one character in conflict with himself, another person, or the natural world, preferably all three simultaneously. The most common type is conflict between two characters. One wants something and the other won't give it to him, or stands in his way to the goal, or both characters want the same thing. As the writer, you need to figure out whose scene it is—which character *drives* the scene? In every scene, the reader looks for a character with whom to identify so that he can experience the scene emotionally. Often, it's the story's protagonist, but this doesn't mean that the protagonist will drive every scene in the script. Sometimes, a scene will *belong* to the antagonist or a secondary character with a subplot. So every dramatic scene with two characters or more will have a *lead* character that drives it and with whom the reader empathizes. Usually, this is the character who has a clear objective and an active strategy for accomplishing it. If a character only reacts to another character's actions, chances are this is not his scene. For example, in *North by Northwest*, when Thornhill meets Vandamm for the first time after being kidnapped, the scene belongs to Vandamm, even though Thornhill is the hero and we identify with him. The reason is that Vandamm controls the scene with the clear objective of wanting "Kaplan" to confess and reveal his secrets, while Thornhill keeps protesting he's not Kaplan and has no strategy for a resolution.

PREVIOUS MOMENT

One of the ways to maintain reader interest is to make sure your scenes follow a cause-and-effect pattern. When you set up an event in one scene, we look forward to its payoff in another scene. This works especially well with character emotions. For instance, if a character discovers he's been betrayed, we look forward to the scene where he confronts the betrayer because we understand the emotions involved and anticipate drama between the two characters. Always be aware of what happened to the character before he enters this scene. Did he lose his job? Fall in love? Become a parent? Discover a lie? The previous moment often gives a character a sense of urgency and immediacy in his present objective.

FEELINGS AND ATTITUDES

Once you figure out the character's previous moment, this will give you his feelings and attitudes, which should be a factor in how the present scene plays out. For instance, if he lost his job, he may be depressed, angry, bitter, and frustrated (or happy depending on the circumstances), whereas if he just fell in love, he may be hopeful and euphoric, without a care in the world.

OBJECTIVES

The simplest way to think of a scene is that somebody wants something badly and is having difficulty getting it. If what he wants is too easy to get, the scene won't be dramatic. The objective is usually the why of a scene, and it involves an immediate desire. Always ask yourself what a character wants to get from the other character right now.

George Bernard Shaw once said that plots are really about how people negotiate and create relationships. This insight gives the writer as many choices for a scene as there are unique people in the world. The more unique the character, the more unique his choices will be to get what he wants. In fact, the objectives in most great scenes are about relationships—to get love, power, sex, friendship, acceptance, a job, money, and because an objective requires a response from the other person in the scene, the best way to phrase it is in a way that involves the other person. For example, rather than say your character wants a job in an interview scene, you should phrase it as, "my character wants the other person to give him the job." This will make the hero active in his goal and the other person reactive, back and forth, making the scene more engaging. Also, try to phrase the objective in the positive instead of the negative. For instance, a character wants to marry to start a family, not to avoid loneliness. A positive goal is clearer and stronger than a negative avoidance.

CHARACTER ACTIONS

A character with a clear objective needs to have a plan to achieve his goal. What actions will he take to carry out his objective? Actions are the mini-goals to accomplish the master goal in the scene, the different approaches and tactics the character takes based on the reactions of the other person in the scene. They may be physical and mental, and are not to be confused with character activity, or "actor business," which involves the mannerisms and behaviors of the character in the scene to add realism or reveal emotional state. Rather, actions are part of the character's strategy to get what he wants. For example, if the objective in the scene is to get an interviewer to offer him a job, his actions throughout the scene may be to charm, to convince, to assure, to impress, to humor, to manipulate, to persuade, or to inspire.

THE MAIN CONFLICT

Conflict is the essence of a dramatic scene. Without conflict, or the promise of conflict through anticipation and tension, a scene will be expository. This is fine if it's the type of scene you want to write, but it can't be a dramatic scene without conflict. Make sure the conflict is internal, external, or interpersonal rather than the superficial argumentative conflict, where two characters simply disagree, as in "Yes, no, yes, no, is so, is not, etc." Real conflict is not a static argument. It's a clear obstacle to a goal with a smooth progression from beat to beat towards a climax.

STAKES

We discussed what's at stake for your character in Chapter 5. In planning a scene, once you focus on the driving character, you need to know what's at stake in the scene. What happens if he fails to achieve his goal? What happens if he succeeds? If your character can walk away from the scene without losing or gaining anything important to him, there's nothing at stake, and the scene will be flat. The more at stake in the scene, the more immediate and urgent his desire to accomplish his objective.

BEATS

The same way scenes are the basic building blocks of a plot, beats are the building blocks of a scene. Don't confuse them with the theatrical term "beat," which indicates a pause in dialogue or action. A scene beat is the smallest unit of dramatic structure, which is made up of a new thought, an action, a reaction, and an emotion. Every time there is any change within a scene, it creates a new beat. Look at a beat as an individual approach to achieve a goal, whether it's a behavior or a line of dialogue. Every beat in a scene should be a dance between action and reaction, with bonus points if the reaction is unpredictable. For a detailed example of beats in a classic scene, refer to the section "On the Page: Scene in Action" at end of this chapter.

EXPOSITION

Storytelling is about how much information you reveal and hide to engage the reader's attention. If you give too much information, your story loses its mystery, and the reader becomes bored. If you don't give enough, the reader becomes confused, frustrated, and unable to follow the story. The challenge, of course, is to find the right balance. You can only discover it in later drafts, so the most common advice is to write too much and trim later. When it comes to planning a scene, once you know its purpose, you should know what information you want to reveal in the scene, and how to reveal it. While description and dialogue are the only methods available to the screenwriter, there are several devices you can use in a scene: a **voice-over narrator** (*Sunset Boulevard, American Beauty*); **breaking the fourth wall** with a character speaking directly to the audience (*Annie Hall, Ferris Bueller's Day Off, High Fidelity*); a **TV or radio news report** (*Casablanca*); a **title card** (*Star Wars*); **meeting or "getting to know you" scenes**, like a job interview where one character comments on another's résumé or biographical file; a **montage** (a first date, prepping a heist, training for a boxing bout); or just simple **images and signs** that can give important information. For example, if I write "A Porsche Boxter speeds down a highway past a sign that reads "Welcome to California," the Boxter establishes the period and the sign tells us the location. The same goes for landmarks, costumes, furniture, hairstyles, etc.

SCENE STRUCTURE

Since a scene is mini-story, it should be structured as such, with a clear beginning, middle complications with conflict, tension, and reversals, all accelerating to a climactic resolution that ends the scene or propels the reader into the next.

SCENE POLARITY

Every action in a scene has a polarity in story terms—positive or negative. An action should never be neutral. This includes character behaviors and dialogue. As you plan a scene, it should either start at a **positive charge**—things are going well for the character, or a **negative charge**—things are going bad. Because the point of a scene is change, the scene should end with the reverse charge of the beginning. For instance, if you start a scene where a character is happy at his job, you'd better end it with a negative event, like losing his job or experiencing a crisis. If the scene starts and ends on the same polarity, there's no change in the scene, and therefore no purpose for existing dramatically. If you start the scene in neutral, you can end it positively or negatively. Sometimes, you can go from negative to negative or positive to positive, but only if there's a wide range the intensity of the actions. For example, you may start a domestic dispute scene with the negative polarity of a wife hitting her husband—negative, and end the scene with the wife stabbing him in a rage—highly negative. The same goes for a positive to highly positive polarity. The key is a clear change from one polarity to another.

CHASE-AND-ESCAPE VS. CHASE-AND-CAPTURE

Similar to scene polarity is the concept of chase-and-escape versus chase-and-capture, two terms that have to do with how a scene ends. Because a scene usually involves a character wanting something from another (the chase), there are only two ways it can end: The character gets what he wants, either outright or in a compromise (capture), or he doesn't (escape).

DESCRIPTION AND DIALOGUE

Once you've given some thought to all the above elements that make up a dramatic scene, you can start writing it through the only two ways visible to the reader—description and dialogue, which will be discussed in depth in the next two chapters. Knowing what makes up a scene, however, doesn't mean you can create a compelling one that will fascinate the reader and be emotionally satisfying. For that, you need scene craft.

THE CRAFT: WRITING GREAT SCENES

What follows are proven dramatic techniques and tricks of the trade designed to inject life into otherwise flat scenes. This doesn't mean all your scenes have to be great, although the more fascinating scenes you have, the better. Jack Nicholson once said that he commits to a project if it has three great scenes and no bad ones. So let's explore how you can craft a great scene.

TECHNIQUES TO CRAFT FASCINATING SCENES

BEGINNINGS AND ENDS

Where to start a scene and where to end it is a challenge most writers face. The most given advice is "Get in late and get out early," but the key factor, as always, is the emotional impact on the reader. Novice writers often begin scenes too early and end scenes too late, giving too much information—like someone driving, parking the car, entering a building, and riding the elevator to enter an office for a job interview. This can only bore the reader. Professional writers would start the scene "**in media res**," meaning "in the middle of things," with the character being asked a provocative question at the interview. This is more immediate, intriguing, and energetic. It engages the reader through the mental stimulation required to understand the dynamics of the scene. Again, this is similar to the way you'd open any story, so for opening techniques, you may refer to the "Opening Hook" section in the previous chapter.

How do you end a scene? Leaving early is one way. But the most common technique is to end the scene with a hit of **visceral emotion**, such as curiosity, anticipation, tension, or surprise. This automatically creates the desire to know what happens next, and propels the reader into the next scene. For example, you could end with **a surprising reversal** that sets back a character and forces him to make an important choice—a choice revealed in another scene. You could end with **a question**, which arouses curiosity and makes us read on to get the answer, or with **an agreement or promise** to meet later, which creates anticipation. For more, you can always go back to the key story emotions we explored in Chapter 6.

THE EMOTIONAL PALETTE

I now want to introduce you to the exciting concept of the "Emotional Palette," which came to me when I considered the analogy of the writer being a painter on the page, using words instead of colors. Just as the painter adds a particular touch of color to the canvas for emotional impact, the writer does the same with words. For me, it goes much further since it's the writer's duty to evoke emotion on the page. This means that instead of words on your palette, you have emotions—the character's emotions (anger, fear, joy, confusion) and the reader's emotions (curiosity, anticipation, tension, surprise). You craft a scene by knowing what the character will feel in the scene and add these emotions to the palette. Then, knowing what emotional responses you want the reader to have, you figure out the techniques you'll use. The key to building a fascinating scene is to jump around the palette for each beat. Let's take a deeper look at this concept:

CHARACTER EMOTIONAL CUES

These are the specific emotions felt by the character. When a man proposes to a woman, and she responds that she found someone else, the man is stung. That's an emotional cue, or hit. It's called a cue because it stimulates, or *cues*, possible reactions. Remember that a scene beat is a contained unit of action and reaction. The woman tells the man she found another man (action); the man is stung (reaction). Great scenes are fascinating because they focus on the unpredictable emotional cues of the characters as they react to events in the scene. If the reader identifies with the character, if he understands the character's objective and cares about the outcome, then he should also feel that character's emotional cues.

Try not to repeat the same emotions. There's a law that says the more we experience something, the less effect it has. To ensure constant interest, move around the emotional palette. If your scene has ten beats, use ten emotional cues, or a progression of ten sub-emotions from one major emotion, like from indifference to anger. If you've purchased a copy of this book, turn to the last page for instructions on how you can receive a free copy of *The Emotional Thesaurus*, in which I gather all the possible character emotions and arrange them by intensity level. This is a valuable tool to design the various beats in your scene from an emotional angle.

You're no doubt aware of the maxim "Show, don't tell." This is important when it comes to emotional cues. Show the emotion; don't tell the reader how a character feels through description or dialogue. Don't say, for example, "I'm angry at you." Show the emotion through an action (a slap) or dialogue ("Don't touch me"). You can go over your scene in the rewrite stage and flag on-the-nose statements that tell and replace them with active actions and subtext that show.

Always remember that emotions are the lifeblood of a dramatic scene, not dialogue, descriptions, or character traits. It's only through emotional cues that you give your characters life and momentum to overcome obstacles and achieve their objectives. For an example of emotional cues in action, refer to the scene analyzed at the end of this chapter.

THE READER'S EMOTIONAL RESPONSE

The same advice applies to the emotional responses of the reader. You can design each beat in the scene for a particular visceral effect, such as curiosity, tension, worry, and hope. Imagine them on your palette, and through the techniques in Chapter 6, you can hold the reader's attention from beat to beat.

THE EMOTIONAL SWITCH-AROUND

Armed with character emotions on one side of the emotional palette and reader emotional responses on the other, you can create different beats by bouncing or switching around from one to the other along an emotional scale. This is where *The Emotional Thesaurus* comes in handy. Many writers who think of a scene in terms of emotional beats have lists of emotions along a ladder of intensity, like a musical scale. For instance, you may pick a feeling for a character, then make a list of all the emotions a person goes through when experiencing that feeling. If someone is resentful towards another character, for example, he may feel frustration, anger, bitterness, and hatred (and more). You then arrange these emotions in order from least intense to most intense, and you have emotional beats to build a scene.

FLIP CLICHÉD EMOTIONS

The mark of amateur writing is in the clichéd emotional reactions in a familiar scene. How many times have we seen a confrontation scene, say, between an angry woman and her husband after discovering he's cheated on her? The scene is typically a one-note of anger one beat after another, which gets old after a while. It's also predictable. Your goal is to craft fresh and unpredictable scenes, and the best way to do so is to flip the expected emotional response into an unpredictable one. Instead of giving the reader the clichéd anger beat when the woman confronts her husband, choose an unexpected emotion such as curiosity ("What does she have that I don't?"), guilt ("I know I'm not good enough for you"), or delight ("Now I can kick your butt to the curb and get half your fortune").

CHARACTER APPEAL TECHNIQUES

Looking back at Chapter 5 on character, you'll recall that one of the keys to maintaining reader interest is through identification with the protagonist. You learned how to achieve this emotional connection through a series of techniques designed to make a character, including villains, instantly appealing, like when the reader feels sorry for him, witnesses his humanity, or recognizes an admirable and coveted quality. You can also use these techniques to build a great scene, since empathy is a satisfying emotional response. In fact, using character pathos techniques, such as underserved misfortune, betrayal, or abuse, often results in a compelling dramatic scene due to the built-in conflict of these techniques.

ACTIVE DIALOGUE

By now, you should probably be aware that something active is stronger than its passive counterpart—an active sentence, character, objective, etc. This includes dialogue in a dramatic scene. Active dialogue, the kind that generates questions and creates curiosity, is always more engaging than passive dialogue, which is reactive, and not as involving. Active dialogue always has as a purpose, whether to give information or get what you want from the other character in the scene. It's the kind of dialogue that feels like an action, but it's not behavior. Sometimes we fight physically to get what we want; sometimes we fight with words. If I want to hurt someone's feelings, I would do so through words designed to insult, scold, or shame. Each line of dialogue would be an attack. On the other hand, if I spew exposition without a clear goal in the scene, that would be passive dialogue. Not as compelling.

CONFLICT

This should be a given by now. To create a compelling dramatic scene, you must include at least one of the three types of conflict: individual vs. self, individual vs. others, and individual vs. nature (which includes the supernatural, God, fate, technology, monsters, machines, etc.) Here are some tricks of the trade to inject conflict into your scene:

THE ACTOR'S STUDIO TECHNIQUE

This technique from the renowned Method-Acting school is used by actors to generate conflict in their scene improvisations. The instructor whispers to each actor in the scene secret directions, which contrast with the other actor's directions. For example, he may say to one actor, "You're a headmaster at an exclusive prep school, and you've just caught a student cheating. Since you have a zero-tolerance policy, you've expelled the student. Now, his mother is coming to discuss his reinstatement. Under no circumstance are you to let him back into the school or you will lose your job." To the actor playing the mother, he'd whisper the following, "You're the mother of the smartest student in the school, who's been mistakenly expelled for cheating. You know he's not a cheater, and you need to meet with the headmaster to address the error. Your son is the first in the family to get a decent education, and since you're poor, his full scholarship is a relief. Under no circumstances can you allow your son to be expelled." And... Action! By giving different scripts, agendas, or contexts to the characters in the scene, you automatically create compelling conflict.

CONFRONTATIONS

Arguments, quarrels, altercations between two characters are always engaging, provided the disagreement has been set up earlier and is interesting. A confrontation is immediate, tense, uncertain, and therefore involving through its inherent drama. Who will win the argument, how, and what will happen next?

INTERROGATIONS

The same goes for interrogations in any setting—police vs. criminal, lawyer vs. hostile witness, enemy vs. captured spy or soldier, mother vs. child—instant drama coming from the conflict, tension, and uncertainty of how the scene will end. You can also add a slew of techniques to an interrogation to increase its appeal—impatience, misunderstanding, dramatic irony, different scripts, etc.

OBSTACLES/COMPLICATIONS/REVERSALS

You can enhance a scene's conflict through mini-obstacles and complications that are quickly overcome, such as extra cars and trucks that get in the way during a car chase, a cell phone ringing during a symphony concert, or having to avoid glass shards when you're barefoot, like in *Die Hard*.

INNER CONFLICT

Here, the conflict comes from the main character, self versus self, usually a flaw that gets in the way of the character's objective in the scene or overall story. Examples include Alvy Singer's inability to experience pleasure in *Annie Hall*; Clarice Starling's screaming lambs in *The Silence of the Lambs*; or Melvin Udall's personality and medical condition in *As Good As It Gets*.

NOT ALL SCENES NEED CONFLICT

It would be a disservice to all aspiring writers to say that all scenes need to have conflict to be emotionally engaging. You've already seen how important it is to have an ebb and flow of tense versus relaxing scenes to maintain reader interest throughout your script. After a compelling crisis, the reader needs a scene of relaxation, relief, or humor, which is devoid of conflict. Too many dramatic scenes in a row will only lead to emotional exhaustion and possible desensitization to additional conflict.

Granted, these types of scenes don't have to be dramatic scenes, but you can still have a dramatic scene without conflict as long as you *promise* conflict through anticipation ("Beware, the conflict will come soon") or rising tension ("Nothing is happening now, but it can come at any time, from anywhere").

Tension, especially the kind generated by dramatic irony in a previous scene, makes up for a lack of conflict. Hitchcock was the master of this, and *North by Northwest* is full of fascinating scenes devoid of conflict, which still could be considered dramatic, like the classic crop-duster scene. Even when Thornhill stands in the middle of nowhere, we are gripped. Why? Because the scene has dramatic irony from us knowing Eve has set him up and tension from what could happen at any time.

Contrast within the scene

As you've seen in previous chapters, contrast can be a powerful device to increase interest in a story or scene. For instance, Hollywood has been fond of **contrasting characters** in "Buddy" or "Odd-couple" films (*Lethal Weapon*, *The African Queen*, *The Odd Couple*, *Rush Hour*), as well as **contrasting character with environment** in "Fish-out-of-water" films (*Beverly Hills Cop*, *City Slickers*, *Splash*). But this is not all. Just as you can contrast scenes in a plot, you can **contrast beats** in a scene, like **beat durations** (long/short) and **beat tempos** (fast/slow). A good example is the Swordsman scene in *Raiders of the Lost Ark*. Not only is the scene funny because it's original and unexpected, but it also contrasts the long build up of the swordsmanship display with Indiana Jones' brief reaction and quick shooting. Another common technique is to **contrast emotions** within a scene, like angry/calm, happy/sad, affectionate/hostile, daring/afraid, etc., and **contrast objectives**, as you just saw with The Actor's Studio technique above.

Discoveries and revelations

Aaron Sorkin (*A Few Good Men*, *The American President*, *The West Wing*) once said, "Tension and discovery—it's what rivets an audience, holds its attention and makes a story absorbing." Whether a character discovers crucial information or others reveal it to him, it's a great way to energize a scene and maintain the reader's interest. In an ideal scene, you want a constant flow of new information, new conflicts, and new twists and turns, at least one per scene. Each discovery should be a tiny reversal that changes the direction of the scene's energy, and should have an emotional impact on both the character and the reader.

First times and last times

Imagine writing a scene where a character who's been dreaming for years about something is about to experience it for the first time or the last. There's something gripping about seeing a character about to do something for the first time—a first kiss, a first day at a new job, a first space walk; or for the last time—saying goodbye to a lover you'll never see again, or to a dying relative, your last day at a job you've had for fifty years, or your last fix as a drug addict.

FLASHBACKS

A lot has been said about using flashbacks in a story, mostly warnings about how readers frown upon them and consider them amateurish and lazy writing, and how they're to be avoided at all costs. Then why do we see them in classic films, both modern and old? Writing flashbacks is not the issue here. Their quality is. The reason readers caution against them is that most beginners write *boring* and *unnecessary* flashbacks that break the tension of the present narrative. Their only purpose is to reveal a character's backstory. A flashback is simply another dramatic scene that simply happened before the present story. It can be fascinating or tedious. So all the techniques for emotional impact you've learned so far may apply to a flashback. This ensures reader interest.

Another important point is to use a flashback only when it's critical for the reader to know what happened in the past. Always wait for the moment when the reader is dying to know the information you will now reveal through a flashback. If you can't find some way to weave this information into the present scene, do so in a short but fascinating flashback scene that moves the story forward or gives insight into the main character. A flashback should always change the present situation of the story. Otherwise, it has no purpose in your script.

HELLOS AND GOODBYES

How you first introduce a main character is another important layer that contributes to emotional impact. Think about your favorite films and how main characters are first introduced, either to the reader or to each other in a meeting scene. More often than not, a character's first appearance is memorable due to its originality, surprise, or anticipation. Think of the dramatic introductions of Darth Vader in *Star Wars*, Hannibal Lecter in *The Silence of the Lambs*, Rick Blaine in *Casablanca*, Axel Foley in *Beverly Hills Cop*, or Jack Sparrow riding into port on a sinking ship in *Pirates of the Caribbean*.

The same goes for dramatic farewells in a scene—how a character says good-bye, either setting out on a journey or dying. The more original, surprising, tense, and thought provoking the departure, the better the effect. Examples of dramatic farewells include Charles Foster Kane in *Citizen Kane*, R. P. McMurphy in *One Flew Over the Cuckoo's Nest*, Obi-Wan Kenobi in *Star Wars*, Jack's frozen death in *The Shining*, and Evelyn Mulwray in *Chinatown*.

INFORMATION SETUP AND EMOTIONAL PAYOFF

We explored setups and payoffs in Chapter 6 as a means to create surprise. Throughout the script, you plant seeds of information, which later pay off in a surprising way, like in *The Silence of the Lambs*, where Hannibal Lecter focuses on the pen (setup) and later uses a part of it to free himself from the handcuffs (payoff). In a scene, you can pay off anything that's been set up earlier—an object, a phobia, a skill, a line of dialogue, etc., preferably in an emotional way. The setup doesn't have to be important—it's just exposition. But the payoff should be emotional, in that it should arouse any of the major reader emotions. For example, let's imagine you've set up the information that a character is a billionaire, and now you have a scene where he loses a thousand dollars in a Las Vegas casino. Nothing interesting about that, since it's not a major loss for the character. But what if you've set up that the character is poor, that the thousand dollars he's just lost was everything he had in the bank and his overdue mortgage payment, and that he has a family of four to support? Now the loss is an emotional payoff. That's what drama is all about.

JUXTAPOSE TWO SIMULTANEOUS EVENTS

If you can create interest in a scene through conflict, think what two simultaneous conflicts could do to increase the reader's attention. You have the one event, which is the main conflict between two characters, and you add a second event, which keeps interrupting the first, and creates additional tension. For example, in *Some Like It Hot*, when Joe, disguised as Shell Junior, meets Sugar at the beach there's one level of conflict—Joe wants her to believe he's the billionaire she's been looking for. But when Jerry joins them and recognizes Joe, there's a simultaneous conflict as he tries to sabotage Joe's seduction.

PROPS

Sometimes a scene can become extra fascinating by using a prop—an object that adds meaning to a scene and makes it more emotionally resonant. Think of the glove in the park scene in *On the Waterfront*, how it increases its fascination from what could have been a simple talking-heads scene. Other examples include the snowflake globe and the sled in *Citizen Kane*, the shoe in *The Gold Rush*, the ring in *Lord of the Rings*, and the matchbook in *North by Northwest*.

REVEAL CHARACTER

Every scene in your script, dramatic or otherwise, is an opportunity to reveal character. Beginners often make the mistake of introducing a character and revealing most of their traits in one long scene. This makes subsequent scenes flat and uninvolving. A better strategy is to reveal whenever possible a new facet of a character in every scene. This gives the reader a smoother interaction with that character over time, rather than all at once at the beginning of the story. Revealing a character's trait, belief, or attitude adds interest to the scene through recognition ("He's just like me" or "I knew he'd feel this way") or surprise ("I had no idea he felt this way"). You can use any of the character revealing devices from Chapter 5 to increase the appeal of a scene, especially when they relate to the main character's emotional arc.

RUNNING GAG

A running gag is anything that repeats itself over the entire course of the story for a humorous effect. It can be a recurring character, a prop, or a line of dialogue. The repetition is what causes the laugh, so including it in a scene is a good way to inject some humor into it. For example, in *Midnight Run*, the "Look behind you!" gag repeats throughout the script and pays off dramatically at the end. In *Airplane!*, Dr. Rumack responds to sentences containing the word "surely" with "Don't call me Shirley." And in the animated TV series *South Park*, whenever Kenny suffers a gruesome death, the children exclaim, "They killed Kenny; you bastards!" Sometimes, a running gag can travel across two films. The swordsman-shooting gag in *Raiders of the Lost Ark* repeats itself with a twist in its sequel, *Indiana Jones and the Temple of Doom*. Jones faces another mighty swordsman and immediately reaches for his gun, but this time it's missing.

SATISFIED OR FRUSTRATED DESIRES

As you saw earlier, a scene can end with a chase-and-capture dynamic (the character achieves his scene objective) or a chase-and-escape (he doesn't get what he wants). A balanced plot line will often include scenes that alternate between the two. Once the writer establishes the central question of whether the protagonist will accomplish his goal, the scenes that answer, "Yes, he will" in a small scene victory should alternate with "No, he won't" in a defeat, back and forth. This alternates the potent visceral emotions of hope and worry. Because a scene is like a mini-story, its beats can also alternate between satisfaction whenever the central character gets a step closer to getting what he wants, and frustration whenever there's a setback, creating a dance between hope and worry within one scene, and thus keeping the reader hooked.

SECRETS

In Chapter 6, you learned how character secrets are an essential tool to generate surprise. Whether it's a story secret that drives the entire script and is revealed in the climactic scene, like in *Chinatown, The Usual Suspects*, and *The Sixth Sense*, or a secret that simply drives a couple of scenes, like Eve working for the bad guys in *North by Northwest*, secrets can be a potent way to increase the emotional intensity of a scene. This is done through surprise, dramatic irony, or curiosity, depending on how much information you reveal to the reader prior to the scene. For instance, when the reader doesn't know the secret, there's curiosity as to why a character (who knows it) behaves in a particular way, followed by surprise when the secret is revealed. When the reader knows the secret and the character doesn't, we have that satisfying feeling of superior position brought about by dramatic irony, and which includes anticipating the moment the secret will be revealed. And when both the reader and the character learn the secret, they're equally surprised.

SHOCKING MOMENTS

Any event that has a high intensity of surprise, revulsion, horror, or violence could be labeled shocking. We can all remember the most shocking moments in our favorite films—the gut busting scene in *Alien*, the head swivel in *The Exorcist*, the shower scene in *Psycho*, the horse's head in *The Godfather*, the gender reveal in *The Crying Game*, Darth Vader admitting he's Luke's father in *The Empire Strikes Back*, or Evelyn's revelation about her father in *Chinatown*. In fact, one could argue that a scene is memorable because of its shocking event, so this is a powerful device to grip the reader, as long as it's a critical part of the story, and not thrown in just for effect.

SHOW, DON'T TELL

This is the most given advice to writers, and for good reason: It makes the scene more engaging because the reader is involved in concluding the meaning of a scene rather than being told about it, which is a passive and dull experience. Seeing a character's anger through his body language or violent behavior will always be more interesting than reading "He's angry." Try to show as much as you can. After all, you're writing for a visual medium. There's an old Hollywood anecdote involving Irving Thalberg working with a playwright on a seven-page dialogue scene designed to show a marriage in trouble. When the writer couldn't trim it down, Thalberg called in an old-time writer from the silent days. His solution: The couple gets into an elevator, and the husband doesn't bother to remove his hat. At the next floor, a pretty woman gets on, and the husband immediately takes off his hat. His wife gives him a dirty look. Fifteen seconds of screen time versus seven minutes. The lesson is that you can show so much without dialogue. Studying silent films is a great way to learn how to show instead of tell.

SPIN A CLICHÉD SCENE

Just as you can flip a clichéd emotion, you can flip a clichéd scene or spin it into something fresher. Marlon Brando once said, "Every scene has a cliché; I always try to find that cliché and get as far away from it as I can." As a writer, you should also avoid clichés. They will break the reader's bond with the page, no matter how much suspense or great dialogue your scene has. Amateurs often make the mistake of writing scenes readers have seen a hundred times. Professional screenwriters constantly try to turn clichéd scenes into something fresh and original. A great example of spinning a clichéd scene is the interrogation scene in *Basic Instinct*. The cliché would have been the detectives questioning Catherine Tremell, harassing her to reveal clues, and getting her to confess. But Joe Eszterhas spins the scene around by having Catherine be in complete control of the interrogation, mesmerizing the detectives with her body language and active dialogue designed to push their emotional buttons.

STRIKING IMAGES OR SPECIAL EFFECTS

Another sure way to inject exhilaration into a scene is through a memorable image or special effect that excites the senses and makes the reader go "WOW!" Think of *Terminator 2*, which would have been a clone of the original chase film without the distinctive special effects of the T-1000 cyborg. How about the striking underwater visuals in *Finding Nemo*, or the fresh stunts and imagery in *The Matrix*? Dazzling visuals and special effects are such intense attention grabbers that they shouldn't be overdone, or be so gratuitous as to break the reading experience.

SCENE SWEETENERS

Just as you add sugar to sweeten a dessert, a scene sweetener is anything that "sweetens" a scene, like a little romance, wit, or humor. Sweeteners are especially visible in film trailers. If you analyze them, you'll discover that most of the shots in a trailer are witty lines of dialogue, humorous situations, and romantic moments, which are the most sought-after visceral feelings audiences pay good money to experience. Sweeteners can be witty lines of dialogue, like in *Casablanca* or *All About Eve*, bits of humor like the swordsman shooting in *Raiders of the Lost Ark*, or a "gotcha" moment of poetic justice, like in *Chinatown*, when Gittes rips the ledger in the Records Office after the clerk gave him attitude. One could also argue that previous devices such as running gags, sexuality, violence, striking images, and special effects are scene sweeteners, as long as they create these sweet feelings of awe, love, happiness, amusement, and laughter.

SUBTEXT: OFF-THE-NOSE SCENES

It's been said that if a scene is about what the scene is really about, it's flat. Although we'll explore subtext in depth in Chapter 10 as it relates to dialogue, a dramatic scene can be fascinating if it has subtext—an underlying meaning implied by the surface of the scene. A scene with subtext is certain to be engaging, if not memorable, because it puts the reader's brain cells to work, as they have to piece together the emotional truth of the scene. Examples of subtextual scenes in great scripts include the eating scene in *Tom Jones*, the first meeting between Neff and Phyllis in *Double Indemnity*, and Grace Kelly talking about jewels in *To Catch a Thief*. There are many techniques you can use to create subtext, all of which I'll present in Chapter 10. One of the most effective, however, is to **contrast a character's dialogue with his actions**. He says something but does another, illustrating the truism that actions speak louder than words. If a character says he loves dogs but then recoils when he sees one, what's the truth of the scene? Clearly, he's afraid of dogs, but he may fear being judged negatively, so he lies. At the end of *When Harry Met Sally*, Sally tells Harry she hates him, but then kisses him. In *Casablanca*, Rick says he sticks his neck out for nobody, but he pockets the transit letters.

TWISTS AND REVERSALS

Just as plot twists are essential to maintaining momentum in a story, a scene twist or reversal is the key to maintaining momentum in a scene. Most well structured stories have at least two major turning points that end the first two acts. Similarly, a dramatic scene will have two turning beats that create surprise, raise the reader's curiosity, reveal insight into the scene or character, or point the scene into a new direction. The best way to grasp this device is to see it in action through the in-depth scene analysis at the end of this chapter.

VISCERAL EMOTION TECHNIQUES

By now, you should be aware that since scenes make up a story, all the techniques discussed in Chapter 6 to evoke an emotional response in the reader, from interest to curiosity, anticipation to suspense to surprise, thrills, and humor, can only be used in scenes. In other words, what you learned is how to create a particular emotional response. The next step is to put them to work in a scene as you design its emotional effect on the reader. For example, in addition to all the techniques in this chapter, I could browse through Chapter 6, decide I want additional tension in a scene, and use "Reader Superior Position" by revealing something a character doesn't know in the scene. Or let's say I want to create anticipation. I would then choose to have a character reveal a plan of action or daydream about something he truly wished. The possibilities are endless. What's most important in a scene, once you've planned its key elements, is its emotional effect on the reader. This is up to you. Now that you have the tools of the craft to make your writing desires a reality, you can spend more of your energy on the creative part—producing something fresh and original.

ON THE PAGE: SCENE IN ACTION

Let's look at a classic scene from the critically acclaimed and audience-favorite *The Silence of the Lambs*, adapted from the Thomas Harris novel by Ted Tally. The scene is where Clarice Starling confronts Hannibal Lecter for the fourth and last time, desperate for one last clue that'll help her catch Buffalo Bill. I chose this scene because it's one of the most fascinating, mesmerizing, and intense scenes I've read and seen. Upon analysis, you'll soon understand why. It also contains many of the techniques presented in this chapter. Since the screenplay is slightly different from the movie, I'll be using a transcription instead of the actual script pages. I suggest you first watch the scene for its emotional effect, and then read the scene a couple of times to see the techniques in action.

In the film, the scene is seven minutes long and yet, because of Clarice's desperation and the tension of the scene's context, it feels like seven seconds. Starting with the basic elements of a dramatic scene, we know the scene takes place in the evening on the fifth floor of the Shelby County Historical Society in Memphis, which has been sealed off to accommodate Lecter's cage. Like in their previous encounters, this is Lecter's scene. Although he's the prisoner, he knows he has all the power because of the information Clarice wants from him. He's also older and wiser, while Clarice is the student. Lecter wants to get inside her head and feed off her childhood's traumatic experiences. Clarice wants to catch Buffalo Bill. She suspects that, prior to this scene, Lecter has given the Senator false clues because Clarice's promise of a view on an island has been a sham. The conflict for both characters is clear. The stakes are high for Clarice. The scene has a clear beginning, middle, and end, with two turning points. Polarity-wise, it starts in the negative for Lecter—still a prisoner, no reward for his help, and still yearning for Clarice's emotional secrets, and ends in the positive—Clarice reveals her traumatic childhood event and what drives her to save Catherine from Buffalo Bill. This is a clear chase-and-capture scene for Lecter. Here are the individual beats that make up the scene:

Inside the cage, Dr. Lecter sits at a table, reading, his back to Clarice.
LECTER (*without turning*): Good evening, Clarice.

Beat #1 – Clarice apologizing and trying to get on his good side again.

Clarice returns his confiscated charcoal drawings, placing them at the edge of the cage.
CLARICE: I thought you might like your drawings back, doctor. Just until you get your view.
LECTER: How very thoughtful... Or did Jack Crawford send you for one last wheedle before you're both booted off the case.
CLARICE: No, I came because I wanted to.
LECTER: People will say we're in love.

Beat #2 – Lecter reprimanding her for her foolish scam.

LECTER (*clucking at her with his tongue*): Anthrax Island. That was an especially nice touch, Clarice. Yours?
CLARICE: Yes.
LECTER: Yeah. That was good. Pity about poor Catherine, though. Tick-tock, tick-tock, tick-tock, tick-tock.

Beat #3 – Clarice turning the tables, showing she's worthy, that she's figured out his false clues.

CLARICE: Your anagrams are showing, doctor. Louis Friend? Iron Sulfide. Also known as Fool's Gold.
LECTER: Oh, Clarice. Your problem is you need to get more fun out of life.

Beat #4 – Clarice wanting more clues on Buffalo Bill. Lecter responding indirectly to challenge her.

CLARICE: You were telling me the truth back in Baltimore, sir. Please continue now.

LECTER: I've read the case files. Have you? Everything you need to find him is right there in those pages.

Beat #5 – Clarice impatient and desperate, time running out.

CLARICE: Then tell me how.

LECTER: First principles, Clarice. Simplicity. Read Marcus Aurelius. Of each particular thing, ask, "What is it in itself, what is its nature?" What does he do, this man you seek?

CLARICE: He kills women.

LECTER (*scolding sharply*): No, that is incidental. What is the first and principal thing he does, what needs does he serve by killing?

CLARICE: Anger… social acceptance, and… sexual frustrations…

LECTER: No! He covets. That is his nature. And how do we begin to covet, Clarice? Do we seek out things to covet? Make an effort to answer now.

CLARICE: No, we just…

LECTER: No. We begin by coveting what we see every day. Don't you feel eyes moving over your body, Clarice? And don't your eyes seek out the things you want?

Clarice: All right, yes. Then, please tell me how…

Beat #6 – Lecter turning the tables, wanting more from Clarice's emotional past. The first turning point in the scene.

LECTER: No. It's your turn to tell me, Clarice. You don't have any more vacations to sell. Why did you leave that ranch?

CLARICE: Doctor, we don't have any more time for any of this now.

Beat #7 – Lecter insisting. Clarice desperate.

LECTER: But we don't reckon time the same way, do we, Clarice? This is all the time you'll ever have.

CLARICE: Later. Now please, listen to me. We've only got five…

Beat #8 – Lecter insisting again. Clarice finally surrendering.

LECTER: NO! I will listen now. After your father's murder, you were orphaned. You were ten years old. You went to live with cousins on a sheep and horse ranch in Montana. And…?

CLARICE: And one morning, I just ran away.

LECTER: Not just, Clarice. What set you off? You started at what time?

CLARICE: Early, still dark.

LECTER: Then something woke you, didn't it? Was it a dream? What was it?

CLARICE: I heard a strange noise.

LECTER: What was it?

CLARICE: It was - screaming. Some kind of screaming, like a child's voice.

LECTER: What did you do?

CLARICE: I went downstairs, outside. I crept up into the barn. I was so scared to look inside, but I had to.

LECTER: And what did you see, Clarice? What did you see?

CLARICE: Lambs. They were screaming.

LECTER: They were slaughtering these spring lambs?

CLARICE: And they were screaming.

LECTER: And you ran away?

CLARICE: No. First, I tried to free them. I... I opened the gate to their pen, but they wouldn't run. They just stood there, confused. They wouldn't run.

LECTER: But you could and you did, didn't you?

CLARICE: Yes. I took one lamb, and I ran away as fast as I could.

LECTER: Where were you going, Clarice?

CLARICE: I don't know. I didn't have any food, any water, and it was very cold, very cold. I thought... I thought if I could save just one, but... he was so heavy. So heavy. I didn't get more than a few miles when the sheriff's car picked me up. The rancher was so angry he sent me to live at the Lutheran orphanage in Bozeman. I never saw the ranch again.

LECTER: What became of your lamb, Clarice?

CLARICE: They killed him.

Beat #9 – Lecter relieved, understanding Clarice at last.

LECTER: You still wake up sometimes, don't you, wake up in the dark, and hear the screaming of the lambs?

CLARICE: Yes.

LECTER: And you think if you save poor Catherine you could make them stop, don't you? You think if Catherine lives, you won't wake up in the dark ever again to that awful screaming of the lambs.

CLARICE: I don't know. I don't know.

LECTER: Thank you, Clarice. Thank you.

Beat #10 – Clarice desperate for what Lecter promised her. But they're interrupted by Dr. Chilton—the second turning point of the scene.

CLARICE: Tell me his name, doctor.

We hear a door opening.

LECTER: Dr. Chilton, I presume. I think you know each other.

Chilton appears with Sgts. Pembry and Boyle beside him.

CHILTON: Okay, let's go.

Beat #11 – Clarice insisting.

CLARICE: It's your turn, doctor,

CHILTON: Out.

CLARICE: Tell me his name.

SGT. BOYLE: Sorry ma'm, I've got orders to put you on a plane.

LECTER: Brave Clarice. You will let me know when those lambs stop screaming, won't you?

CLARICE: Tell me his name, doctor.

Beat #12 – Lecter thanking Clarice for letting him into her head, and saying goodbye appropriately—the scene's climax.

LECTER: Clarice! Your case file.

Clarice struggles, pulling free to rush back to Lecter. As she reaches between the bars to take the file from Lecter's extended hand, he strokes her finger.

LECTER: Goodbye, Clarice.

Clarice hugs the case file to her chest, staring back at Lecter as the men push her away.

What makes this scene so fascinating is, of course, the unlikely relationship between the two characters. Some have even suggested this is a love story, and this scene is a like a **love scene**—Lecter climaxing at Clarice's intimate revelation about the screaming lambs, and reaching out to her in a final physical touch through the brief stroke of his finger (a **shocking moment**)—clearly a lot of **subtext** in this scene. But there are other obvious techniques at play that add emotional impact to this otherwise expository scene. At the hands of an amateur writer, this could have been a dull scene. Instead, Thomas Harris in the novel, and Ted Tally in the adaptation, used the following techniques:

The Emotional Palette: For **character cues,** we have Clarice's desperation for Lecter's help, rising in intensity throughout the scene, and her surrendering to his demands, as she purges out her demons. For Lecter, his emotional drive is his initial frustration at having been fooled, followed by his willingness to help Clarice, but still challenge her, as a good mentor would, and finally, his intense curiosity about Clarice's past. The writers are also mindful of the **reader's emotional response** to the scene's dynamics, creating **conflict** through the context of the scene—Clarice desperately needs valuable clues to catch Buffalo Bill and prove her worth; Lecter may not want to share them after she conned him earlier.

This alone is enough to make the scene interesting, but there's more: Certainly **anticipation** at whether Lecter will finally reveal an important clue, and **interest** at Clarice's past traumatic event, which is revealed bit by bit through **interrogation** and **active dialogue**, question and answer, and showcases Clarice's **inner-conflict** and Lecter's **deep curiosity.** We also have a **flipping of clichéd emotions,** since it's the prisoner who interrogates the FBI agent.

Contrast is evident throughout the scene—between values (free Clarice, incarcerated Lecter), between characters (good vs. evil), between behaviors (Lecter's violent nature vs. his soft caress of Clarice's finger), and between scene beats (Clarice's desperation vs. her slow and long revelation). Her revelation about the screaming lambs is a **discovery** for both Lecter and the audience. It's also a **character reveal** and a **secret** that shed light on Clarice's motivations for becoming an FBI agent and rescuing the vulnerable. This information serves as the **emotional payoff** to the **setup** established in Clarice and Lecter's previous meeting, where she began to share her past in their Quid Pro Quo agreement.

Lecter's charcoal drawings, which Clarice returns to him after Chilton confiscated them, can be seen as **props** that add meaning to the scene. They can be viewed as a peace offering, a token of Clarice's compassion for Lecter, or a bribe to make him more willing to help her.

There's a well-crafted balance between **satisfied and frustrated desires** in the scene beats. Look at each beat and notice how Clarice initially gets what she wants—Lecter helping her, but not in the way she expected—Lecter challenging her to come up with the answer of what the killer covets. Lecter is also frustrated when Clarice initially refuses to divulge her secret, but he insists and becomes satisfied by her surrendering. A couple of these beats are **reversals** and **turning points** in the scene—going from Lecter helping Clarice to demanding she reveal the secret of the screaming lambs, and Dr. Chilton interrupting their mentor-student connection.

Finally, the way Clarice and Lecter separate, their **goodbye**, is also gripping—having Dr. Chilton and the police officers forcefully escort Clarice out of the room, but not before a brief rebellious return to Lecter to get her file back. Chilton's interruption is also a **juxtaposition of two simultaneous conflicts**—Chilton vs. Clarice and Clarice vs. Lecter.

And this how you craft a fascinating scene.

You now have a collection of techniques to elevate your writing to the professional level. You've read about them and seen them in action in a classic scene. Now it's time to put them to good use in your screenplays. It's time to explore the last two essential elements of the craft, and the only two the reader will experience directly—description and dialogue...

DESCRIPTION

Riveting Style

> *"All the words you need are to be found in the dictionary. All you have to do is put them in the right order."*
>
> -EMMA DARCY

Description is not about what you say, but how you say it—how to shape your words to create specific emotions and moods. This chapter is about good writing. As the quote above implies, good writing is about putting words together repeatedly until they evoke the intended emotional response in the reader. William Goldman once said, "No one really knows what will be commercial, but everybody knows good writing from bad writing."

THE BASICS: WHAT YOU NEED TO KNOW

Always remember that when you're writing a script, it's meant to be read. This means it should be as exciting to read as the movie will be to view. If 95 percent of current spec scripts are awful to mediocre, this means 95 percent of writers ignore this essential factor. As screenwriters, we don't have the luxury of cameras, lights, actors, computer graphics, or music scores to generate emotions; we only have words. Because we chose to write for a visual medium, we have to tell a story with pictures, using as few words as possible, in order to make the reading of our script as engaging as possible. In the industry, we call it a "good read." To separate your work from the thousands of scripts making the Hollywood rounds, your description must be visually poetic in its brevity to be as riveting as possible.. Still, you don't want your writing to get in the way of your story and distract the reader. Remember, you want the reader to lose himself in the experience of the new world you created. You want your words to seep into the bones and soul of the first reader to get that coveted "Recommend." You'll learn how to accomplish this soon. That's what craft is all about. It also tells the reader from page one that he's in the hands of a great storyteller. Great writers do it consistently, others do it accidentally, most fail to do it, and readers reject their script. Have you ever read a William Goldman or Shane Black script? Regardless of the merits of the story, no one will argue that the *reading experience* wasn't unique and entertaining.

Although some may disagree, this chapter proposes that if you are a serious wordsmith, every single page, paragraph, sentence, and word in your script is important. No description in your script should be "just okay." Each sentence should have some sort of emotional impact. Sure, it's a lot to ask, but this is the professional standard you should aspire to. Novice writers worry so much about their story, structure, and characters that they ignore the emotional effect of their descriptive sentences. They take them for granted, especially after reading other mediocre scripts. The bottom line is that if you've mastered the other essential elements of the craft, your writing style probably won't be a deciding factor in whether it's recommended or passed on. But why take the risk? If you can control the emotional impact of your sentences, why not take advantage of it? I promise you it's not that difficult once you discover the techniques professionals use to create a riveting reading experience. But first, let's take a brief look at the most common faults that can sink a script.

COMMON AMATEUR MISTAKES

From my experience covering and consulting on hundreds of scripts, I've grouped the most common flaws into three categories: *Appearance*, which includes formatting, as well as spelling and grammatical errors; *over-description*, which involves unnecessary and bloated narrative; and simply *bad writing*, coming from individuals who clearly have no business being writers.

APPEARANCE, FORMAT, AND SPELLING

Let me state something right off the bat: If William Goldman submitted his best screenplay hand-written on toilet paper, no reader in his right mind would pass on it because it wasn't formatted correctly. Recommending a script is still dependent on its *overall* emotional impact. The reason script formatting gets so much attention is because it separates the pros from the amateurs, that is until a script is written with *Final Draft* or *Movie Magic Screenwriter.* Readers know what a professional script looks like, and they can spot an amateur a mile away. A flawed format immediately tells the reader that if the writer doesn't know basic formatting, chances are he doesn't know craft. The irony is that professional script formatting is the simplest and fastest element to master, especially with all the readily available software and virtually every screenwriting book on the market devoting a chapter to it. Because there is so much out there on the subject, there's nothing to add. Get the software and learn the basic formatting rules so that you can focus on the more important issues of the craft. As to spelling and grammatical errors, they disrupt the flow and take the reader out of the fictive dream, so check your script a couple of times. Don't rely on your spell checker, which will ignore typical reader pet peeves such as *it's* and *its*, *their*, *they're* and *there*, and *you're* and *your*.

OVER-DESCRIBED ACTION AND MINUTIAE

The second most common issue I see in amateur scripts is too much description. Because many aspiring screenwriters come from a fiction background, they tend to overwrite at every level, describing too much, using complex sentences and long paragraphs. Well-written doesn't mean over-written. The best example I've seen of overwriting comes courtesy of script consultant John Rainey, which he posts on his website: "The bovine, heavy with fatigue from its jaw-grinding day of harvesting fresh shoots of redtop and horsetail, swinging its milk-laden udder to and fro with its languorous gait, gingerly steps its way over the sun-baked and deeply-rutted dirt road on its way to relieve its lactate burden in the secure confines of the farmer's dairy barn." This could have been easily communicated with only five words: "The cow crosses the road." I'm not saying the above is bad writing, just that it belongs in a novel, not a screenplay.

Screenwriting, unlike novel writing, is not about writing long, stylish descriptions of settings, character thoughts, clothes, or hair color. It's not about describing every nuance of a character's expression, every hand gesture or raised eyebrow, every inflection and cadence of his dialogue, or the fluctuations of light and shadow. It's about verb-driven, visual, and active sentences that move. Most of all, it's about succinctness, saying the most with the least amount of choice words. This is why great screenwriting is often called "visual poetry." Your craft is to *evoke* images, not necessarily describe them. Scott Frank (*Out of Sight, Minority Report, The Interpreter*) says, "I usually write very few stage directions. I think a lot of that is a waste of time. The art of screenwriting is in its terseness, saying a lot with a little. I have no patience when I read a script where the writer describes this guy and what he's wearing and his glasses and his hair."

In today's Hollywood, the goal is a fast read, an easy read, which means narrative must be kept to a minimum through concise writing—sentences that are short, often one-word and fragmented, and paragraphs no longer than four lines.

BAD WRITING

It may be shocking to learn that 95 percent of amateur scripts, and even professional ones, are poorly written by writers who seem to forget someone has to read their bland writing. Either they haven't mastered the craft, or they don't have the aptitude to communicate through the written word. The sad truth is that many who attempt screenwriting have no business being a writer. In *101 Habits*, Ron

Bass says it best: "For some reason, there's a notion that writing is something anyone could do. Because everybody owns a computer and everybody knows the English language and likes to go to the movies or read books and think about stories, everybody thinks they could do it. The key is: Can everybody not only do it well, but do it well enough that you'd want to pay money to go see that story? Every woman in the world puts on makeup, but how many could become a supermodel? Nobody can stop you from putting on makeup. You just never make it on the covers of magazines because someone has to ask you to model for them. It's the same with the desire to become a screenwriter. You don't need anyone's permission. It doesn't cost you anything. All you have to do is write 120 pages and print them. Starting is easy. Making it is another story. There's a certain ability needed to do anything, be it natural talent, intelligence, passion, desire, experience, whatever it is that makes people good at anything that needs to be done at a high enough level for other people to want to support it. When you get down to somebody spending $80 million to make a movie out of a script, do we really think anyone could do it?"

If you feel writing is your calling, you need to become an expert at using your only tool of the trade—words. You already know that screenwriting calls for a concise type of narrative writing, so let's explore its basics before tackling the craft of description for emotional impact.

THE BASICS OF SCREENWRITING NARRATIVE

Before you submit your screenplay to agents and producers, its presentation should be flawless. This means perfect format, no spelling errors and typos, and no wasted words. This is my standard for clients and for my own writing. It's possible to reach this standard if you make the effort in the polishing stage.

The following prescriptions are not rules set in stone, just common sense advice from professional readers and screenwriters to make your script a fast and easy read. To do this you must avoid the distractions that shatter the fictive spell. Since you don't want to remind the reader he's reading text on the page, here's what to avoid whenever possible:

AVOID CAMERA DIRECTIONS

There are two pieces of advice in this category: Avoid directing the director with camera directions (unless you're also directing the script), and avoid directing the actors in a scene. Your job is to tell the story, not direct the movie with camera directions such as ANGLE ON, CLOSE UP, PAN TO, TRACK ALONG WITH, CUT TO, INSERT, etc. These clutter the script and distract the reader, and directors don't want to be told how to direct the movie. The only acceptable directions are FADE IN at the beginning of your script and FADE OUT at the end, with the occasional DISSOLVE TO in between if you wish to indicate a long passage of time. You can still direct the movie subtly without actually using camera shots. You'll see how soon using a technique called "Virtual close-ups."

Similarly, don't direct actors by describing the details of every physical action and emotional reaction—every look, frown, or eyelid twitch. Some details are fine, but don't overdo it. If the context of the scene and the character's emotions are clear, the reader will fill in the rest. Leave it to the actors to decide the best way to convey physically what the character is feeling.

AVOID THE PASSIVE VOICE

For some reason, the passive sentence sounds better in the writer's mind than its active counterpart, but it doesn't read better on the page. The passive voice, for those who have forgotten their grammar lessons, combines the verb "to be" with the past participle of an action verb, which actually weakens the action and often reverses the subject and object of the sentence. For example, "The car is driven by John" or "The food is eaten by Jane" are passive voices. But it's better to write in the active voice, such as "John drives the car" or "Jane eats the food." Whenever possible, use the active voice over the passive.

AVOID THE NEGATIVE

Similar to the active voice, a positive description is often more potent than its negative version. For example, rather than write, "He's not a generous man," try "He's a miser." Or instead of, "He's not graceful person," try "He's a klutz." It's often better to show what you want to show the reader, not what you don't want him to see. You'll also use fewer words.

AVOID PARENTHETICALS

Parentheticals are the instructions you see in parenthesis between the character heading and his dialogue, such as (laughing), (coldly), (distressed), or (whispering). Just like an actor's physical direction, the writer tells the actor how to feel and say his lines. Thus, they're frowned upon by readers, directors, and actors, who often go through a script and erase them so that the writer does not influence their interpretations. As you go through your script, you should delete any parenthetical that includes an emotional reference, except when there's ambiguity, and clarity is essential to the subtext of the scene. For instance, if there's no other way for the reader to know what the emotion is from the context or the dialogue, like when a character is hurt and says "Hello" in a cold and detached manner, you may want to add the parenthetical (cold) or (icy). Otherwise, a character's emotions should be clear from the context and from the character's speech.

Parentheticals are only acceptable in the following cases: When they specify the dialogue should be spoken in **a particular accent or foreign language**, like (in Spanish); when they **indicate to whom a line of dialogue is addressed** when there are more than two characters in a scene, like (to John); and when the parentheticals describe **a particular character action** if it's quick enough, such as (lighting a cigarette)—this saves you space on the page instead of wasting an entire line for three words. Again, only do this if the action is crucial to the scene. Most readers tend to read vertically down the dialogue column, skipping the narrative description. So this is a good way to make sure essential behavior is not overlooked.

AVOID ADVERBS

Adverbs are verb modifiers, and they're often used by writers too lazy to search for the right verb. For instance, they may use a generic verb like "run" and add the modifier "quickly," instead of using the more appropriate "sprint." Novice writers tend to overuse and misuse common adverbs. This leads to weak and clichéd writing. The good news is that it's not difficult to go through your first draft, flag out weak verbs with adverbs such as "quickly, slowly, softly, loudly, quietly, gently, etc.," and replace them with more dynamic action verbs. This is when you can put your thesaurus to good use. For example, you could replace "walks slowly" with "strolls;" "runs quickly" with "darts, dashes, sprints, or scurries;" "looks cautiously" with "peeks," "looks angrily" with "glares;" and "looks longingly" with "gazes." Think of how many words you'll save. Adverbs not only weaken your writing but they take up space and waste ink. Also, pay attention to "intensifiers"—words that modify adjectives, such as "very, extremely, really, generally, usually, basically, awfully, quite, ultimately, mostly, etc."

AVOID "STARTS TO" AND PRESENT PARTICIPLES

When possible, eliminate "starts to" and "begins to" from your draft. You can easily replace, "She starts to cry" with "She cries," or, "It begins to melt" with "It melts." Again, less words and more impact on the page. Also, pay attention to your present participles, which are verbs in the "ing" form, such as "walking, eating, staring, or driving." It's better to write, "He walks, he eats, he stares, or he drives." Always think of the simplest sentence construction: subject and active verb.

AVOID "THERE IS" AND "THERE ARE"

Another unnecessary use of words I see often in amateur scripts is, "There is" and "There are," as in "There is a house" or "There are cars in the street." Better to write, "A house" or "Cars in the street." Or even better, make the subjects active to give them life, as in "The house overlooks the bay" or "Cars zoom by."

AVOID "WE SEE" AND "WE HEAR"

This is a bit controversial because even professional screenwriters often use these words. When you think about it, however, they're not only unnecessary, they also break the fictive bond between reader and page by referring to the audience.

"We see" and "We hear" are an audience's point of view, and therefore take the reader out of the experience. Keep in mind that a screenplay communicates only two kinds of information: sight and sound. Every single element down to the last detail is either a visual or a sound. When I write, "A house," we can clearly see a house. I don't have to write, "We see a house." The same goes for, "We hear." Everything that's heard in the script, we hear. Everything described, we see. Cut out all references to "We see" and "We hear." It's redundant.

THE CRAFT: WRITING THAT MOVES

Now that you know how to trim the fat from your narrative, it's time to get to the good stuff—the craft of writing description that pulses and sings and mesmerizes the reader with its vividness. Never forget that good description is carefully worded. You want to charge your language to make the reading so electric, palpable, and so vibrant that the reader can *feel* it. Great writers are never happy until they find the right words to communicate their vision. When they do, the result is visual poetry—lean, clear, and emotionally effective.

COMMANDING ATTENTION

One effective way to punch up your writing is to command attention on the page, and control the reader's eye for the intended visual effect. In fact, this is how professional screenwriters direct on the page without actually telling the director where to place the camera. Here are several tricks of the trade so you can do the same:

VERTICAL WRITING - LEADING THE EYE ON THE PAGE

Prose writers tend to write horizontally from left to right. Screenwriters write vertically down the page, which creates a dynamic pace that speeds up the reading. The reason it does is that our eyes are trained to jump to the left side of the page, for the start of a new sentence, which means new information. To take advantage of this, screenwriters begin a new sentence in a new line for every new shot. Every time you imagine a new camera angle with new visuals, you start a new line of action, no matter how long each line may be. The following example is a page from the Walter Hill and David Giler draft of *Alien*, which is a perfect illustration of vertical writing[1]:

LAMBERT
What's the matter?
KANE
I don't know... I'm getting cramps.

The others stare at him in alarm.
Suddenly he makes a loud groaning noise.
Clutches the edge of the table with his hands.
Knuckles whitening.

---

1   *For readability and space, script examples are not in standard format.*

                                ASH
                        Breathe deeply.

Kane screams.

                                KANE
                Oh God, it hurts so bad. It hurts. It hurts.
                        (stands up)
                Ooooooh.

                                BRETT
                What is it? What hurts?

Kane's face screws into a mask of agony.
He falls back into his chair.

                                KANE
                Ohmygooaaaahh.

A red stain.
Then a smear of blood blossoms on his chest.
The fabric of his shirt is ripped apart.
A small head the size of a man's fist pushes out.
The crew shouts in panic.
Leaps back from the table.
The cat spits, bolts away.
The tiny head lunges forward.
Comes spurting out of Kane's chest trailing a thick body.
Splatters fluids and blood in its wake.
Lands in the middle of the dishes and food.
Wriggles away while the crew scatters.
Then the alien being disappears from sight.
Kane lies slumped in his chair.
Very dead.
A huge hole in his chest.

Note how each line is a new visual or shot in the reader's mind. With vertical writing, you never need to write a camera angle, such as INSERT, CLOSE UP, or ANGLE ON. You're actually directing the scene by the way you place your sentences, and controlling the pace by their length. Long sentences feel like lengthy shots; short sentences, even one word sentences, feel like quick cuts.

ISOLATE WORDS FOR VIRTUAL CLOSE-UPS

Isolating a word so it stands out on its own in a line creates an automatic close-up in the reader's mind and visual impact. In professional scripts, you see many pages like the following, written by Tom Mercer, the 1998 winner of the Screenwriting Group's Page One Contest. For your benefit, I've bolded the close ups:

EXT. AN OLD OIL DERRICK, SOUTH TEXAS - DAY

A barren eyesore. Not a drop of crude pumped since the 80's. A brisk wind whistles through the holes of a surrounding chain link fence, as

BENJAMIN FRANKLIN

on a hundred dollar bill hits the fence with a wet slap. It is soon joined by others. A few at a time, then several.

Dead presidents on currency, striking the fence like locusts.

A HANDWRITTEN SIGN - NO TRESPASSING

It violently rocks in the wind, so much it falls off the fence striking the ground.

Where it joins a blood-soaked body.

BENJAMIN CASTILLO

AKA Baby B, the baby-faced LT. CASTILLO of the Laredo Police Dept. Right now, he is doing a great imitation of a dead guy staring fish-eyed in the blistering midday sun.

The wind licks his body. His tattered jacket billows in the wind, releasing a chain of blood soaked money in the air.

An errant bill is lifted in the desert breeze. A fiver. Lincoln looking his usual grim between two crimson drops of blood.

A HAND, well-manicured and feminine, picks it up, and lifts it to a very pretty face of a WOMAN. She takes in the scent of blood and currency.

WOMAN
I do love the smell of Texas blood money.

Castillo is in no position to argue.

This technique is especially common in action scripts to make action sequences easier to read, visualize, and understand.

INTRA-SCENE LOCATION HEADINGS

Making your pages easy to read is a key factor in the overall reader satisfaction. You already know you should avoid camera and other technical directions. There is, however, one technical element you can't avoid—the slug line, or location heading, such as "INT. RESTAURANT – NIGHT," which establishes location and time. The problem with slug lines is that too many of them can get in the way of the flow of a scene and can take the reader out of the fictive spell. This is especially a problem if a character moves through a series of locations in a short period, like in a house, moving through several rooms. The amateur writer would write, "INT. MIKE'S HOUSE – BEDROOM – NIGHT," then as the character moves to another room, "INT. MIKE'S HOUSE –BATHROOM– NIGHT," and then, "INT. MIKE'S HOUSE –KITCHEN– NIGHT." The pro would establish Mike's house with one slug line, then simply keep the other rooms to one word, thus making the reading experience smoother, like in the following example, from *48 Hrs. (Roger Spottiswoode, Walter Hill, Larry Gross, Steven E. DeSouza)*:

DOORWAY

The portal slams open revealing a man holding a huge pistol, JACK CATES, S.F.P.D., a large and powerful man... He stealthily moves up a stairwell.

CORRIDOR

He stops at the top of the stairs... Listens, gun still ready. A continuous sound of running water... Cates moves toward the bathroom. Rips the door open.

BATHROOM

The shape behind the shower curtain freezes. Cates, gun held level, moves forward... Rips the shower curtain open. Revealing a young and very beautiful woman, ELAINE MARSHALL.

CATES

Inspector Jack Cates, S.F.P.D. And you're
wanted.

[scene continues]

BEDROOM

Cates in bed with Elaine. She wears his shirt.

GET SPECIFIC

More often than not, choosing a concrete detail over a generalization adds impact to your writing. For instance, if I read in a newspaper that a dog attacked a girl, it's not as compelling as a Doberman Pinscher that attacked a girl. Which do you see better? The dog or the Doberman Pinscher? A car or a red 2005 Corvette? A gun or a Smith & Wesson .38? Look at your writing and see where you can be more specific. The trick is to name things that target any of our five senses. Instead of "eating ice cream," you're now enjoying a "double-fudge Rocky Road with a cherry on the top." Look at the following example from *The Shawshank Redemption (Frank Darabont)*, details in bold:

> He opens the glove compartment, pulls out an object wrapped in a rag. He lays it in his lap and unwraps it carefully --
>
> -- revealing a **.38 revolver**. Oily, black, evil.
>
> EXT. **PLYMOUTH** - NIGHT (1946)
>
> His **wingtip shoes** crunch on gravel. Loose bullets scatter to the ground. The **bourbon bottle** drops and shatters.

REPLACE WEAK WORDS

Remember your basics, how you should avoid verb modifiers and choose active, dynamic, high-energy verbs that pop off the page? The same goes for weak, sluggish words that don't add impact to your narrative. Whenever possible, replace these flat words with more vivid ones. For example, rather than say, "She is a mean woman," write, "She's a shrew." Instead of, "He's a generous and thoughtful man," try "He's a saint." Again, think visual poetry—saying the most in a vivid way with the least amount of well-chosen words.

LESS IS MORE

Most seasoned readers can tell by the end of page one whether a writer is a pro or an amateur, especially through the writer's narrative abilities—how competent he is in evoking vivid images through a limited amount of words. As you saw earlier, most amateur scripts tend to be overwritten because the writers think of them the way they think of novels, and thus write highly detailed prose. The result is a blur of black lines on the page, when "white space" is the ideal (more on this soon). This is a turnoff for the overworked reader who reads scripts full-time. Sure, it's great for novels, but unacceptable for scripts. The bottom line is that writing a script is more like writing poetry—vivid simplicity, brief and clear. Every word counts. The less amount of words you use to contain a thought or an image, the more impact that thought or image will have. This advice is especially effective when it comes to describing characters and locations, as you'll see later in this chapter.

TRIM THE FAT OF REDUNDANCY

Pablo Picasso once said, "Art is the elimination of the unnecessary." One way to command attention and convey as much information as possible in as little words as possible is to eliminate unnecessary words and clauses, especially when they're redundant. For instance, instead of following the maxim "Show, don't tell," novice writers often do both—they show *and* they tell. They tell the reader how the character feels, and then show us the behavior that actually indicates the feeling, like in the following: "Sally is happy. She smiles." In this case, always choose the behavior over the feeling. Show us; don't tell us. Every line should contribute to character and plot advancement. If it doesn't, consider cutting it.

WEAVE INFORMATION INTO THE ACTIONS AND REACTIONS OF A CHARACTER

Getting information across in a subtle way is another challenge for writers—how much is enough, when to tell it, and more important, how not to bore the reader with it. It's difficult to involve the reader with static description. First, you should decide whether the information you're about to describe is essential to the story or the character. Usually, physical details other than a character's age are irrelevant to the story, unless they contribute to that character's unique essence. This means, we don't need to know a character's hairstyle and color, what type of eyes he has, how tall he is, or what he's wearing. Next, if a detail is essential to the plot or the character's attitude and personality, such as a deformity or the fact that he's wearing thick glasses, the solution is to have the character *interact* with that detail. For example, rather than say, "The apartment is filthy—empty beer cans everywhere, fast food wrappers, a total mess," write, "Mike looks for a place to sit, wipes off empty beer cans and fast food wrappers off the sofa." The details of the apartment's filthiness are embedded in Mike's actions. This works better because the reader is focusing on Mike, so the description registers in a more subtle way. Whenever possible, don't simply describe things; show a character interacting with or reacting to them.

WHITE SPACE

If you execute most of the above techniques on the page, it should have what most readers call "white space," which is an overall look caused by short paragraphs, short sentences, virtual close-ups, and no camera directions, as opposed to dense blocks of black text, which are hard to read. Many readers have told me that before reading a script, they flip through it to see how much text is on the page. White space gives them confidence that the read will be fast and easy. Large blocks of description do not, causing them to choose another script in the pile.

When possible, break your description paragraphs into blocks of one to four lines maximum to achieve that lean and clean look. And don't forget to apply any of the techniques above to command attention on the page.

CREATING MOTION

Another way to achieve emotional impact through your narrative is to create motion. Never forget that movement is the essence of films. It's no accident that they're called "movies" and "motion-pictures." This means your screenplay must move, and I don't mean just your characters. You want active words and sentences, charged language that creates momentum and makes the reading vivid, not flat. When your writing is active, description leaps off the page, and the reader can feel it. Here are some techniques to help you do that:

ALWAYS CHOOSE ACTIVE INSTEAD OF STATIC

The most given piece of advice for beginners is "Show, don't tell." Showing is active; telling is static and flat. Most writers, however, don't know how to do this on the page. So here's the trick, which is worth more than price of this entire book, in my humble opinion. I say this because when I finally learned this technique, it drastically improved my writing. So here it is:

Always describe something through its actions, rather than tell the reader about it through adjectives and adverbs. For example, rather than say, "Sally is happy," you write, "Sally smiles." Instead of, "John is nervous," try, "John paces back and forth." Go through your manuscript, and for every adjective you find, see if you can replace it with an active verb. For everything that is, ask yourself what it does. Use actions that imply the adjectives. Look at your adjectives that tell and turn them into verbs that show. Instead of "Her eyes are bright," try,

"Her eyes sparkle." "A loud man" becomes "The man roars." And "a happy dog" turns into "The dog wags its tail."

Look again at the Page One winning page on page 155, and note how the writer could have easily said, "It's windy." But look at what he wrote instead, which made the description palpable: *A brisk wind whistles, a hundred dollar bill hits the fence with a wet slap, striking the fence like locusts, violently rocks in the wind, the wind licks his body, jacket billows in the wind,* and *errant bill is lifted in the desert breeze.* Note the active verbs instead of adjectives. Always think movement. Don't describe things; describe things that do something. It doesn't mean a thing has to move from point A to point B. Just that things are *doing* something instead of *being* something.

SET THE RIGHT PACE

Pace, which is the rhythm and speed of your scenes, can also be a factor in creating motion. A scene's pace can be slow or fast, pastoral or chaotic, leisurely or rushed. Setting the right pace depends on your script's genre and story. In general, an action thriller will move faster than a period drama. Look at the following two examples, and see how their pace differs from each other using words, length of sentences, and the characters' actions and speech:

THE GODFATHER (FRANCIS FORD COPPOLA, MARIO PUZO)

By now, THE VIEW is full, and we see Don Corleone's office in his home. The blinds are closed, and so the room is dark, and with patterned shadows. We are watching BONASERA over the shoulder of DON CORLEONE. TOM HAGEN sits near a small table, examining some paperwork, and SONNY CORLEONE stands impatiently by the window nearest his father, sipping from a glass of wine. We can HEAR music, and the laughter and voices of many people outside.

> DON CORLEONE
> Bonasera, we know each other for years, but this is the first time you come to me for help. I don't remember the last time you invited me to your house for coffee...even though our wives are friends.

> BONASERA
> What do you want of me? I'll give you anything you want, but do what I ask!

ALIEN

> RIPLEY
> Wait.

They stop quickly, almost stumbling.

> RIPLEY
> It's within five meters.

Parker and Brett heft the net.

Ripley has the prod in one hand, tracker in the other.
Moves with great care.
Almost in a half-crouch, ready to leap back.
Prod extended, Ripley constantly glances at her tracker.
The device leads her up to a small hatch in the bulkhead.
Perspiration rivers down her face.
She sets aside the tracker.
Raises the prod, grasps the hatch handle.
Yanks it open.
Jams the electric prod inside.
A nerve-shattering squall.
Then a small creature comes flying out of the locker.
Eyes glaring, claws flashing.
Instinctively, they throw the net over it.
Very annoyed.
They open the net and release the captive.
Which happens to be the cat.
Hissing and spitting...it scampers away.

USE DYNAMIC HIGH-ENERGY VERBS

Now that you know you should replace adjectives with active verbs whenever possible, you should also pay attention to the kinds of verbs you choose. To create motion, spend some time selecting the perfect verb for each sentence—verbs that move, dynamic verbs that have high-energy and are more potent than regular active verbs. For example, the bell **clangs** instead of *rings*; sludge **oozes** instead of *drips*; the parasol **sways** instead of *moves*; the woman **sobs** instead of *cries*; the man **sprints** instead of *runs*. Here's a professional example from the master of dynamic verbs, Shane Black:

LETHAL WEAPON

Lloyd **blinks**. **Swallows**. Another moment. Finally—
He **lowers** the gun. **Sighs**.

LLOYD
...What do you want to know...?

Murtaugh relaxes visibly. And that's when two things happen. The picture WINDOW GLASS suddenly **COLLAPSES**. Falls **TINKLING** into a million shards.

And the carton of milk in Lloyd's hand **pops**, **spurting** milk all over the front of his black suit.

He **frowns**. Stares at the dribbling milk. **Blinks**. And his eyes **snap** open wide, as blood **seeps** out of his shirt, **spattering** the floor.

LLOYD
Roger -- !

With his dying breath, he **leaps** in front of Murtaugh. Takes the SECOND BULLET. The one meant for Murtaugh. It **blows** him into Roger, takes them both to the floor in a breath-crushing impact.

More BULLETS **CHOP** the kitchen. China PLATES **BURST** into a glassy spray. Food **spatters** and **gushes**, staining the walls.

GENERATING A RIVETING READING EXPERIENCE

Commanding attention on the page and creating motion through active description alone will dramatically increase the emotional effectiveness of your narrative style. But there are additional tricks of the trade that can generate a riveting reading experience regardless of your genre. Remember, you only have one chance to impress the reader. Why not make it a great one that resonates emotionally on all levels, including your description?

SENSORY WORDS

You know that great description is carefully worded. It is also sensory. Professional writers who care about how their words affect the reader emotionally pick simple but interesting words, words that glow, pulse, bleed, and kick, specifically words that appeal to our five senses—sight, hearing, smell, taste, and touch. When it comes to description, the thesaurus is your most valuable tool. After writing your first draft without worrying about word choices, replace your static words with sensory words, such as *peer, snoop, bark, snap, fragrant, musky, bitter, juicy, caress* or *kiss*. Look again at the Page One winner (p. 155), and note how many sensory words are evident: *barren eyesore... brisk wind whistles... hits the fence with a wet slap... like locusts... violently rocks in the wind... blood-soaked body... staring fish-eyed in the blistering midday sun... wind licks his body... tattered jacket billows in the wind... blood-soaked money... breeze... crimson drops of blood.* The more sensory words on the page, the more palpable and vivid the reading experience.

SOUND BURSTS

Sound bursts, also known as *onomatopoeia,* are words that mimic natural sounds, such as *whomp, whap, clang, screech,* specifically sensory words that appeal to our hearing. Often, these sounds become verbs because their sound reflects their meaning. For example, it is recommended to match certain nouns with their corresponding onomatopoeic verb—bells *clang*, birds *chirp*, wolves *howl*, winds *whistle*. Here are a couple of professional examples:

BLADE RUNNER (HAMPTON FANCHER, DAVID PEOPLES)

> BATTY
> My eyes... I guess you designed them, eh?
> CHEW
> You Nexus? I design Nexus eyes.

SMASH! Leon, infuriated by the unblinking eyes, smashes the tank and the insolent eyes pour out onto the floor. Batty smiles and points to his own eyes.

> BATTY
> Ah, Chew...

> **(squish, squish)**
> If only you could see the things I have seen with
> your eyes.

Squish! Squish! The squishes are Batty's feet stepping in eyeballs as he paces in front of Chew.

SE7EN (ANDREW KEVIN WALKER)

> He reaches to the nightstand, to a wooden, pyramidical metronome. He frees the metronome's weighted swing arm so it moves back and forth. Swings to the left -- **TICK**, swings to the right -- **TICK**.
>
> **Tick... tick... tick...** measured and steady.

Emotional cues revisited

As you saw in Chapter 8, emotional cues are the emotions a character feels in a scene. Applying the "Show, don't tell" maxim, you can show these emotions by describing a character's actions, which cue the reader to the character's emotions in a scene. They're often more expressive than the actual telling of the emotion. For instance, great writers show how a character is angry by writing **specific actions that suggest this emotion.** They would never write, "She is angry." Instead, they would write, "She throws a pot through the window." Be aware that actions are always more truthful than what a character might say to describe an emotion. In *When Harry Met Sally*, when Sally says to Harry, "I hate you," then kisses him, which is the truth? The line or the action? Right, the action. We are what we do. Since dialogue should be subtextual, the truth of a scene is not in the dialogue but in its emotional cues, which are visual. Look at the following example from *The Long Kiss Goodnight*, and how Shane Black conveys the little girl's fears without ever mentioning it on the page:

> INSIDE, a bed, dappled with moon shadow.
>
> A LITTLE GIRL, fast asleep. The wind whistles and sighs outside. She DREAMS... Eyelids closed, eyes roving beneath... then suddenly they SNAP open. A stifled cry. She thrashes for her STUFFED BEAR, as a soft voice says:
>
> > VOICE
> > Shhhhh.
>
> And there's MOM, kneeling beside her. Vague shape in the dimness. The full moon throws light across one sparkling eye.
>
> > LITTLE GIRL
> > Mommy, the men on the mountain...
> > MOM
> > Shhhh. Gone, all gone now.
> > (strokes her hair)
> > I'm here. Mommy's always here and no one can

ever hurt you. Safe now... safe and warm... snug
as a bug in a rug.
(beat)
I'll sit with you, think you can sleep?
LITTLE GIRL
Turn on the nightlight.

TALKING DESCRIPTIONS

This advanced technique uses *unspoken dialogue* as straight description to convey
a character's reaction to an event or previous line of dialogue. It can also convey
a character's thoughts without actually telling the reader what the character is
thinking. On the page, it would look like this:

JOHN
I was at the movies.

Yeah, right.

JOHN
I swear!

Most writers get away with communicating thoughts by writing something
like, "He gives her a look that says, 'Yeah, right.'" Talking description, on the
hand, is a shorter and more effective "Yeah, right" without the previous seven
words. Here are more examples:

ALIENS (JAMES CAMERON)

HICKS
Not that tunnel, the other one!

CROWE
You sure? Watch it...behind you. Fucking move,
will you!

Gorman is ashen. Confused. Gulping for air like a grouper. **How could the situation
have unraveled so fast?**

RIPLEY
(to Gorman)
GET THEM OUT OF THERE! DO IT NOW!

GORMAN
Shut up. Just shut up!

SOMETHING'S GOTTA GIVE (NANCY MEYERS)

HARRY
This is crazy. I can't remember the last time I
cried. I think I'm overwhelmed.

ERICA
(crying with him)
Me too. That's the perfect word.

> HARRY
> Baby, I had sex three days after a heart attack
> and I didn't die.

Erica pauses. **Oh. That kind of overwhelmed.**

SIDEWAYS (ALEXANDER PAYNE, JIM TAYLOR)

> MILES
> (suppressing his panic)
> But I like a lot of wines besides Pinot too. Lately
> I've really been into Rieslings. Do you like
> Rieslings? Rieslings?

She nods, a Mona Lisa smile on her lips. **Come on, Miles.** Finally –

> MILES
> (pointing)
> Bathroom over there?

A similar technique is the **talking parenthetical**. Here, the *meaning* of the line is in parentheses as the dialogue is spoken. Just like a regular parenthetical, this shouldn't be overdone. Only use it when the actual dialogue is so general that the reader couldn't possibly understand its true meaning, and when the dialogue's true meaning is crucial to the scene's dynamics. Here's an example from *American Beauty (Alan Ball)*:

> LESTER
> Oh really, do you need a ride? We can give you a
> ride. I have a car. You wanna come with us?

> ANGELA
> Thanks... but I have a car.

> LESTER
> Oh, you have a car. Oh. That's great! That's
> great, because Janie's thinking about getting a
> car soon too, aren't you, honey?

> JANE
> **(you freak)**
> Dad. Mom's waiting for you.

EMOTIONALLY EVOCATIVE VERBS AND ADJECTIVES

Just as we explored dynamic high-energy verbs to evoke a sense of motion on the page, you can use verbs that connote emotion. For instance, the verb *to walk* is a generic action, but *to stride*, *to march*, *to pace*, and *to amble* evoke the feelings of purpose, anger, anxiety, and contentment respectively. When possible, see if you can replace a generic, emotionless verb with an emotionally evocative verb. It can only make your description more riveting to read. You may also use emotionally evocative adjectives. For example, a room can be *dingy, sterile, homey, busy, inviting, silent, tacky*, etc.

VISUAL SYMBOLISM

Visual symbolism is another effective way to add emotional depth to your narrative. This is an advanced technique because it's difficult to master, and it's something that works at the subconscious level. When it comes to symbolism, techniques include *metaphors and similes, symbols and leitmotifs, colors, and weather patterns.*

METAPHOR AND SIMILES

One of my favorite techniques to punch up description is to use metaphors and similes. Since this is an advanced writing book, I assume you know what these literary terms mean, but if you don't, both are figures of speech that compare two things. A simile says something is *like* something else, as in "Life is like a river of emotions," whereas a metaphor says something actually *is* something else, as in "Life is a river of emotions." When used in scripts, metaphors and similes can make your narrative more colorful and fresher than the flat writing readers endure on a daily basis. Look at this example from *Big Fish (John August)*: "On EDWARD as his heart falls 20 floors." This, of course, is an implicit metaphor comparing Edward's heart to a loose elevator falling down to evoke a sense of extreme disappointment without actually saying so. It's a fresher way to write it than, "Edward's heart feels like an elevator that falls 20 floors." Here are more examples:

TAXI DRIVER (PAUL SCHRADER)

Betsy doesn't quite know what to make of Travis. She is curious, intrigued, tantalized. **Like a moth, she draws closer to the flame**.

Travis' cold piercingly eyes stare out from his cab parked across the street from Palantine Headquarters. He is **like a lone wolf** watching the **warm campfires of civilization** from a distance.

AMERICAN BEAUTY

> CAROLYN
> I will sell this house today.

She says this as if it were **a threat**, then notices a smudge on the mirror and wipes it off.

EXT. SALE HOUSE - FRONT YARD – LATER

The front door opens to reveal Carolyn, greeting us with **the smile she thinks could sell ice to an Eskimo**.

SIDEWAYS

The phone RINGS and both men look at it, silenced by the ominous sound.

> MILES
> Don't answer it.

But Jack is drawn to it as though **enticed by a strange game of Russian roulette**.

SYMBOLS AND LEITMOTIFS

A symbol is a visible thing that by association or convention represents an invisible thing, like the eagle, which symbolizes the United States of America. A leitmotif is a musical term that describes a melodic phrase that comes along every time a character or situation reappears, like the "DAA DUM" in *Jaws*. But when it comes to writing, a leitmotif is a **reoccurring symbol** attached to a corresponding event or character, such as the red rose petals in *American Beauty*. Symbols are a powerful way to tell your story with pictures, especially when they're used to reflect your themes. For example, look at the opening image of *Rocky*—a picture of Jesus on a sign that says "Resurrection Athletic Club," which clearly symbolizes Rocky's resurrection from bum to champion. In *Body Heat*, the opening image is flames in the night sky, which symbolize the heat of passion. The leitmotif in *Casablanca* is the airport's beacon light sweeping across the exterior of Rick's café, which resembles a prison's circular searchlight and represents the forced confinement of everyone in the city.

COLORS

Colors can be considered symbols and leitmotifs, as you saw above in the *American Beauty* example—red symbolizing excitement, energy, desire, and passion. Red can also represent heat, love, danger, violence, and all things intense. It's no accident that the color red is prominent throughout *American Beauty*. Yellow represents happiness, idealism, imagination, and hope. Blue represents peace, tranquility, harmony, cold, technology, and depression. Green represents nature, health, renewal, youth, fertility, jealousy, and misfortune. And let's not forget black and white—white representing purity, simplicity, innocence, birth, winter, sterility, marriage (in Western cultures), and death (Eastern cultures), while black represents power, elegance, wealth, mystery, evil, anonymity, mourning, and death (Western cultures).

WEATHER ELEMENTS

The weather and other natural patterns are also a powerful way to symbolize themes and emotions. Think of waves, the wind, heat, and fog, which elicit emotions such as love, passion, hate, and fear respectively.

Keep in mind that visual symbolism adds power to your narrative but should not be explicit. All of the above techniques work their magic in a subtle way, registering in the reader's mind subconsciously. Some perceptive readers may recognize them and appreciate your craft. Most, however, will not even realize there are symbols embedded in your description.

SET THE RIGHT MOOD OR TONE

Mood is the emotional climate of your story or scene. Therefore, it's an ideal way to engage the reader through evocative words that will guide him toward experiencing a particular emotional state. A great example of setting the right mood for the type of story told is *Body Heat*, which starts with the phrase, "Flames in a night sky." This provocative visual establishes a sense of foreboding and symbolizes the passion and evil Racine is about to encounter. Later, and throughout the script, Kasdan peppers his description with words like *burning, dripping, dressed in undershorts, fire, hot, air conditioner, blasts of hot hair, infernal heat, sweaty, sizzling, relief, the hottest January in fifty years* to evoke heat, matching the subject matter of this classic thriller. Now, if you were writing a comedy, you'd want the tone to be lighter and faster paced. You'd choose the right words to suggest a humorous climate.

MATCH YOUR STYLE WITH GENRE

Just as you want to match mood to the subject and genre of your script, your narrative style should match your genre. For instance, if you're writing a thriller, your style should be terse and thrilling. If your script is an action, your style should be active, and if it's a comedy, it should be funny. The key is that style matches genre. Too many beginners learn a particular style through an article or a professional script and adapt it to their own project regardless of genre. This often creates an emotional dissonance. The script may be well written but *something* just isn't right. Match style with genre. A great tip is to read the best professional scripts in the particular genre you're writing in and pay attention to how the narrative is constructed.

DESCRIBING CHARACTERS

The best place to apply the "Less is more" maxim is in describing characters and locations. Avoid the clichéd and generic adjectives like *beautiful, pretty,* or *tall, dark, and handsome.* Instead, while using the least amount of choice words, give the reader a more interesting vision of your character—the essence of their personality traits and attitudes. This means you shouldn't waste words to describe what a character is wearing, how tall or skinny he is, or what the color of his hair is, unless it's crucial to the story, like a deformity or disability. In fact, the ideal character description should be a brief, hopefully interesting and original sentence that conveys the essence of your character. The record for the least amount of words to describe a character used to be held by Lawrence Kasdan who managed to describe the Mickey Rourke character in *Body Heat* with only four words— "TEDDY LAURSON, rock n' roll arsonist." It's all there. All we have to know about Teddy is there—his occupation, attitude, even what he wears, including tattoos and piercings. The new record is three words, held by Steve Barancik in *The Last Seduction*: "BRIDGET GREGORY, bitch-ringmaster-goddess." Remember that in screenwriting, a hint is always more engaging than an explanation. Too little is better than too much. Here are more examples of how the pros do it:

SIDEWAYS

> The NEW HUSBAND. He exudes the quiet confidence of a successful businessman who played college football, takes expensive skiing and sailing vacations, and hasn't read a novel since high school.

THELMA AND LOUISE (CALLIE KHOURI)

DARRYL comes trotting down the stairs. Polyester was made for this man, and he's dripping in "men's" jewelry.

AMERICAN BEAUTY

This is RICKY FITTS. He's eighteen, but his eyes are much older. Underneath his Zen-like tranquility lurks something wounded... and dangerous.

THE LOST WORLD: JURASSIC PARK (DAVID KOEPP)

MRS. BOWMAN, painfully thin, with the perpetually surprised look of a woman who's had her eyes done more than once.

THE MATRIX (ANDY WACHOWSKI, LARRY WACHOWSKI)

NEO, a young man who knows more about living inside a computer than living outside one.

THE SHAWSHANK REDEMPTION

WARDEN SAMUEL NORTON strolls forth, a colorless man in a gray suit and a church pin in his lapel. He looks like he could piss ice water.

DESCRIBING LOCATIONS

The same goes for describing locations—getting the essence of a setting with the least amount of words. My all-time favorite setting description comes from *The Shawshank Redemption* by Frank Darabont, who describes the prison as "A malignant stone growth on the Maine landscape." Here are more examples to give you an idea of what's possible. This is the standard you'll have to compete against to make it as a professional screenwriter:

BLADE RUNNER

INT. HOTEL ROOM - NIGHT

The room is dark and ominous, full of danger.

It's clean in contrast to the littered hallway. A bed, a wardrobe, a small desk, a chair. Spartan, almost military.

LETHAL WEAPON

CLIFFSIDE HOUSE – DAY

A sprawling, expensive villa nestled on the side of a bluff overlooking the ocean. Terraces, verandahs, gazebos. Architecture that merits three syllables. The ocean looks cheap by comparison.

ENTRAPMENT (RON BASS)

INT. IMPERIAL HOTEL BAR – LATER

Graceful, timeless room, designed by Frank Lloyd Wright in the '20s. Burnished. Elegant. Way cool. A place to drink, to deal, to dream.

BONUS PROFESSIONAL TIPS

There you have it, a set of professional techniques and tricks of the trade to drastically improve your narrative description and turn your script into an exhilarating reading experience. Keep in mind that all these techniques are not mandatory. I've read plenty of scripts whose characters, plot, and dialogue were so fascinating it didn't matter that the narrative was average. But my view is that every single page in your script should stir up some sort of emotional impact, so writing with a riveting style is a smart move. It certainly can't hurt. To help you master the craft of description, consider the following:

GET A THESAURUS

If you don't already own a thesaurus, stop reading right now, head to the bookstore, and buy a copy. A writer without a thesaurus is like a painter without paint.

STUDY THE WRITING OF SUCCESSFUL WRITERS

Reading the work of professional screenwriters is the best education you'll ever get. When it comes to narrative, check out the writing of Shane Black, William Goldman, Walter Hill, James Cameron, Ron Bass, David Koepp, Richard Price, Frank Darabont, Lawrence Kasdan, Paul Schrader, Terry Rossio & Ted Elliott, Alexander Payne & Jim Taylor, and Cameron Crowe, among others.

STUDY THE SPORTS PAGES

An old-time writer once advised me to study the newspaper's sports pages because they're full of dynamic, high-energy active verbs, such as *kick*, *blast*, *strike*, and *pummel*. The writer would highlight these verbs and reuse them in his screenplays when appropriate.

STUDY POETRY

Similarly, study poetry for its evocative language and for the emotional impact it achieves with its succinctness.

ON THE PAGE: DESCRIPTION IN ACTION

Because I've presented so many examples to highlight narrative techniques, it would be redundant to include another page of description. If you wish to experience most of these techniques in action, however, revisit the Page One Contest winner on page 155, and see how many techniques you can recognize on that one page. To this day, it's one of the few script pages that made me go "Wow!" after reading it. This is my standard of excellence as a writer. It should be yours too. All that's left to master is, of course, the most challenging element for all screenwriters—dialogue...

10
DIALOGUE
Vivid Voices

"Good dialogue illuminates what people are not saying."
-ROBERT TOWNE

Dialogue presents an interesting paradox: it's the most important and least important part of the screenplay. Huh? Let me explain. Great dialogue is essential because it makes your characters leap off the page, creating a more riveting reading experience through empathy. It's crucial to attracting talent. It can cover weak areas in your script, thereby increasing the chances of a reader recommendation. Dialogue is also important because it's the trickiest element to master. Well-crafted dialogue sells scripts, and it sells the writer. Talented scribes who excel in this area are highly sought-after to the tune of six figures per week for dialogue rewrites.

That said, however, dialogue is not as important as character development or structure because you're not writing a play. Screenwriting is mostly about what you see, not hear. You're writing motion pictures, not visual radio. Silent movies were doing fine without much dialogue for twenty years before sound changed the industry. William Goldman says that dialogue "is among the least important parts of a screenplay... if movies are story, and they are, then screenplays are structure." Alfred Hitchcock said, "Once the picture is set, we add the dialogue." Walt Disney used to leave out the dialogue right up to the point in a sequence where he could see how little was needed. Dialogue isn't as important if everything else in your script is outstanding and the dialogue is mediocre because producers know they can always punch up the dialogue. So dialogue isn't everything. All the witty dialogue in the world won't sell your script if it fails on everything else. It will, however, make you that sought-after writer who is hired to polish the flawed dialogue of other writers.

Bottom line, you want as little dialogue as possible, and tell the story as visually as possible. But whatever little dialogue is on the page, it should be great. Those of you who have written several scripts know how difficult dialogue is to master. In fact, most aspiring writers who otherwise have solid elements fail because of flat, "on-the-nose" dialogue (more on this soon). Because of this, I'll present effective dialogue techniques (the most you'll find in one chapter) that will help you turn dull speeches into fresh, striking ones that affect the reader emotionally.

THE BASICS: WHAT YOU NEED TO KNOW

How-to books and screenwriting seminars discuss dialogue superficially. Their treatment is more often prescriptive rather than enlightening. They focus on what dialogue must do but neglect discussing specific techniques on how to do it. Maybe it's because many believe dialogue can't be taught, that writers either have an "ear" for it or not. There's a bit of truth to that—*great* dialogue can't be taught, but *good* dialogue can. By analyzing how seasoned pros craft good dialogue, aspiring writers can train themselves to recognize it in scripts and apply the same techniques to their own dialogue in the rewriting process.

CHARACTERISTICS OF GREAT DIALOGUE

So what constitutes great dialogue? Not wanting to rely on my subjective opinion alone, I surveyed additional resources on dialogue—books, seminars, magazine and Internet articles, as well as interviewed readers, producers, agents, actors, and professional screenwriters. I believe the result is a definitive checklist that goes beyond the traditional trio of dialogue requirements—to advance plot, reveal character, and deliver exposition.

CONVEYS A SENSE OF REALISM

The first requirement of great dialogue is that it sound real, as though characters were really speaking. It should be believable, ring true, feel natural, not forced or mechanical. Readers shouldn't be conscious that someone has written it. Keep in mind, however, that dialogue is not actual speech. Real speech is repetitive, speakers ramble on with run-on sentences and unnecessary words. Film dialogue only *resembles* actual speech, the same way film resembles life. It's not an actual recording of chaotic and meaningless life, only a structured, concentrated, and meaningful slice of life. Similarly, film dialogue conveys realistic speech because it's distilled and refined. It's everyday speech without the redundancies and incoherencies, without the pauses, interruptions, grammatical errors, and missing words. Using the tools of dialogue craft, a character can say the same thing in a more compressed and focused form while maintaining realism.

DEFINES AND REVEALS CHARACTER (BOTH SPEAKER AND OTHERS)

This is a big factor in making characters leap off the page and luring A-list talent to your project. What writers need to understand is that when characters speak, they become. Because the way people speak defines who they are, great dialogue should communicate a character's personality, attitudes, values, and social background, rather than telling the reader about them through description.

CONVEYS INFORMATION INDIRECTLY AND ADVANCES THE ACTION

This is the most common use of dialogue, and often the only aspect in amateur scripts. As a result, it can become flat and labeled "on-the-nose" when the exposition is direct and obvious. To be considered great, information that advances the action and carries the plot forward should be delivered in a subtle way that engages the reader. We'll explore various techniques to help you do this in the "Subtle Exposition" section.

REFLECTS CHARACTER EMOTIONS AND CONFLICT

Great dialogue also reveals conflict and what the characters are feeling, adding tension to a scene. This is important because conflict in a scene happens through either action (physical aggression, obstacles) or dialogue. Since you can't have constant aggression, even in an action-adventure script, dialogue is the remaining choice to inject conflict into a scene, and therefore keep the reader engaged. In fact, dialogue that reveals the speaker's emotions is ideal because it shows rather than tells, especially if it's revealed through subtext.

REVEALS OR HIDES CHARACTER MOTIVATION

Great dialogue gives the reader a hint of the speaker's motivation in the scene, or it creates curiosity about it by hiding it. For greater effect on the reader, the motivation should be implied through subtext rather than stated directly, which would then be on-the-nose dialogue. We'll explore specific techniques to create subtext later in this chapter.

REFLECTS THE RELATIONSHIP OF SPEAKER TO OTHER CHARACTERS

Because characters tend to speak differently to various people based on their relationship, good dialogue should reflect the speaker's relationship to the listener. For instance, a man will speak differently to his teenage daughter than to his wife or colleagues at work. A convict will talk one way to his mother, another to his girlfriend, and yet another to a fellow inmate. We tend to have several vocabularies and switch between them depending on who we're talking to and what we're talking about.

CONNECTS PRIOR SPEECH AND LEADS INTO NEXT

One of the joys of great dialogue is when each line of dialogue effortlessly leads into the other, back and forth, creating a smooth and rhythmic flow throughout a scene. Imagine a chain with each link connecting one to the other. Great dialogue is like a chain, where each line leads to the other, link to link, usually through a trigger word that compels the other character to repeat it, expand upon it, or object, thus connecting the two speeches. For example, the following exchange from *Casablanca* has impact because they're linked by the common words "impress" and "half." Rick says, "Well, he's succeeded in impressing half the world." Renault answers, "It is my duty to see that he does not impress the other half."

FORESHADOWS WHAT'S TO COME

Great dialogue can evoke anticipation in the reader by hinting at future events in a subtle way. This is one of the most effective ways to foreshadow what's to come, especially when it reminds the reader of what's at stake.

IS APPROPRIATE TO THE GENRE

Great dialogue should also be appropriate to the script's genre. For instance, if you're writing a comedy, most of the dialogue should be funny and witty. If you're writing a thriller or horror script, the dialogue should be terse, visceral, and add tension to most scenes.

IS APPROPRIATE TO THE SCENE

Not only is great dialogue appropriate to the script's genre, but also to its individual scenes. There are several types of scenes, as you saw in Chapter 8, but dialogue-heavy scenes are usually driven by three elements: *conflict, circumstance*, or *beliefs and attitudes*. In the **conflict-driven** scene, the dialogue clashes with conflicting objectives, which are clearly established early on, and emerges from action, character, and the obstacles in the scene. In the **circumstance-driven** scene, dialogue emerges from the characters' reactions to prior events, such as the ghost or backstory, reactions to events that occur in the actual scene, or to impending events, where the dialogue is anticipatory. Lastly, in the **belief-driven** scene, the dialogue often reflects theme, beliefs, ideas, and a character's personal attitudes.

IS ACTIVE, HAS PURPOSE

Above all else, great dialogue engages the reader by being active and purposeful in the scene, rather than passive, thus making it the immediate level of drama. To raise the effectiveness of your dialogue, remember that a dramatic scene is about one thing—a character who wants something and is having difficulty getting it. This character has an objective and can only accomplish it through two means—action and dialogue. Therefore, look at active dialogue as a form of dramatic action. Words become actions, the means to get what the character wants in a scene. Most amateur scripts with flawed dialogue have too many scenes with passive dialogue—dialogue that's purposeless, doesn't contribute to the character's objective, and is mainly expositional, conversational, and civil. In other words, dead wood on the page. Now, there's nothing wrong with a little passive dialogue here and there—you do need a balance with the more active and dramatic dialogue. But if you make your dialogue active, you'll dramatically increase its appeal because it has impact. It creates conflict by forcing another character to react emotionally. This means active dialogue is manipulative. Never forget that most great scenes are about characters manipulating each other to get what they want. They negotiate, exploit, coerce, inquire, seduce, irritate, provoke, impress, blackmail, warn, or create a power struggle through forceful and confrontational dialogue rather than be sympathetic, agreeable, or conversational. Therefore, look at active dialogue as a form of dramatic action. Words become actions, the means to get what you want in a scene.

HAS EMOTIONAL IMPACT

Emotional response is by far the most critical aspect of great dialogue. Unfortunately, it's also the most neglected in beginners' scripts. Great dialogue always contributes to the reader's overall satisfaction. The dialogue you find in great scripts, written by masters of the craft, has punch, wit, and sparkle. It crackles and pops off the page because it's interesting, unpredictable, and evokes curiosity, laughter, tension, and anticipation in the reader.

AVOIDING THE MOST COMMON DIALOGUE FLAWS

Now that you know what great dialogue must accomplish in your script, let's look at the most common dialogue flaws found in amateur scripts, and more important, how to avoid them.

DIALOGUE IS WOODEN OR STIFF

This is dialogue that lacks ease and grace. It doesn't flow smoothly because it doesn't sound real. Exposed to this dialogue, the reader can tell it's been written by a beginner who doesn't have an ear for the manner people speak. The way to fix this problem is to eavesdrop on real conversations, analyze the work of dialogue masters, especially plays, and apply any of the techniques you'll learn in the "Individual Dialogue" section.

DIALOGUE IS STILTED

This is dialogue that seems artificial and contrived. It uses a formal vocabulary, which seems academic and highbrow. Here, characters speak in complete sentences with proper grammar and no contractions. This is fine if the speaker happens to be highly educated. Most characters, however, don't speak this way, so stilted dialogue often brings attention to itself and takes the reader out of the reading experience. Again, using specific techniques from the "Individual

Dialogue" section, such as favorite expressions, fragmented and incomplete sentences, repetitions, bad grammar, as well as jargon and slang, will often correct this type of dialogue.

DIALOGUE IS TOO EXPOSITORY

How to present important information without seeming awkward and obvious, how to disguise it to keep the reader engaged, how to reveal without explaining, is a huge challenge for writers. This is probably the most common flaw in amateur scripts, even professional ones. If you've ever watched a daytime soap opera where characters convey huge amounts of information through dialogue, you've probably heard lines like "—I just saw Kimberly at the mall. –You mean the same Kimberly whose father was tried for murder, then he got off by claiming insanity because he ate too many Twinkies, and whose mother used to be married to the prosecutor, then she married his brother, but is pregnant with his son Jake's baby? –Yes." This is also known in writing circles as *"As you know, Bob"* dialogue—from the line, "As you know, Bob, I'm your father." Sounds phony and contrived, doesn't it? People who know each other don't usually remind each other of who they are or where they come from. The trick to handling exposition is to misdirect the reader's attention, usually through conflict, which lets him absorb expository information without noticing it. We'll explore other powerful techniques in the "Subtle Exposition" section.

DIALOGUE IS "ON THE NOSE"

Another constant issue with beginning scripts, and a close second to overt exposition is "on-the-nose" dialogue, a term many of you have probably heard before. If you haven't, this is dialogue that is obvious and explicit, where characters speak directly, stating what they think, mean, and feel. "Off-the-nose" dialogue, on the other hand, illuminates what the characters are not saying, revealing the emotion *behind* the words. Like expository dialogue, the way to solve this problem is to disguise it, providing multiple levels of depth, which ultimately give the reader a satisfying experience. You do this through subtext, to be discussed later.

DIALOGUE IS PREDICTABLE

If you've ever watched a badly written TV show and were able to predict a line of dialogue in response to another, you know what this is about. For instance, when someone says, "I love you," nine times out ten, the other character will respond... you got it, "I love you, too." Make it a game the next time you watch a bad movie or TV show. My record is four accurately guessed lines in a row. Predictable dialogue is an example of lazy writing. Great dialogue evokes an emotional response in the reader by being unpredictable, and we'll soon discuss techniques to help you write it.

CHARACTERS TALK TOO MUCH

Director John Lee Hancock once said, "Good actors want fewer words, and bad actors want more words." Words of wisdom to all amateur writers who often write long dialogue speeches. Few writers, actors, or directors have the skill to carry a long speech, which can be deadly onscreen. This is not a rule set in stone— you can find many exceptions in great scripts, but you should consider trimming, cutting, or breaking up any dialogue running more than five or six lines. Because great dialogue tends to be short and lean, professional writers always compress bloated dialogue to its bare bones—cutting, cutting, and cutting some more in the rewrite, getting rid of unnecessary words, and shortening sentences wherever they can. Generally, no character will speak more than two or three lines, and rarely more than four. In an interview, a writer once spoke of a producer's strict standard, "The Finger Rule:" If the dialogue was thicker than her index finger, it was too long. Although a challenge, the finger rule forced the writer to make the dialogue work. It kept the pace fast and the dialogue interesting.

CHARACTERS SPEAK ALIKE

Another common problem found in spec scripts is that all characters have the same voice, which is, not surprisingly, the writer's. This often shows that the writer hasn't developed his characters fully. The more you understand your characters, the more realistic and unique their dialogue will become. Lazy writers often attempt to give characters distinctive voices through regional accents or dialects, but this is not enough. It's also unrealistic if the setting doesn't call for it. In addition to fully developing their characters, great writers also pay attention to speech rhythms, cadences, and emotional tempos, among other techniques, which I'll discuss in the "Individual Dialogue" section.

REPEATED FIRST NAMES

"Look, Tara... Don't tell me what to do, Bob... Listen to me, Tara!" Sometimes, names are necessary to reveal character, balance rhythms, indicate a recipient when there are more than two characters in the scene, or have an emotional impact. But first names become a problem when they're repeated too often. First, it can be redundant information. If the reader can see Bob is talking to Tara, you don't have to mention their names. Second, it makes the dialogue stiff and unrealistic, because real people don't add names after each line of dialogue. The fix is easy: Go through your dialogue, and whenever possible, delete names.

FILLERS OR HANDLES

Examples of dialogue fillers, also known as "handles," include *Nevertheless, I mean, well, so, look, you know, by the way, still, anyhow, the point is, as I see it,* etc. Like names, eliminate these unnecessary fillers from your dialogue to make it leaner and crisper. Again, if you need one to balance the rhythm of a character's speech, that's fine, but more often than not, you'll be amazed how much sharper dialogue becomes when you delete fillers.

CHITCHAT (SMALL-TALK)

These are the routine exchanges of ordinary conversations, like "Hello... Hi... How are you? Fine." Often found at the beginning of scenes, these types of small talk don't contribute anything to the scene, and you should cut them. Because good dialogue is specific and concise, there's no room in a scene for undramatic chitchat. In real-life conversations, people go off on tangents. One thing leads to another, and next thing you know, the conversation has gone off-track. This is okay when you have a whole lifetime. When you have only two hours to tell a story, you have to get right to the point and stay on point. You don't want your dialogue to look planned, so every conversation needs conflict built in. There needs to be a struggle for information, so that even if we get directly to the point, we don't get the information directly. Your characters have to fight for it.

OBVIOUS REPETITION (SHOW AND TELL)

There's also no room for redundant information if you're aiming for tight dialogue. You know you should *show*, not *tell*, but when you show *and* tell, it's redundant. For example, if a character says, "I think you're a moron," the first two words are unnecessary because if he says something, clearly he's thinking it too. A better choice would be, "You're a moron," or simply, "Moron." Likewise, if you show that a character is angry, and tell us in the dialogue that's he's angry, or show us a gun and have a character say, "Look, a gun!" this would be repetitive.

DIALECT PHONETICS

To individualize characters, many writers tend to give them accents by spelling out the pronunciations of a particular accent. What they fail to realize is how this affects readers. Phonetics frustrates them because it slows down the reading by having to decipher it. This takes them out of the reading experience. Let the actor figure out dialect pronunciations. What you want to do is capture the texture of foreign or regional speech by focusing on expressions and speech patterns instead of word spellings. You'll see examples in the "Individual Dialogue" section.

FOREIGN LANGUAGES

Writers also like to present foreign characters by actually writing out their dialogue in their native tongue. They either include the English translation afterwards, or leave it up to the reader to figure out the meaning. Both tactics are hazardous to the reader's experience. The only acceptable format when it comes to foreign languages is to write them in English, and either write in the narrative that the characters speaks in, say, French, or write "in French" in the parenthetical below the character's name.

THE CRAFT: WRITING VIVID DIALOGUE

You're now aware of the high standards your dialogue must meet to be considered great and the most common mistakes you should avoid. Now, we'll explore how to do it right by using professional techniques that will elevate your dialogue to the next level. In the following pages, I divide these techniques into four categories: *emotional impact, individuality, subtle exposition,* and *subtext.*

TECHNIQUES FOR EMOTIONAL IMPACT

Most amateurs neglect the emotional impact great dialogue must have. They focus instead on dialogue that provides information about the plot and the characters. This leads to flat, wooden, and dull dialogue, which ultimately makes the whole script look bad. On the other hand, emotional impact, which makes the reader laugh, cry, feel tension, and experience a variety of other emotions, can elevate a mediocre script and even propel the writer toward lucrative dialogue rewrites. Here are more than twenty-five techniques to give your dialogue a more emotional punch:

THE COMEBACK ZINGER

A zinger is a quick, scathing, or witty response to a character's question or comment. To be considered a zinger, it should always be better than the original comment. It's common in buddy films, where two people who dislike each other constantly insult one another. If you have access to buddy action comedies, such as *Lethal Weapon, 48 Hrs., Rush Hour,* or critically-acclaimed television sitcoms, such as *Cheers, Frasier,* and *Seinfeld* to name a few, you'll find many examples of witty comebacks for inspiration. Again, for the sake of space, the formatting for the following dialogue examples is non-standard:

ALIENS
> HUDSON: Hey, Vasquez, have you ever been mistaken for a man?
> VASQUEZ: No, **have you**?

ALL ABOUT EVE (JOSEPH L. MANKIEWICZ)
> BILL: Is it sabotage, does my career mean nothing to you? Have you no human consideration?
> MARGO: **Show me a human** and I might have!

REAL GENIUS (NEAL ISRAEL, PAT PROFT, PETER TOROKVEI)
> KENT: Oh, you're the new stud, are you? Or is it dud?
> MITCH: How do you mean?
> BODIE: Stud. Hot shot. Brain. You're the twelve-year-old, right?
> MITCH: I'm fifteen.
> CARTER: **Does your body know that?**

ANNIE HALL (WOODY ALLEN, MARSHALL BRICKMAN)

ANNIE: So you wanna go into the movie or what?

ALVY: No, I can't go into a movie that's already started, because I'm anal.

ANNIE: **That's a polite word for what you are.**

PUSH-BUTTON DIALOGUE

This is one of my favorite dialogue techniques. As the name implies, this type of dialogue pushes another character's emotional buttons. It's verbal shrapnel. Pure fireworks. And it always causes an emotional reaction in the receiver, which also creates a strong emotional hook for the reader. Think of your favorite lines of dialogue, and I'll bet most of them fit this criterion. "You're not too smart—are you? I like that in a man" (*Body Heat*); "Frankly, my dear, I don't give a damn" (*Gone with the Wind*); "You can't handle the truth!" (*A Few Good Men*). With push-button dialogue, words come out of a character's mouth as weapons with a specific purpose—to hurt, spite, confuse, charm, delight, seduce, amaze. Always think of the purpose of a character's line. If there isn't one, consider deleting it.

AMERICAN BEAUTY

CAROLYN: Honey, I watched you the whole time, and **you didn't screw up once**!

ALL ABOUT EVE

MARGO: Nice speech, Eve. But I wouldn't worry too much about your heart. You can always put that award **where your heart ought to be.**

SOMETHING'S GOTTA GIVE

HARRY: Wow. It's the perfect beach house.

MARIN: I know. My mother doesn't know how to do things that aren't perfect.

HARRY: **Which explains you.**

THE SILENCE OF THE LAMBS

LECTER: Why do you think he removes their skins, Agent Starling? Thrill me with your acumen.

CLARICE: It excites him. Most serial killers keep some sort of trophies from their victims.

LECTER: I didn't.

CLARICE: **No. You ate yours.**

AS GOOD AS IT GETS (MARK ANDRUS, JAMES L. BROOKS)

CAROL: Oh, come on in and try not to **ruin everything by being you.**

CAROL: When you first came into breakfast, when I saw you -- I thought you were handsome... Then, of course, **you spoke...**

SARCASM

Sarcasm is another way to liven up flat dialogue, as long as it fits the character, since it's often a personality trait. Like humor, it's difficult to teach if the writer is not himself sarcastic. Because sarcasm is used primarily to insult another character or show scorn, it's often compared to push-button dialogue. Keep in mind, however, that although sarcasm always pushes a character's emotional buttons, push-button button dialogue is not always sarcastic or negative.

THELMA AND LOUISE

LOUISE: Why are you actin' like this?

THELMA: Actin' like what?! How am I supposed to act? **'Scuse me for not knowing what to do after you blow somebody's head off!**

MILLER'S CROSSING (JOEL COEN, ETHAN COEN)

VERNA: Where're you going?

TOM: Out.

VERNA: **Don't let on more than you have to.**

WHO'S AFRAID OF VIRGINIA WOOLF? (ERNEST LEHMAN)

Martha walks in wearing a pair of tight stretch pants and displaying a lot of cleavage.

GEORGE: **Why, Martha! Your Sunday chapel dress.**

AMERICAN BEAUTY

LESTER: You don't think it's weird and kinda fascist?

CAROLYN: Possibly. But you don't want to be unemployed.

LESTER: Oh, well, **let's just all sell our souls and work for Satan, because it's more convenient that way.**

CAROLYN: **Could you be just a little bit more dramatic, please, huh?**

FRASIER (TV) (DAVID ANGELL, PETER CASEY, DAVID LEE)

FRASIER: Dad, what do you think of the view? Hey, that's the Space Needle there!

MARTIN: Oh, **thanks for pointing that out. Being born and raised here, I never would have known.**

COMIC COMPARISON

Humor is obviously a skill that makes any dialogue shine. I won't even attempt to teach the comedic draft in depth, other than present three common techniques that can make your dialogue funnier. The first is comic comparison, where you compare two things for comic effect.

FRASIER (TV)

DAPHNE: Nice to meet you. Oh, and who might this be?

FRASIER: That's Eddie (*the dog*).

MARTIN: I call him "Eddie Spaghetti."

DAPHNE: Oh, he likes **pasta**?
MARTIN: No, he has **worms**.

NOTTING HILL (RICHARD CURTIS)

SPIKE: There's something wrong with this **yogurt**.
WILLIAM: It's **mayonnaise**.
SPIKE: Oh.

SILVERADO (LAWRENCE KASDAN, MARK KASDAN)

(Paden has gotten his horse back and they're "kissing" each other.)
MARSHALL: How do I know this is your horse?
PADEN: Can't you see this **horse** loves me?
MARSHALL: I had a gal do that to me. It didn't make her my **wife**.

ANNIE HALL (WOODY ALLEN)

ANNIE: It's so clean out here!

ALVY: That's because they don't throw their **garbage** away, they turn it into **television**.

COMIC CONTRAST

The second humor technique is to contrast, rather than compare, two opposite things, which creates a comic effect.

FRASIER (TV)

NILES: Dad doesn't get along with Maris.
FRASIER: Who does?
NILES: I thought you liked my Maris!
FRASIER: I do. I... I like her from a distance. You know, the way you like the sun. **Maris** is like the **sun**. Except **without the warmth**.

L.A. STORY (STEVE MARTIN)

HARRY ZELL: Three ideas in town I'd like to try you on. One: a **comedy. Dark night, girl gets raped two months before her wedding night.**
HARRIS: Did you say comedy?

COMIC DOUBLE MEANING

A third method for humor is *double meaning*, which I'll also discuss in the subtext segment. Here, it's dialogue that can be understood two different ways.

REAL GENIUS

ATHERTON: I want to start seeing **a lot more of you** in the lab.
CHRIS: You want me to **work nude**?

THE THIN MAN (ALBERT HACKETT, FRANCES GOODRICH)

NORA: They say you were shot in **the tabloids**.
NICK: They never got near **my tabloids**.

CAROLINE IN THE CITY (TV)

CAROLINE: Annie, I thought you were in Atlantic City. When did you get back?

ANNIE: Last night.

CAROLINE: Well, how'd you do?

ANNIE: I got **Lucky**. (*Lucky enters. They kiss. Lucky exits.*) Mmm. See you, **Lucky**. So what's going on with you, huh?

CAROLINE: Del and I had a big fight and broke up.

ANNIE: Get out of here. How could you break up with Del, he has such great **hair**.

CAROLINE: I know Annie, but I wanted **a little more**.

ANNIE: He could **grow it**.

THE SILENCE OF THE LAMBS (TED TALLY)

LECTER: I do wish we could chat longer, but I'm **having an old friend for dinner**.

WIT

Like humor and sarcasm, you're either witty or you're not. This is another of these "talent" areas that cannot be taught, but you can develop it by being exposed to and practicing it. Here are some great examples:

48 HRS.

FRIZZY: Aw, you guys were in last week. You better ask around. I'm not supposed to be hassled... I got friends.

VANZANT: Hey, **park the tongue** for a second, sweet-pants, we just want to search a room.

NORTH BY NORTHWEST (ERNEST LEHMAN)

THORNHILL: I don't think I caught your name

PROFESSOR: I don't think I pitched it.

THORNHILL: You're police, aren't you? Or – is it FBI?

PROFESSOR: **FBI... CIA... ONI... we're all in the same alphabet soup**.

FROM DUSK 'TIL DAWN (QUENTIN TARANTINO)

SETH: You. Plant yourself in that chair.

HOSTAGE: What are you planning on doing with--

SETH: **I said plant yourself. Plants don't talk**.

DRAWING ATTENTION TO SOMEONE OR SOMETHING

Bringing attention to something focuses the reader's interest and can arouse curiosity, anticipation, and tension. For example, in the classic crop-duster place scene in *North by Northwest*, the reader goes from curiosity in seeing Thornhill in the desolate and treeless farmland to anticipation and tension when the man says, "That plane's dusting crops where there ain't no crops." The reader's attention is now focused on the plane. This technique is also used in *The Silence of the Lambs*, in the autopsy scene where Clarice examines the first victim. Note our emotional change when Clarice says, "She's got something in her throat." Our attention focuses on her throat, anticipating what that something will be.

EXAGGERATION

Exaggeration, like its counterpart *Understatement*, is a good device to amuse the reader. As you can see from the following examples, it's not meant to be taken literally but metaphorically.

THELMA AND LOUISE

THELMA: I just don't see what it would hurt just to give somebody a ride. Did you see his butt? Darryl doesn't have a cute butt. **You could park a car in the shadow of his ass.**

ANNIE HALL

After Annie parks the car.
ALVY: Don't worry. **We can walk to the curb from here.**

ALVY: Honey, there's a spider in your bathroom **the size of a Buick.**

AS GOOD AS IT GETS

CAROL: An ear infection can send us to the emergency room—maybe five, six times a month where I get whatever **nine-year-old they just made a doctor**. Nice chatting with you.

SHAMPOO (ROBERT TOWNE)

JACKIE: Don't look over, it's Lenny Silverman.
JILL: Who is that?
JACKIE: A real swinger. He's been trying to do me for about **two hundred years**.

UNDERSTATEMENT

Whereas exaggeration amplifies the truth, understatement downplays it, usually in ironic contrast to the situation. You may see examples of this in disaster movies, where in response to a major crisis or life-or-death situation, a character utters an ironic line, like "Houston, we have a problem."

BUTCH CASSIDY AND THE SUNDANCE KID (WILLIAM GOLDMAN)

BUTCH: What happened to the old bank? It was beautiful.
GUARD: People kept robbing it.
BUTCH: **It's a small price to pay for beauty.**

ALMOST FAMOUS (CAMERON CROWE)

Anita shakes hands with Mom, and exits. As the car takes off:
ELAINE: She'll be back.
In the distance, we hear the whoop of her daughter.
ANITA: YEAHHHHH-HOOOOOOOO.
ELAINE: **Maybe not soon...**

PSYCHO (JOSEPH STEFANO)

NORMAN BATES: Mother... **isn't quite herself** today.

THE LAST BOY SCOUT (SHANE BLACK)

The two men approach the door. Jimmy takes out his key ring.

HALLENBECK: The cops are gonna want to check this place out, so don't disturb anything.

JIMMY: Yes, massah.

Jimmy opens the door. Flips on the lights. Stops in his tracks.

The room has been systematically torn to pieces. Broken furniture, shredded clothing. Everywhere. It looks like a combat zone.

JIMMY: I think **someone disturbed some stuff**, Joe.

GOING OFF ON A TANGENT

This technique is like taking a sudden and unexpected exit off the freeway. Here, you have a character go off on a tangent with a reply that's off the subject discussed.

AMERICAN GRAFFITI (GEORGE LUCAS)

TERRY: I bug out a lot. When I graduate, I'm going to join the Marines.

DEBBIE: They got the best uniforms. But what if there's a war?

TERRY: With the bomb, who's going to start it? We'd all blow up together. Anyway, I'd rather be at the front. I'm like that--rather be where the action is, you know. Once I got in a fight with--

DEBBIE: I love Eddie Burns.

Terry stops, trying to figure out where their conversation went.

TERRY: Eddie Burns--oh, yeah, Eddie Burns. I met him once, too.

DEBBIE: **You really think I look like Connie Stevens?** I like her--Tuesday Weld is too much of a beatnik, don't you think?

CHEERS (TV)

NORM: Women! Can't live with 'em, **pass the beer nuts**.

ALL ABOUT EVE

LLOYD: She wanted to explain about her interview, wanted to apologize to someone - and didn't dare face Margo... She started to tell me all about it - and she couldn't finish, she cried so...

He's over by a window, his back to her. Karen eyes him curiously, waiting for the payoff...

LLOYD (*finally*): **You know, I've been going over our financial condition - if you'll pardon the expression...**

KAREN: That's quite a change of subject.

INAPPROPRIATE COMMENT OR RESPONSE

This involves a character telling another something, or responding to something, in a way that inadvertently offends them or seems inappropriate to the situation.

BEDAZZLED (2000) (LARRY GELBART, HAROLD RAMIS, PETER TOLAN)

CAROL: I'm a lesbian, Elliot.

ELLIOT (*laughs nervously*): You are not.

Carol opens her wallet and flashes a picture.

ELLIOT: **Who's he?**

CAROL (*evenly*): That's Diane, my partner.

ELLIOT: Oh, sorry. It's just—**those are some shoulders.**

FOUR WEDDINGS AND FUNERAL (RICHARD CURTIS)

CHARLES: How's that gorgeous girlfriend of yours?

JOHN: Oh, she's not my girlfriend anymore.

CHARLES: **That's probably for the best. Rumor had it she had sex with every guy she ever met.**

JOHN: She's my wife now.

L.A. STORY (STEVE MARTIN)

HARRIS: Hey, so some weekend sailors lost some boats. Big deal. If they were rich enough to have a boat, they were rich enough to lose it. **And what kind of an asshole sailor would trust the wacky weekend weatherman, anyway?**

TOD: This one. You're fired.

INTERRUPTIONS

Interrupting another character is a good way to add tension and excitement to the dialogue.

THELMA AND LOUISE

THELMA (*taking map*): Well, it looks like we can get on this road 81 that heads down towards Dallas, then cut over to--

LOUISE: **I don't want to go that way. Find a way that we don't have to go through Texas.**

BASIC INSTINCT (JOE ESZTERHAS)

NICK: I'm Detect--

CATHERINE (*evenly*): **I know who you are.**

She doesn't look at them. She looks at the water.

You can also use interruptions to complete a thought for comic effect, such as:

THE SHAWSHANK REDEMPTION

Andy and Red play checkers. Red makes his move.

RED: King me.

ANDY: Chess. Now there's a game of kings. Civilized...strategic...

RED: ...**and totally fuckin' inexplicable.** Hate that game.

LISTS

This technique uses lists of specific items for dramatic effect, often prompted by a character's frustration.

ERIN BROCKOVICH (SUSANNAH GRANT)

ERIN: Which number do you want, George?

GEORGE: You got more than one?

ERIN: Shit, yeah. I got numbers coming out of my ears. Like, for instance, **ten**.

GEORGE: Ten?

ERIN: Sure. That's one of my numbers. It's how many months old my little girl is.

GEORGE: You got a little girl?

ERIN: Yeah. Sexy, huh? And here's another: **five**. That's how old my other daughter is. **Seven** is my son's age. **Two** is how many times I been married and divorced. You getting all this? **16** is the number of dollars in my bank account. **454-3943** is my phone number. And with all the numbers I gave you, I'm guessing **zero** is the number of times you're gonna call it.

MILLER'S CROSSING

TOM: 'Lo, Terry. You weren't aiming at me, were you?

TERRY: **In the first place**, I don't know what you're talking about. **In the second place**, if I had been aiming at you, I'd've hit you. **In the third place**, I don't know what you're talking about in the first place.

BEDAZZLED (2000)

THE DEVIL: There's nothing sinister here. Paragraph one states that I, the Devil, a not-for-profit corporation with offices in Purgatory, Hell and Los Angeles, will give you seven wishes to use as you see fit.

ELLIOT: Why seven? Why not eight?

THE DEVIL: Why not six? I don't know, seven sounds right. It's a magical mystical thing. **Seven days of the week, seven deadly sins, 7-up, seven dwarves**, okay?

SOMETHING'S GOTTA GIVE

HARRY: Can we talk tomorrow?

ERICA: What for? I saw your friend you were having dinner with, if that's what you want, it's never going to work with me. Look at me. I'm a middle-aged woman, don't let this brown hair fool you, I don't have real brown hair on my head, I'm almost all grey... that would freak you out, wouldn't it? And I have **high cholesterol** and my **back hurts** every morning and I'm **post menopausal** and I have **osteoporosis** and I'm sure **arthritis** is just around the corner and I know you've seen my **varicose veins**. Let's face it man, that's not quite the buzz you're looking for.

METAPHORS AND SIMILES

Just as you can apply metaphors and similes to your narrative description, you can also use these two literary tools in dialogue to punch it up.

ALMOST FAMOUS

Mom drives William to the San Diego Sports Arena. She looks out the window at the adrenalized concert-goers.

ELAINE: Look at this. An entire generation of **Cinderellas and there's no slipper coming**.

BUTCH CASSIDY AND THE SUNDANCE KID

SUNDANCE (*chuckling*): You just keep thinkin', Butch. That's what you're good at.

BUTCH: Boy, I got vision, and **the rest of the world wears bifocals.**

CRUEL INTENTIONS (ROGER KUMBLE)

KATHRYN: Don Juan is moving with **the speed of a Special Olympics hurdler.**

BULL DURHAM (RON SHELTON)

EBBY: Is somebody gonna go to bed with somebody or what?

ANNIE: You're a regular **nuclear meltdown**, honey-slow down.

AUSTIN POWERS: THE SPY WHO SHAGGED ME (MIKE MYERS, MICHAEL MCCULLERS)

DR. EVIL: You're not quite evil enough. You're semi-evil. You're quasi-evil. You're the **margarine** of evil. You're the **Diet Coke** of evil, just **one calorie**, not evil enough.

BODY HEAT (LAWRENCE KASDAN)

RACINE: Are you all right?

MATTY (*laughs*): Yes. My temperature runs a couple degrees high. Around 100 all the time, I don't mind it. It's the **engine** or something.

RACINE: Maybe you need a **tune-up.**

MATTY: Don't tell me -- you have just the **right tool**.

PARALLEL CONSTRUCTION

This technique creates rhythm in dialogue to make it more appealing. It means two or more sentences in a row are built the same way. It's a common technique used by public speakers because it lulls the listener, much like music does. Thus, it's a pleasure to hear. Most of the memorable lines from classic speeches, such as Martin Luther King's "I have a dream," and JFK's "Ask not what your country can do for you," are examples of parallel construction.

APOCALYPSE NOW (JOHN MILIUS, FRANCIS FORD COPPOLA)

KURTZ: **We must** kill them. **We must** incinerate them. **Pig after pig. Cow after cow. Village after village. Army after army.**

DOUBLE INDEMNITY (BILLY WILDER, RAYMOND CHANDLER)

WALTER NEFF: You were pretty good in there for a while, Keyes. **You said** it wasn't an accident. **Check. You said** it wasn't suicide. **Check. You said** it was murder. **Check.** You thought you had it cold, didn't you?

ON THE WATERFRONT (BUDD SCHULBERG)

TERRY MALLOY: You don't understand! **I could've** had class. **I could've** been a contender. **I could've** been somebody, instead of a bum, which is what I am.

GASLIGHT (JOHN VAN DRUTEN, WALTER REISCH, JOHN L. BALDERSTON)

PAULA: But **because I am mad**, I hate you. **Because I am mad**, I have betrayed you. And **because I'm mad**, I'm rejoicing in my heart, **without a shred of** pity, **without a shred of** regret, watching you go with glory in my heart!

GILMORE GIRLS (TV) (AMY SHERMAN-PALLADINO)

RORY: So, Grandpa, how's the insurance biz?

RICHARD: **People** die, **we pay. People** crash cars, **we pay. People** lose a foot, **we pay**.

PROGRESSIVE DIALOGUE

As the name implies, this is dialogue that progresses upward in intensity, as in "I was in an accident. I smashed my head. I may die!" Or the dialogue can progress downward. Note how the first example has an upward progression, followed by a downward one:

MONTY PYTHON'S FLYING CIRCUS SKETCH

INTERVIEWER: So, in three years you've spotted no camels.

CAMEL SPOTTER: Yes, in **three** years. Er, I tell a lie, **four**, be fair, **five**. I've been camel spotting for just the **seven** years. Before that, of course, I was a Yeti spotter.

INTERVIEWER: A Yeti spotter, that must have been interesting...

CAMEL SPOTTER: You've seen one, you've seen them all.

INTERVIEWER: And have you seen them all?

CAMEL SPOTTER: Well, I've seen **one**. Well, a **little one**... a **picture of a**... **I've heard of them.**

AS GOOD AS IT GETS

MELVIN: Thanks for being on time... Carol, the waitress, this is Simon, the fag.

CAROL: Hello... Oh, my God, who did that to you?

SIMON: I, uh... I was... attacked. Walked in on **people robbing me**. I was **hospitalized**. I almost **died**.

ALMOST FAMOUS

PENNY LANE: How old are you?

WILLIAM: **Eighteen**.

PENNY LANE: Me too. (*beat*) How old are we really?

WILLIAM: **Seventeen**.

PENNY LANE: Me too.

WILLIAM: Actually I'm **sixteen**.

PENNY LANE: Me too. Isn't it funny? The truth just *sounds* Different.

WILLIAM (*confesses*): I'm **fifteen**.

GLENGARRY GLEN ROSS (DAVID MAMET)

BLAKE: We're adding a little something to this month's sales context. As you all know, **first prize** is a **Cadillac Eldorado**. Anybody want to see second prize? (holds up prize) **Second prize** is a **set of steak knives**. **Third prize** is **you're fired**.

(*Note: also an example of the List technique*)

REVERSALS

This is when a character takes an opposite turn in the middle of a thought process, which obviously creates surprise in the reader, and often humor. Using this technique, you set the reader up with an expectation, and then twist it with an unexpected response, which is the opposite of what he'd expect.

WHEN HARRY MET SALLY (NORA EPHRON)

HARRY: I've been doing a lot of thinking, and the thing is, I love you.

SALLY: What?

HARRY: I love you.

SALLY: How do you expect me to respond to this?

HARRY: How about, you love me too.

SALLY: **How about, I'm leaving.**

(*Note: also an example of Parallel Construction*)

BUTCH CASSIDY AND THE SUNDANCE KID

BUTCH: I think we lost 'em. Do you think we lost 'em?

SUNDANCE: No.

BUTCH: **Neither do I.**

RAISING ARIZONA (JOEL COEN, ETHAN COEN)

NATHAN: Who the hell are you?

BIKER: Name of Leonard Smalls. My friends call me Lenny... **Only I ain't got no friends.**

DOUBLE INDEMNITY

LOLA: There he is. By the bus stop. He needs a haircut, doesn't he? Look at him. No job, no car, no money, no prospects, no nothing. (*pause*) **I love him.**

AS GOOD AS IT GETS

CAROL: You wanna dance?

MELVIN: I've been thinking about that for a while.

CAROL (*rising*): And?

MELVIN: **No...**

MONTY PYTHON'S FLYING CIRCUS SKETCH

    CHARACTER A: I say... Are you implying something?

    CHARACTER B: No, no, no, no, no, no. (*Beat*) **Yes**.

SETUPS AND PAYOFFS

As in a plot setup, where a prop or character gesture that may seem insignificant at first is set up early in the story and then paid off, a line of dialogue can also be set up so that it can be paid off with a stronger impact on the reader. The best-known example is in *Casablanca*, where the line "Here's looking at you, kid" is set up in the Paris flashback and later paid off with more emotional impact at the climactic farewell. And then, of course, there's the memorable line, "Round up the usual suspects," which is set up earlier, and then takes on multiple emotional layers at the end. Here are some more examples:

RAIDERS OF LOST ARK (LAWRENCE KASDAN)

    INDY: Give me the whip.

    SATIPO: Throw me the idol. No time to argue. Throw me the idol. I throw you the whip.

    Indy tosses the idol across the pit to Satipo.

    INDY: Give me the whip.

    SATIPO: **Adios, senor.** (*Setup*)

    Satipo drops the whip and rushes out toward the entrance.

    Later, Indy finds himself face-to-face with a dead SATIPO, spikes protruding from his bloodied head. Indy retrieves the golden idol from the ground.

    INDY: **Adios, estupido.** (*Payoff*)

BASIC INSTINCT

    LT. WALKER: The maid came in an hour ago and found him. She's not a live-in.

    GUS: **Maybe the maid did it.** (*Setup*)

    LT. WALKER: She's 54 years old and weighs 240 pounds.

    CORONER (*deadpan*): There are no bruises on his body.

    GUS (*grins*): **It ain't the maid.** (*Payoff #1*)

    LT. WALKER: He left the club with his girlfriend about midnight. That's the last time anybody saw him.

    NICK (*looks at body*): What was it?

    CORONER: Ice pick. Left on the coffee table in the living room. Thin steel handle. Forensics took it downtown.

    HARRIGAN: There's cum all over the sheets -- he got off before he got offed.

    GUS (*deadpan*): **That rules the maid out for sure.** (*Payoff #2*)

TRIGGER WORD OR PHRASE

This is the best way to maintain a consistent dialogue flow in a scene. You'll recall that one characteristic of great dialogue is when each line of dialogue leads into the other, back and forth, creating a rhythmic flow throughout the scene.

Applying this technique is like creating a chain, where each line leads to the other, link to link, through a trigger word or phrase that compels the other character to repeat it, expand upon it, or object. Because of its effectiveness on dialogue rhythm, it's one of the most common dialogue techniques in professional scripts.

SLEEPER (WOODY ALLEN, MARSHALL BRICKMAN)

> LUNA: It's hard to believe that you haven't had sex for **two hundred years.**
>
> MILES: **Two hundred and four,** if you count my marriage.

CASABLANCA (JULIUS J. EPSTEIN, PHILIP G. EPSTEIN, HOWARD KOCH)

> LASZLO: This is a very interesting cafe. **I congratulate you.**
>
> RICK: **And I congratulate you.**
>
> LASZLO: What for?
>
> RICK: Your work.
>
> LASZLO: Thank you. **I try.**
>
> RICK: We all **try.** You succeed.

CHINATOWN (ROBERT TOWNE)

> GITTES: A memorial service was held at the Mar Vista Inn today for Jasper Lamar Crabb. He passed away two weeks ago.
>
> EVELYN: Why is that **unusual**?
>
> GITTES: He passed away two weeks ago and one week ago he bought the land. **That's unusual.**

NOTTING HILL

> ANNA: Can I stay for **a while**?
>
> WILLIAM: You can stay **forever.**

APOCALYPSE NOW

> WILLARD: I was sent on a **classified** mission, sir.
>
> KURTZ: It appears that it's **no longer classified**, is it? What did they **tell** you?
>
> WILLARD: They **told** me that you had gone totally insane and that your **methods were unsound.**
>
> KURTZ: Are my **methods unsound**?
>
> WILLARD: I don't see **any method at all**, sir.

THE AFRICAN QUEEN (JAMES AGEE, JOHN HUSTON)

> ALLNUT: A man takes a drop too much once in a while, it's only human **nature.**
>
> ROSE: "**Nature,**" Mr. Allnut, is what we are put into this world to **rise above.**

UNEXPECTED RESPONSE

Because humor is based on surprise and the unexpected, this technique is often used for comic effect. As the name suggests, it involves a character countering with a surprising response. This is one way to fix predictable dialogue and simultaneously highlight a character's trait and attitude.

ALMOST FAMOUS

> WILLIAM: Don't you understand? He sold you for a case of beer!
>
> (*after a pause, through tears*)
>
> PENNY LANE: **What kind of beer?**

MOONSTRUCK (JOHN PATRICK SHANLEY)

> RONNY: I'm in love with you!
>
> LORETTA: **Snap out of it!**

THE LONG KISS GOODNIGHT

> *Some LITTLE KIDS have wandered over, intrigued by the sweet-looking lady with the high-powered broomstick.*
>
> KID#1: Hey, lady, that thing for real?
>
> SAMANTHA (*without looking up*): Nope. It's a toy.
>
> *Hennessey nods, clears his throat:*
>
> HENESSEY: Yeah, this is Muriel Nintendo, the president of the company. She's doing research for a game.
>
> *KID #2 scowls at Hennessey:*
>
> KID#2: **Is not, nimrod. The president of Nintendo is Minoru Arakawa, he's a man in his forties.**
>
> HENESSEY: **Look, fuck you, junior--**
>
> SAMANTHA: Shhh. Quiet!

SNEAKERS (PHIL ALDEN ROBINSON, LAWRENCE LASKER, WALTER F. PARKES)

> COSMO: I cannot kill my friend. (*to his henchman*) **Kill my friend**.

Visceral dialogue

This is the kind of dialogue that shoots adrenaline into the reader's bloodstream. It's specifically designed to tense, frighten, or excite the reader. Although overused in action films during intensely suspenseful situations, you can also use it to titillate, like in the following example from *Basic Instinct*:

> CORRIGAN: Would you tell us the nature of your relationship with Mr. Boz?
>
> CATHERINE: I had sex with him for about a year and a half. **I liked having sex with him.**
>
> She has control of the room: she looks from one man to the other as she speaks.
>
> CATHERINE (*continuing*): He wasn't afraid of experimenting. **I like men like that. I like men who give me pleasure. He gave me a lot of pleasure.**
>
> A beat, as they watch her. She is so matter-of-fact.

ALIENS

> HUDSON: Let's get the fuck out of here!

HICKS: **Not that tunnel, the other one!**

CROWE: You sure? Watch it...behind you. Fucking move, will you!

Gorman is ashen. Confused. Gulping for air like a grouper. How could the situation have unraveled so fast?

RIPLEY (*to Gorman*): **GET THEM OUT OF THERE! DO IT NOW!**

GORMAN: **Shut up. Just shut up!**

EXECUTIVE DECISION (JIM THOMAS, JOHN THOMAS)

CAHILL: **We're losing the seal! Hurry!**

The HISSING INCREASES, the seal threatening to go. Travis looks up, realizing...

TRAVIS: **Close the hatch!**

Grant hesitates, still extending his arm.

TRAVIS: **We're losing it! Close the goddamn hatch...**

WORD REPETITION (ECHOING)

This technique is about repeating certain keywords to create rhythm and emphasis. You can use it to evoke a particular emotion, like Gerard's awe at the train's destruction when he says in *The Fugitive (Jeb Stuart and David Twohy)*, "My, my, my, my, my, what a mess," Leo's nervous excitement in *Lethal Weapon 2 (Jeffrey Boam)* when he keeps saying, "Okay, okay, okay," or Dr. Szell's cryptic question "Is it safe?" in *Marathon Man (William Goldman)*. Echoing a word or phrase can also emphasize wit by turning a line around, like when President Kennedy said, "Ask not what your country can do for you; ask what you can do for your country." Other examples include:

SUNSET BOULEVARD (CHARLES BRACKETT, BILLY WILDER, D.M. MARSHMAN, JR.)

JOE GILLIS: You used to be in **pictures**. You used to be **big**.

NORMA DESMOND: I am **big**. It's the **pictures** that got small.

DUCK SOUP (BERT KALMAR, HARRY RUBY)

RUFUS: **I could dance with you 'til the cows come home.** On second thought, **I'd rather dance with the cows 'til you came home.**

PATTON (FRANCIS FORD COPPOLA, EDMUND H. NORTH)

GEN. PATTON: Now, I want you to remember that **no bastard ever won a war by dying for his country. He won it by making the other poor dumb bastard die for his country.**

ALL ABOUT EVE

KAREN'S VOICE: When was it? How long? It seems a lifetime ago. Lloyd always said that in the theater **a lifetime was a season**, and **a season a lifetime.**

CLICHÉ ALTERNATIVES

This is about turning clichés to your advantage by providing alternatives to them, while still keeping the original pattern. For example:

LETHAL WEAPON

RIGGS: Oh, by the way: Guy who shot me?

MURTAUGH: Yeah.

RIGGS: Same guy who shot Lloyd.

MURTAUGH: Jesus... You sure?

RIGGS: I never forget an **asshole**.

IT HAPPENED ONE NIGHT (ROBERT RISKIN)

ELLIE: Well, I proved once and for all that **the limb is mightier than the thumb**.

REAL GENIUS

Atherton is returning from his daily jog. He's decked out in an expensive designer jogging suit and has all the appropriate accessories. He also has all the silly habits of the trendy runner for cooling down and stretching.

CHRIS: You wanted to see me, **your joggingness?**

YES/NO ALTERNATIVES

Asking a question is often the easiest way to deliver exposition, but most responses tend to be "Yes" or "No" answers. Sometimes, these simple answers provide an emotional punch, but more often, they generate flat and repetitive dialogue the reader can easily anticipate. For more impact, you have two choices: whenever possible, either replace a question with an open ended one that reveals character, or vary the reply, using creative alternatives to "Yes" and "No" answers, such as *Piece of cake, No problem, You wish, In your dreams,* or *As if!*

SIDEWAYS

JACK: Been checking your messages?

MILES: **Obsessively.**

MILLER'S CROSSING

CASPAR: So it's clear what I'm saying?

LEO: **...As mud.**

CITY SLICKERS (LOWELL GANZ, BABALOO MANDEL)

MITCH: Hi, Curly, kill anyone today?

CURLY: **Day ain't over yet.**

CLERKS (KEVIN SMITH)

RANDAL: You called Caitlin again?

DANTE: **She called me.**

RANDAL: Did you tell Veronica?

DANTE: **One fight a day with Veronica is about all I can stomach, thanks.**

TERMS OF ENDEARMENT (JAMES L. BROOKS)

AURORA: Would you like to come in?

GARRETT: **I'd rather stick needles in my eyes.**

TECHNIQUES FOR INDIVIDUAL DIALOGUE

One of the essential functions of dialogue is that it fit the speaker's personality and attitudes, thus revealing that character's essence. David Mamet says in *True and False*, "there is no such thing as a character in a script, only words on a page. An actor speaks these words of dialogue, and so the reader forms a sense of an actual person, though the character himself is an illusion." Dialogue is an essential tool to create and maintain this illusion. Because every character is unique, their dialogue should sound unique as well, not like the writer's voice, as is often the case in amateur scripts.

A script reader's common feedback is that *all the characters sound alike*—same speech pattern, same vocabulary, even the same cadence in their dialogue. In real life, and especially in screenplays, people speak differently from each other, not just in terms of dialect, but also in their rhythms, sophistication, verbal expressions, and word choice. Therefore, to give each character a distinct voice, you must consider with *each* line of dialogue how a character expresses a thought through his own personal rhythm, vocabulary, and style of speaking. The writer must also make sure that this voice remains consistent throughout the script.

To help you develop distinct ways of speaking for each character, here are various tricks of the trade:

CONTRAST DIALOGUE WITH CONTEXT

You're already aware of the power of contrast in engaging the reader—contrasting character traits and attitudes in a scene, contrasting values within one character, or even character and setting for a fish-out-of-water effect. Here, we contrast the context of the scene with a character's emotion as revealed through dialogue. For example, a character may speak in a slow, calm voice amid an intense and chaotic event, or he could tell a joke and laugh at a funeral. In *Chinatown*, Evelyn stammers and trembles when she's asked about her father during a leisurely meal at a fancy restaurant, which engages the reader through curiosity—why is she so nervous, and what is she hiding from Gittes? In *The Last Boy Scout*, Hallenbeck is threatened by two hit men, Chet and Pablo, and yet exhibits complete cool in this life or death context, while Pablo, who's expected to be in control, freaks out:

THE LAST BOY SCOUT

Hallenbeck strikes with a flattened palm. Breaks Chet's nose. Drives it up into the brain. Chet stands, pole-axed. Blinks once. Pitches over dead.

And suddenly Pablo isn't laughing. He stares at Hallenbeck, incredulous. Stares at Chet, lying on the carpet.

PABLO: Jesus Christ. (*draws his gun*) You son-of-a-bitch. Jesus Christ!! You killed him! 'Fuckin' A, you killed him, he's fuckin' dead!!!

Hallenbeck says nothing. Calmly returns to his seat.

At that moment, a door opens, and Milo enters.

Slick. Well-dressed. Utterly composed.

MILO: Is there a problem?

PABLO (*still dazed*): He killed Chet, Milo. The motherfucker just killed him!

Milo looks toward Hallenbeck. Hallenbeck says nothing. Instead, he calmly leans forward and picks up Chet's lighter from the carpet. Lights his cigarette. Blows smoke.

A tense moment... and then Milo does something unexpected: He starts to laugh. Advances into the room, chuckling.

MILO: Oh, my. Oh, Goddamn. Joseph, Joseph, you don't disappoint me.

He draws a Walther PPK and approaches Hallenbeck, smiling and cheerful.

MILO: You seem to have killed one of my men.

HALLENBECK (*shrugs*): I needed a light.

CONTRAST EMOTIONAL TEMPO

This is one of the most effective ways to individualize a character's dialogue, while creating conflict within a scene. Tempo is a musical term, which means the speed of a melody. Here, it means the speed of a character's dialogue, which conveys his emotion—fast evoking happiness, excitement, or anger; slow and pained evoking sorrow, for instance. And when you contrast emotional tempos—fast with slow, angry with calm, it highlights the emotions and makes the scene more interesting. In the first example, note how Sonny's emotional tempo contrasts with Hagen's; in the second, how Henessey's contrasts with Nathan's and Samantha's:

THE GODFATHER

HAGEN: We should hear what they have to say.

SONNY: No, no Consiglere. Not this time. No more meetings, no more discussions, no more Sollozzo tricks. Give them one message: I WANT SOLLOZZO. If not, it's all out war. We go to the mattresses and we put all the button men out on the street.

HAGEN: The other families won't sit still for all out war.

SONNY: Then THEY hand me Sollozzo.

HAGEN: Come ON Sonny, your father wouldn't want to hear this. This is not a personal thing, this is Business.

SONNY: And when they shot my father...

HAGEN: Yes, even the shooting of your father was business, not personal...

SONNY: No no, no more advice on how to patch it up Tom. You just help me win. Understood?

THE LONG KISS GOODNIGHT

Now they're on the open road. Doing 110 mph. Henessey is trembling; Samantha comatose. Both will freeze soon.

Nathan steals a glance at the rear view mirror. Gets his first good look at Samantha. React, stunned.

NATHAN: Charly, Jesus Christ. I don't believe what I'm seeing, you're so fat.

This is not what she expected to hear.

SAMANTHA: I'm... Um, I mean... What?

NATHAN: What in pluperfect hell have you been eating, you look positively bovine!

Henessey's still back a few steps:

HENESSEY: WE JUMPED OUT OF A BUILDING!

NATHAN: Yes, it was very exciting. Tomorrow we'll go to the zoo. Shut up.

They squeal through a hairpin turn. Burn rubber.

SAMANTHA: You're Windeman.

NATHAN: Nathan Windeman. There. The fog lifts, eh? Look, if I talk in front of him, you may be asked to kill him later. Works for me, your call.

HENESSEY: WE JUMPED OUT OF A GODDAMN BUILDING!

NATHAN: Charlene, darling--

FAVORITE EXPRESSION

Another effective tool to individualize characters is to give each of them a favorite expression. When you hear how different people speak—a great exercise for all writers—you may notice that they have at least one speaking quirk, whether it's a favorite phrase or slang buzzword. Giving a character a *signature* line, if you will, or *tag* line at the end of his sentences—such as "Know what I'm saying?" or "Okay?"—will differentiate him from other characters. Note how the following signature lines individualize the characters throughout the script:

FARGO (ETHAN COEN, JOEL COEN)

WAITRESS: Can I warm that up for ya there?

ANDERSON: **You bet.**

SOME LIKE IT HOT (BILLY WILDER, I.A.L. DIAMOND)

OSGOOD: **Zowie!**

SWINGERS (JON FAVREAU)

TRENT: **You're so money.**

LETHAL WEAPON 2

LEO: **Okay, okay, okay...**

TOY STORY (JOHN LASSITER, ANDREW STANTON)
> BUZZ LIGHTYEAR: **To infinity and beyond!**

ROCKY (SYLVESTER STALLONE)
> ROCKY: I think I'm gonna take a steam. Shoulda seen me fight. Did good, **y'know.**

FRAGMENTED, CONTRACTED, SHORT SENTENCES

If you were to record an actual conversation, you'd find few complete sentences. Real speech tends to be jumpy. We often stumble, interrupt, hesitate, use weak words, and don't complete sentences. We also tend to contract nouns and verbs, saying, for instance, "I'm... you're... shouldn't... I'd" instead of "I am... you are... should not... I would." And we often drop words, making our sentences sparse. Look at this perfect example from *American Graffiti*:

AMERICAN GRAFFITI
> JOHN: That's Freddy Benson's Vette... he got his head on with some drunk. Never had a chance. Damn good driver, too. What a waste when somebody gets it and it ain't even their fault.
>
> CAROL: Needs a paint job, that's for sure.
>
> *John doesn't hear her and walks on.*
>
> JOHN: That Vette over there. Walt Hawkins, a real ding-a-ling. Wrapped it around a fig tree out on Mesa Vista with five kids in it. Draggin' with five kids in the car, how dumb can you get? All the ding-a-lings get it sooner or later. Maybe that's why they invented cars. To get rid of the ding-a-lings. Tough when they take someone with them.

This is all about making the dialogue as tight as it can be. By dropping words, like when John says, "Damn good driver, too," instead of *"He was a* damn good driver, too" and contracting words, his dialogue sounds real, unforced, and spontaneous, as if he's just making it up as he goes along.

Fragmenting and contracting also helps to fix stilted dialogue, which as you saw earlier in this chapter, is artificial, formal, and grammatically correct dialogue. Go through your dialogue and when appropriate, see if you can fragment, contract, and drop words, usually the first in a sentence, to make your character sound more realistic and unique.

WORD CHOICE: JARGON AND SLANG

Just as you can give a character a favorite expression, you can focus on his vocabulary, and make his dialogue more colorful through jargon and slang. Jargon is the terminology and shorthand particular to a certain profession or cultural subgroup. If you listen to the way real people talk in various jobs, or different age groups, particularly teenagers, you'll find that different trades have different ways of speaking. For instance, a police officer, a university professor, and a doctor will have very different manners of speech. This type of dialogue can give your characters a sense of authenticity, while making their voice unique.

BLADE RUNNER

DECKARD: Great complexion! Suit looks really nice. Who's your tailor?

HOLDEN: A big fucking skin **job put the smash on me, wrecked me up**! Looka me, for Chrissake!

SPORTS NIGHT (TV) (AARON SORKIN)

WOMAN'S VOICE: Stand by audio, stand by tape.

MAN'S VOICE: Georgia Dome's **hot**.

ANOTHER WOMAN: You're **hot**, Atlanta.

MAN'S VOICE: Somebody, Arrowhead, then back to Mile High, is that how it goes?

FIRST WOMAN: **We're live** in 60 seconds.

SECOND WOMAN: Arrowhead **bounces to** Mile High.

Different age groups can have their own jargon, especially teenagers:

AMERICAN BEAUTY

JANE: I need a father who's a role model, not some horny **geek-boy** who's **gonna spray his shorts** whenever I bring a girlfriend home from school. (*snorts*) **What a lame-o.** Somebody really should put him out of his misery.

AMERICAN GRAFFITI

JOHN: I don't like that surfing **shit**. Rock 'n Roll's been going downhill ever since Buddy Holly died.

CAROL: Don't you think the Beach Boys are **boss**!

JOHN: You would, you grungy little **twerp**.

CAROL: Grungy? You big **weenie**, if I had a boyfriend he'd pound you.

SOMETHING'S GOTTA GIVE

PRETTY GIRL: I'm **totally** excited about this audition... there's this **totally** hilarious scene where she's dating this **like** chauvinist older guy and just as they're about to do it, he moans and she thinks he's just really into her, **right**? Except he's having a heart attack and she's **like so creeped out** and her mother, who basically despises the guy, rushes in, gives him CPR, and saves his life.

Slang is a type of informal jargon, often specific to an uneducated, urban, vulgar, or criminal crowd, but not exclusively. To avoid clichés, you can make it up entirely, as long as it sounds authentic and the reader understands its meaning. This makes your dialogue fresh, colorful, and entertaining.

MILLER'S CROSSING

TOM: Gimme a stiff one.

TONY: No small talk, uh? They shoot your **nag**?

ROCKY

ROCKY: The **juice** is climbin' every week.

FATS: I know the juice is climbin'. I been workin' six months just to pay the damn interest.

ROCKY: Ya still **light** seventy.

RESERVOIR DOGS (QUENTIN TARANTINO)

MR. PINK: I gotta **take a squint**, where's the **Commode** in this **dungeon**?

If you chose to **make up words** and phrases, make sure they sound realistic so that the meaning of the conversation is clear, and the characters know what they're talking about. You often see this technique in science fiction and fantasy genres, such as *A Clockwork Orange (Stanley Kubrick)*:

ALEX: There was me, that is Alex, and my three **droogs**, that is Pete, Georgie and **Dim** and we sat in the **Korova milkbar** trying to make up our **rassoodocks** what to do with the evening. The Korova Milk Bar sold **milkplus**, milk plus **vellocet** or **synthemesc** or **drencrom** which is what we were drinking. This would sharpen you up and make you ready for a bit of the old ultra-violence.

Galaxy Quest (David Howard, Robert Gordon) actually pokes fun at this technique with this bit of dialogue:

BRANDON: Mr. Kwan? In episode nineteen, when the reactor fused, you used an element from Leopold Six to fix the quantum rockets. What was that called?
FRED: Bivrakium.
BRANDON: The blue sheath it was encased in-?
FRED: A bi-thermal krevlite housing.
Brandon makes a note, thanks him and exits with his group.
GUY: How do you remember this stuff?
FRED: Oh, I make it up. Use lots of k's and v's.

Own Agenda

Dialogue is always a function of what a character wants or needs in a scene, even when spouting exposition. And when they stubbornly cling to their agenda, their dialogue becomes interesting. The characters listen and respond to each other, but their agenda remains steadfast and clear. A perfect example is the "Quid pro quo" scene between Clarice and Lecter in *The Silence of the Lambs*, where each character has a clear agenda: Clarice wants information that will lead to Buffalo Bill's capture, and Lecter wants to get inside her head by making her disclose her past. The scene is too long to include here, but as you read it or watch it, note the power play between them, as each character clutches to their own agenda, using sharp orders like:

LECTER: Quid pro quo. I tell you things, you tell me things.
LECTER: Tell me. Don't lie, or I'll know.
CLARICE: Quid pro quo, Doctor.
CLARICE: No. Tell me why.
LECTER: After your father's death, you were orphaned. What happened next?
CLARICE: No...! Quid pro quo, Doctor.

And for a completely lighter mood, this classic example:

SOME LIKE IT HOT

JERRY: Look, Osgood--I'm going to level with you. We can't get married at all.

OSGOOD: Why not?

JERRY: Well, to begin with, I'm not a natural blonde.

OSGOOD (*tolerantly*): It doesn't matter.

JERRY: And I smoke. I smoke all the time.

OSGOOD: I don't care.

JERRY: And I have a terrible past. For three years now, I've been living with a saxophone player.

OSGOOD: I forgive you.

JERRY (*with growing desperation*): And I can never have children.

OSGOOD: We'll adopt some.

JERRY: But you don't understand! (*He rips off his wig; in a male voice*) I'm a man!

OSGOOD (*oblivious*): Well--nobody's perfect.

OWN TRACK

This is similar to the technique above, except here, one character is completely oblivious to the other character, ignoring what the other is saying and continuing on his own track. Both are in their own world instead of listening to each other and reacting.

SOME LIKE IT HOT

Sugar has screwed the cap back on the flask, and now slips it under her garter.

SUGAR: Are my seams straight?

JERRY(*examining her legs*): I'll say.

SUGAR: See you around, girls. She waves and exits into the Pullman car.

JERRY: Bye, Sugar. (*to Joe*) We been playing with the wrong bands.

JOE: Down, Daphne!

JERRY: How about the shape of that liquor cabinet?

Joe spins him around, and unbuttoning the back of his dress, starts to fix the slipped brassiere.

JOE: Forget it. One false move, and they'll toss us off the train - there'll be the police, and the papers, and the mob in Chicago...

JERRY: Boy, would I like to borrow a cup of that Sugar.

JOE (*whirling him around, grabbing the front of his dress*): Look - no butter, no pastry, and no Sugar!

TWO AND A HALF MEN (TV) (LEE ARONSOHN, CHUCK LORRE)

ALAN: Charlie, I need to talk about this.

CHARLIE: Me too. If I don't do anything about this website, I'm gonna have to move to Pennsylvania and chase Amish broads.

ALAN: Judith wants to reconcile. I've dreamed about this happening but now that it's here, I wonder if it's what I truly want.

CHARLIE: I'm thinking whoever put up this website has to be somebody I went out with at least once.

ALAN: It would be great for Jake to have both his parents in one house again, not to mention without alimony, I would stop getting my hair cut at the barber college.

CHARLIE: I'm thinking I could eliminate the married chicks, the ones that don't speak English, and the handful to whom I was never properly introduced.

ALAN: I should make a list, the pros and cons of getting back together with Judith.

CHARLIE: You know what, I'm gonna need to make a list.

ALAN: I'm glad we talked this out.

CHARLIE: I'm always here for you, bro.

ALAN: Me too.

REGIONAL/FOREIGN ACCENTS AND FOREIGN LANGUAGES

Another effective way to give each character his own voice is to use regional or foreign accents and speech patterns, also known as *vernacular*. For instance, a Southern country boy would speak in a rural vernacular, such as "I reckon that ain't no lie," while a university professor in an urban setting might use an academic and intellectual one—"I presume this is no fabrication." You can combine this with jargon and slang for a highly unique character voice. Masters of this technique include David Mamet (con men and street vernacular) and the Coen Brothers (rural speech).

RAISING ARIZONA (JOEL COEN, ETHAN COEN)

ED: Gimme here.

He hands her the infant.

ED: Oh, he's beautiful!

HI: He's awful damn good. I think I got the best one.

ED: Don't you cuss around him.

HI: He's fine, he is. I think it's Nathan Jr.

ED: We are doin' the right thing, aren't we Hi?-I mean, they had more'n they could handle.

HI: Well now honey, we been over this and over this. There's what's right and there's what's right, and never the twain shall meet.

ED: But you don't think his momma'll be upset? I mean overly?

HI: Well, a course she'll be upset, sugar, but she'll get over it. She's got four little babies almost as good as this one.

REVEALING ATTITUDES AND TRAITS

Since no two people have exact experiences or physical attributes, no two characters in a script should view the world in the same way. What they say to others, and how they say it, defines their attitudes and values and shows the reader who they are. In fact, every line of dialogue is an opportunity to reveal personality and attitude. Vocabulary choices and speech patterns should suggest a character's personality in addition to his current emotion.

Before you can expose a character through dialogue, however, you must know who they are, which is why the basic character work in Chapter 5 is essential for this technique to be effective. Once you know a character's feelings on issues, his fears, hopes, and values, his dialogue will become more distinctive. The trick is simple, though the execution must be creative: Pick a trait or attitude, and "translate" it into dialogue, reflecting it through word choice or manner of speaking, under different contexts. For example, let's say you have a character who's frugal and values saving money. You may reveal this trait when he says to his wife, "Hope you didn't throw away the coupons," or to the waiter at a restaurant, "Separate checks, please." Not the best dialogue, but you get the idea. This is the quintessential technique used in TV sitcoms, where writers repeat well-defined characteristics through different episodes and different jokes over years. Looking at classic films, in *Chinatown*, Noah Cross's superior attitude is exposed through his mispronouncing Gittes' name and ignoring his corrections. In *One Flew Over the Cuckoo's Nest*, Nurse Ratched's controlled language, which constantly orders people, reveals her sense of superiority, while Billy's stuttering exposes his low self-esteem. And in *Who's Afraid of Virginia Woolf*, Martha's and George's bitter attitudes toward each other are revealed throughout their dialogue. Here's another great example of personality and attitude revealed through the dialogue of a fast-talking, obnoxious, and sexist traveling salesman in *It Happened One Night (Robert Riskin):*

> SHAPELEY: Shapeley's the name - and that's the way I like 'em! You made no mistake sitting next to me. Just between us, the kinda mugs you meet on a hop like this ain't nothing to write home to the wife about. You gotta be awful careful who you hit up with, is what I always say, and you can't be too particular, neither. Once when I was comin' through North Carolina, I got to gabbin' with a good-lookin' mama. One of those young ones, you know, and plenty classy, too. Kinda struck my fancy. You know how it is. Well, sir, you could'a knocked me over with a Mack truck. I was just warming up when she's yanked offa the bus. Who do you think she was? Huh? Might as well give up. The girl bandit! The one the papers been writin' about. (He pulls out a cigar) What's the matter, sister? You ain't sayin' much.

SENSORY PREFERENCES

According to Neuro-Linguistic Programming (NLP), a psychological model of how we communicate to ourselves and others, we represent the world through the five senses—visual, auditory, kinesthetic, gustatory, and olfactory. We also tend to have one predominant representational system, which often shows up in our speech. For instance, if we're a visual person, we respond to images and use words like *Good to see you, See you later, Let me look at it, Focus on it, Watch it, Be clear, It's still foggy, Picture this, Notice, It appears that,* or *Looks good to me.*" An auditory person responds to sounds and tends to use words like, *Listen, Talk to you later,* or *I've been hearing good things about it.* A kinesthetic person is predominantly sensitive to touch and internal feelings, and will say things like, *I've got a good feeling about this, I'll be in touch, Hold on, I can't grasp the premise,* or *I'll handle it later."* There are also olfactory people sensitive to smells (*Smells fishy to me*), and gustatory people sensitive to tastes (*I'm so close, I can taste it*). But the most common ones are visual, auditory, and kinesthetic. I must admit this is a minor technique seldom used by writers because these sensory clues tend to be dialogue fillers that are often cut in the rewrite. However, they can add uniqueness and veracity to a character, especially when you contrast sensory preferences within a scene. Like many other techniques in this book, this is one that works subconsciously. The reader shouldn't be conscious of it.

SPEECH RHYTHMS

In his book *On Writing Well*, William Zinsser says, "Bear in mind, when you are choosing words and stringing them together, how they sound. This may seem absurd: readers read with their eyes. But actually, they hear what they are reading, in their inner ear, far more than you realize." This is where having "an ear" for dialogue comes in handy—being able to hear the "sound" of dialogue. Dialogue is like music. You can actually hear it. It has rhythm and pace, crescendos, pauses, and silences. Aaron Sorkin, best known for his dialogue in TV shows such as *Sports Night* and *The West Wing*, once said, "I don't have stories to tell. What I love is the sound of dialogue and the music of dialogue. It's what I like to write." Other masters of dialogue, like Paddy Chayefsky, David Mamet, and Quentin Tarantino would probably agree since they're known to rewrite dialogue until the rhythms are right.

So how do you develop this skill? You have to develop an ear for it, there's no other way. You do this by listening to how others speak, eavesdropping on as many different subgroups as you can—rural, city, street, African-American, Hispanic, beach, Southern, teens, etc., until you can pick out all the different speech patterns, cadences, and vocal nuances. Another useful tip is to explore scripts with great dialogue, preferably in different genres and from different writers. Finally, you can improve your dialogue by having others read it out loud, while you sit back and listen. Here are examples of different rhythms:

RAISING ARIZONA

HI: I was in for writing hot checks which, when businessmen do it, is called an overdraft. I'm not complainin', mind you; just sayin' there ain't no pancake so thin it ain't got two sides. Now prison life is very structured—more than most people care for...

MILLER'S CROSSING

LEO: You pay off for protection, just like everyone else. Far as I know--and what I don't know in this town ain't worth knowing--the cops haven't closed any of your dives and the DA hasn't touched any of your rackets. You haven't bought any license to kill bookies and today I ain't selling any. Now take your flunky and dangle.

BULL DURHAM

> CRASH: And you, Larry Hockett, should recognize me 'cause five years ago in the Texas League when you were pitching for El Paso and I was hitting cleanup for Shreveport, you hung a curve on an 0-2 pitch of a 3-2 game in bottom of the 8th and I tattooed it over the Goodyear Tire sign, beat you 4-3--and I got a free wheel alignment from Goodyear.

TECHNIQUES FOR SUBTLE EXPOSITION

Although exposition is best revealed visually, the easiest and most common way is through dialogue. Expressing it "invisibly," however, in a manner that's interesting and entertaining, not awkward, obvious and lifeless, is one of the hardest challenges facing the amateur writer. This includes how much information to reveal in a scene. Beginners often cram too much information into a character's dialogue. The key, like any other script element, is to present it emotionally. This is why the most frequent advice regarding exposition is to deliver it through conflict. While the reader responds to the conflict, any information revealed by the characters is absorbed unconsciously. That's invisible, or subtle exposition—feeding information while distracting the reader emotionally. Humphrey Bogart is known to have said that if he ever had to spout exposition, there'd better be two camels humping in the background to distract the audience. There are, of course, other techniques to weave in exposition seamlessly through dialogue.

BITE-SIZED: PRESENT IT IN SMALL DOSES

This is about presenting information sparingly, feeding it to the reader via an eyedropper, rather than a ladle. Revealing too much information too soon is a common error among inexperienced writers. Think about delivering exposition the way you would dole out candy to a child—just enough to make him happy, but not enough to make him sick. Too much exposition at once can become clumsy and dull. This is why you often see technical information in action scripts spread through several characters, like several engineers in a room explaining scientific data, each giving out a small dose.

ARMAGEDDON (JONATHAN HENSLEIGH, J.J. ABRAMS)

> GOLDEN: Okay guys, one of the worst days in N.A.S.A. history just got worse. Ten million to one. The stuff that hit this morning was the collision's forward-thrown matter, mere pebbles from what's about to come. Walter?
>
> CLARK: A big asteroid. E.T.A., eighteen days. A lot bigger than the five mile one that obliterated the dinosaurs.
>
> GOLDEN: The size of Texas.

THE BOURNE SUPREMACY (TONY GILROY)

> *Everything stops, as THE PHOTO -- blurry, oblique -- begins materializing on HALF-A-DOZEN MONITORS around the room.*

PAMELA (to Nicky): Is it him?
Looking closer -- she nods...
CRONIN: He's not hiding, that's for sure.
ZORN: Why Naples? Why now?
KURT: Could be random.
CRONIN: Maybe he's running.
ABBOTT: On his own passport?
KIM: What's he actually doing?
CRONIN: What's he doing? He's making his first mistake...
And then, from behind them --
NICKY: It's not a mistake. *(everyone looks over)* They don't make mistakes. And they don't do random. There's always an objective, always a target. (beat) If he's in Naples, on his own passport, there's a reason.

FORESHADOW

Foreshadowing is when things are said that appear to be innocent, but in the context of the story often have a sinister implication of events to come. In short, it's a hint of future danger or the promise of things to come through a twist, a clue, or character nuance. This creates anticipation and tension, worry, and intrigue.

CITY SLICKERS

MITCH: Hi, Curly, kill anyone today?
CURLY: **Day ain't over yet.**

BASIC INSTINCT

NICK: What's your new book about?
CATHERINE: A detective. He falls for the wrong woman.
NICK: What happens to him?
CATHERINE *(looks him right in the eye)*: **She kills him.**

THELMA AND LOUISE

MAX: We don't have a whole lotta choice, do we? I can't figure out if they're real smart or just really, really lucky.
HAL: It don't matter. Brains will only get you so far and **luck always runs out.**

ALIENS

RIPLEY: How long before we're declared overdue can we expect a rescue?
HICKS: Seventeen days.
HUDSON: Seventeen days? Look man, I don't wanna rain on your parade, but we're not gonna last seventeen hours! Those things are gonna come in here just like they did before. And they're gonna come in here...
RIPLEY: Hudson!
HUDSON: ...and they're gonna come in here AND THEY'RE GONNA KILL US!

GLAZE IT WITH EMOTION

Exposition can be made more palatable to the reader when it's glazed, or coated, with emotion. This can be any character emotion, like anger, joy, fear, or impatience. It can also be any of the reader emotions we've explored so far—curiosity, anticipation, tension, surprise, or humor. For instance, in *Chinatown*, Robert Towne glazes his heavy exposition with curiosity and anticipation when we follow Gittes' investigation of Mulwray's affair. While we anticipate evidence that Mulwray is indeed cheating, in the background we're given exposition on L.A.'s drought, the politics of water management, and the plight of the farmers. In fact, this is an effective technique is mystery films, which are driven by curiosity and tension. The clues and revelations the reader encounters throughout the story are the actual exposition. In *Basic Instinct*, Joe Eszterhas glazes exposition with tension and curiosity, like in the interrogation scene where Catherine is interrogated by all the detectives at the police station, and she's in complete control. In *Charade*, there's a long exposition scene in a restaurant as Bartholomew tells Reggie the backstory of why five men are after the missing $250,000. Here the exposition is glazed with the emotion of impatience and humor, caused by the waiter's interruptions and Reggie's eccentric behavior. In fact, glazing exposition with impatience is an effective trick of the trade. For example, a character wants to learn something very important. He approaches another character who has that information, but for whatever reason the man talks about everything else but that particular subject. "Everything else" the man talks about is the exposition you need to reveal to the reader.

Here's another example that glazes the dullest exposition—scientific information—with humor and sensual titillation:

REAL GENIUS

SHERRY (*between kisses*): Talk smart to me.

CHRIS: What?

They are lying in the middle of the dish. Passion mounts, fingers cope with belts and buttons, clothing falls away; my God, these people are having sex.

SHERRY: Please I need it. What was your favorite course?

CHRIS: I guess right now I'd have to say Fluid Mechanics.

SHERRY: Oooooooooh...

CHRIS: And Gym.

SHERRY: Please.

CHRIS: Sorry.

SHERRY: What's your research with Artherton?

CHRIS: Ultra-high power laser as an energy force for fusion. Tremendous boon to all mankind. And womankind, too.

SHERRY: Fusion, more fusion.

CHRIS: It's the process for obtaining enormous amounts of energy from forms of hydrogen, like Deuterium and Tritium.

SHERRY: Oh, my God, more.

CHRIS: Extracting the fuels is no problem.

SHERRY: Hmmmm.

CHRIS: Getting them to combine and release the energy is the problem.

SHERRY: Oohh, yes.

CHRIS: It takes temperatures of 100 million degrees Celsius.

SHERRY: Oh, God.

CHRIS: So, I'm...

SHERRY: Yes.

CHRIS ...building...

SHERRY: Yes.

CHRIS: ...a laser...

SHERRY: Oh, yes.

CHRIS: ...that pulses...

SHERRY: Hmmmmmmmm.

CHRIS: ...very hot...

SHERRY: Ohhh...

CHRIS: ...and causes...

SHERRY: Yes.

CHRIS: ...Fusion...

SHERRY: Ahhhhhhhhhhh.

IMPLY INFORMATION

Implied information is always more interesting than direct information for one important reason: the reader is actively involved in trying to figure out the information rather than passively being spoon-fed. This is equivalent to on-the-nose dialogue versus subtext, which is implied emotions and thoughts. We'll explore subtext in depth later in the chapter, but here are a few examples of exposition where the information is implied instead of direct:

BLADE RUNNER

BRYANT: You're gonna spot 'em an' you're gonna air 'em out.

DECKARD: Not me, Bryant. I won't work for you anymore. Give it to Holden, he's good.

BRYANT: I did.

DECKARD: And?

BRYANT: **He can breathe okay... as long as nobody unplugs him.**

ALL ABOUT EVE

MAX: Answer me this. What makes a man become a producer?

ADDISON: **What makes a man walk into a lion cage with nothing but a chair?**

MAX: This answer satisfies me a hundred percent.

ERIN BROCKOVICH

ED: This is the only thing you found?

ERIN: So far. But that place is a pigsty. I wouldn't be surprised if there's more.

ED: I know how those places are run. They're a mess. What makes you think you can just walk in there and find what we need?

ERIN: **They're called boobs, Ed.**

GILMORE GIRLS (TV)

LORELAI: Michel. The phone.

MICHEL: It rings.

LORELAI: Can you answer it?

MICHEL: No. People are particularly stupid today. I can't talk to any more of them.

LORELAI: You know who's really nice to talk to? **The people at the unemployment agency**.

Michel picks up the phone.

PRESENT IT WHEN THE READER IS EAGER TO KNOW IT

One of the most common problems with exposition is offering it before its time, before we're eager to know it. This follows the basic principle that information is more interesting when we want to know it. If you set up the desire to know first, thus establishing curiosity, the reader will become eager to have his questions answered. When you answer his questions, it doesn't feel like exposition. This is why information that's kept secret for as long as possible is more interesting than if it's blurted out all at once, as demonstrated by Evelyn's secret in *Chinatown*. Other examples of this technique include the "I can't swim" scene in *Butch Cassidy and the Sundance Kid*. There's no better time to reveal the exposition that Sundance can't swim than when we're eager to know why he won't jump off the cliff. In *Raiders of the Lost Ark*, we find out Indiana Jones hates snakes when he's faced with one. In *Casablanca*, the Paris flashback appears when we're eager to know why Rick is so bitter towards Ilsa.

SURROUND IT WITH CONFLICT

As mentioned earlier, most professional writers advise to make exposition a by-product of conflict. In other words, there should never be any boring exposition in your script, only interesting discovery through conflict, such as fights, arguments, complications, or life-or-death situations. For example, in *North by Northwest*, all the information Thornhill reveals about himself is in conflict with the men who are trying to kill him. In *The Terminator*, there is a ten-minute scene of pure exposition where Reese, who has just saved Sarah from the Terminator, lays out all the information we need to know—where he comes from, what the Terminator is, and all the foreshadowing designed to create anticipation. Yet, the scene doesn't feel like an exposition scene because of the conflict and excitement generated by the police and the Terminator chasing after Reese and Sarah. Imagine what this exposition would have felt like if it were presented in a ten-minute restaurant scene without any conflict surrounding it. Conflict is the best way to camouflage exposition.

ADD DRAMATIC IRONY

In Chapter 6, we explored this most effective tool to arouse anticipation and tension, thereby creating forward movement in a story. Always keep in mind that it is this anticipation which causes reader engagement, not the freshness of the dialogue, or the action in a scene. This means you simply can't rely on hip and edgy dialogue or character actions to keep the reader's attention. When you add dramatic irony, or Reader superior position, to a scene, you can have the dullest exposition (not recommended, of course) and still have a compelling scene. This is a proven technique when conveying flat information. Look at the scene following the crop duster attack in *North by Northwest*, where Thornhill returns to the hotel to face Eve, whom we know is working for the bad guys and has betrayed him (dramatic irony). The dialogue couldn't be more mundane and expository, and yet because we know something Eve doesn't, this becomes another fascinating scene where we're at the edge of our seats. We wonder what Thornhill will do to Eve, how he'll react, and whether he'll explode and confront her.

MAKE THE EXPOSITION ACTIVE

This technique is similar to those that make anything active—a word, sentence, character, or line of dialogue. Active has always more impact than passive. This is no different with exposition. To make it active, give the information purpose when the characters interact. Thus, the exposition becomes part of a character's agenda. When the character *needs* to give this information, it comes with an emotional edge, and is therefore interesting. For example, on a first date, most of the perfunctory exposition given by one character may be designed to impress, charm, or seduce. So it shouldn't feel dull. In *Some Like It Hot*, when Joe disguises himself as the Shell millionaire Junior and runs into Sugar at the beach, his basic exposition has purpose. It is active information because he needs to convince Sugar he's the millionaire she's been looking for all her life. Always make sure there's a valid reason for a character to deliver this information right here, right now. This will make it ring true to the scene.

TWIST A CHARACTER'S EMOTIONS TO GET IT

Nothing is duller than information being forced on you, and nothing is more intriguing than information someone's trying to hold out. Therefore, if you make characters *need* the information, and have them fight for it, boring exposition turns into taut confrontation. How do you do this? One effective way is to twist the other character's emotions to get at the truth. You keep your hero active in trying to get the information out, rather than passively listening to it. The fun comes from the clash of wills (conflict) and the way the other's emotions are manipulated. A character can squeeze information out of a reluctant character by exploiting their baser human motives—greed, jealousy, fear, anger, impatience, or desire. For instance, you can take advantage of another's greed by giving them money for the information. How many times have we seen the clichéd $20 slip to a reluctant bartender in detective TV shows? Or a detective threaten a reluctant witness with being an accessory to a crime? It's your job to be creative. In *Chinatown*, note how Robert Towne has Gittes irritating Yellburton's secretary, thus exploiting her impatience to get valuable information on Noah Cross and his involvement with the water department.

PRESENT IT IN A UNIQUE WAY

If you find a unique way to present exposition, one the reader hasn't seen in countless screenplays, he'll be receptive to it because it will be glazed with the emotion of freshness, coolness, and originality. Think of how Princess Leia's hologram delivers crucial exposition in *Star Wars*, how E.T. presents information through objects floating in the air as if they were planets, and the self-destruct tape in the *Mission Impossible* TV show. In *Annie Hall*, background information on the character's childhoods is presented by the adult characters interacting with their childhood versions in their home and classroom. The more unique the presentation, the more receptive the reader will be to it.

TECHNIQUES FOR SUBTEXT

On-the-nose dialogue is probably the most common flaw in amateur scripts. When dialogue tells the reader directly what's going on in a scene or what the characters are thinking or feeling, it's often dull and ultimately unsatisfying. Great dialogue, on the other hand, is *off the nose*—it illuminates what the characters are thinking without saying it. This is "subtext," which a writer once called, "The river of emotion that flows beneath the words." For instance, a man and a woman might be having an innocent conversation about a movie they saw the night before, but what they're really expressing are their feelings about their first date. In *The Godfather*, the meaning of the memorable line, "I'll make him an offer he can't refuse" is clear to all of us, although it's not spelled out. But the best example of subtext has to be the meeting scene in *Annie Hall*, where Alvy and Annie talk about mundane topics while subtitles clue us in as to what they're really thinking.

The challenge with subtext is how to disguise character thoughts and emotions without resorting to subtitles. This is what this section is all about. Before we go over subtext techniques, however, we should analyze why subtext is so important in dramatic scenes, and when it is necessary. There are times when subtext is preferred, and times when on-the-nose dialogue is actually a more direct dramatic choice. As with any other element in your script, a balance of direct and subtext dialogue is the ideal.

WHY SUBTEXT IS SO IMPORTANT

For the longest time, I didn't think there was anything wrong with simple and direct dialogue. After all, I saw it in professional scripts and in great movies. I also thought on-the-nose dialogue would make my scenes clearer, since I didn't trust readers would be sharp enough to grasp any subtleties. It wasn't until I became a more experienced writer that I realized where and when subtext was called for. There are two specific reasons why subtext is necessary: characters have too much to lose if they're direct, and you want the reader to experience the scene actively rather than passively.

IT'S THE WAY WE TALK WHEN EMOTIONAL STAKES ARE HIGH

This is a psychological issue. In relationships, when dealing with intense emotions like anger, hate, love, or desire, we're often afraid to expose ourselves emotionally. So we usually hide our true feelings and desires. Think back when you were angry at a friend, shopped around for an expensive item, dealt with a boss you disliked, or went out on a date. Didn't you disguise your intentions, speak indirectly, only gradually working your way up to what you truly wanted? The reason is that communicating what we want directly could get us into trouble. It's simply too much to risk emotionally. So when it comes to your characters, ask what they're in conflict about in the scene. What do they have to risk? What's at stake for each one? What are they afraid to reveal outright? It's this underlying fear that leads them to speak indirectly through subtext. They prefer to hide the thoughts and feelings they don't dare say to another because they're either too personal, private or inappropriate for the moment. Robert Towne once said, "The more it means to the character, the more difficult it is to say. If there's no restraint, no inhibitions, no guilt, no shame, there's no drama."

IT ACTIVELY ENGAGES THE READER

The other reason readers welcome subtext is that, like a good crossword puzzle, it's challenging. It involves them and makes them active in the reading experience. Because subtext has more substance, it makes the reader think more by bringing him into the conversation. Therefore, to engage the reader in our characters and their dialogue, you can't just tell him what's going on directly. The reader would rather find out for himself. When you tell him something on the nose, you deny him the opportunity to collaborate in creating the meaning of the exchange for himself. This makes for a passive reading experience, and less reason to invest himself in your material.

You can engage the reader by allowing him to fill in what's left unsaid. In his book, *The Dramatist's Toolkit*, Jeffrey Sweet uses the example of writing "2+3=5" and the reader acknowledging with a bored look that this is true. But if you write "2+x=5," the reader's immediate impulse is to fill in that x. This reaction is an *active* participation—the reader is *involved* in the equation. Subtext is the dramatic equivalent of letting the reader fill in the x for himself. With subtext, the reader becomes an active participant in the scene, rather than a passive reader being pounded with obvious dialogue.

To use subtext well, you must first know what's really going on in a scene, and why. Who are the characters, what do they truly feel, and what's at stake if they express these feelings directly? You can then write the dialogue as simply and directly as you'd like. Don't worry about it being on the nose. It's a first draft. Nobody's reading it except you. Think of subtext as levels of dialogue. The first level is what the character is truly thinking or wants in the scene. Then, in rewrites, you can decide if subtext is necessary, and how much of the true meaning will show on the surface. Each rewrite is another level until the real meaning is implied, rather than stated directly. To do this, you can apply any of the following techniques:

ACTION AS RESPONSE

This is a simple but proven technique where a character's action is the response to a question, request, or declaration, instead of a straight line of dialogue. For example, if someone said "I love you," and the other slapped him instead of saying "How dare you?" or "Well, I hate you," the slap would have subtext. Imagine another action as response to "I love you"—crying, leaving the room, simply staring at the person for a long beat, going back to reading the newspaper, each a specific action, each saying something else without actually uttering a verbal on-the-nose response. Here's a perfect example from *Network (Paddy Chayefsky)*:

> MAX: Listen, if we can get back for a moment to that gypsy who predicted all that about emotional involvements and middle-aged men, what're you doing for dinner tonight?
> DIANA *pauses in the doorway, and then moves back briskly to the desk,* **picks up the telephone receiver, taps out a telephone number,** *waits for a moment--*
> DIANA (**on the phone**): I can't make it tonight, luv, call me tomorrow.
> *She returns the receiver to its cradle, looks at MAX; their eyes lock.*

CHANGE THE SUBJECT, EVADE

Another clear technique that implies rather than states is having a character abruptly change the subject of conversation, thus evading a topic that could bring about uncomfortable emotional stress. For example:

AMERICAN GRAFFITI
> STEVE: Where was I?

LAURIE: Um, how you thought high school romances were goofy and we started going together just because you thought I was kinda cute and funny, but then you suddenly realized you were in love with me, it was serious...and ah...oh, you were leadin' up to somethin' kinda big.

STEVE: You make it sound like I'm giving dictation. Well, seriously, what I meant was, that ah...since we do care for each other so much, and since we should really consider ourselves as adults. Now, I, ah...**could I have a couple of those fries**?

FRASIER (TV)

FRASIER: Well, the rest of the show was pretty good. (*Roz says nothing*) It was a good show, wasn't it?

ROZ (*tears him a piece of notepaper*): **Here, your brother called**.

FRASIER: Roz, in the trade we call that "avoidance." Don't change the subject, tell me what you think.

ROZ (*points at her console*): **Did I ever tell you what this little button does?**

FRASIER: I am not a piece of Lalique. I can handle criticism. How was I today?

ROZ (*turns her chair to face him*): Let's see... you dropped two commercials, you left a total of twenty-eight seconds of dead air, you scrambled the station's call letters, you spilled yogurt on the control board, and you kept referring to Jerry–with the identity crisis–as "Jeff."

Frasier considers the criticism.

FRASIER (*takes the notepaper*): **You say my brother called...**

GILMORE GIRLS (TV)

LORELAI: So.

RORY: What?

LORELAI: Tell me about the guy.

RORY: **You know what's really special about our relationship?** The total understanding about the need for one's privacy. I mean, you really understand boundaries.

THELMA AND LOUISE

Louise looks down the road and sees a highway patrol car coming down the road towards them. She glides along as the cop car passes on the other side without seeing them. J.D. and Louise look at each other.

J.D.: Maybe you got a few too many parking tickets?

LOUISE: **We'll take you on to Oklahoma City, then you'd best be on your way.**

CONTRAST DIALOGUE WITH ACTION

Briefly discussed in the Subtext section of Chapter 8, this is one of the best ways to create subtext in a scene. The dialogue itself doesn't reveal the true meaning of the exchange, the contrasting action does—like when a character says he loves dogs, but then recoils when he sees one. The subtext comes from the action, not the dialogue. This is why we say actions speak louder than words. To create subtext, make a character say something that's counter to what he does, like at the end of *When Harry Met Sally*, when Sally tells Harry she hates him, but then kisses him, or in *Casablanca*, when Rick says he sticks his neck out for nobody, but then pockets the transit letters.

DIFFICULTY REVEALING EMOTION

Dialogue is rarely the best way to express emotion unless it's forced out into the open. Remember in the previous section on exposition, how information that's forced out is always more engaging than information freely given? The same goes for subtext when you have a character who tries to avoid a sensitive issue or has trouble finding words to express his feelings. Here, you can convey an emotion by having a character struggle with its expression, like in these two great examples:

SEX, LIES, AND VIDEOTAPE (STEVEN SODERBERGH):

> ANN: You just ask them questions?
> GRAHAM: Yes.
> ANN: And they just answer them?
> GRAHAM: Mostly. Sometimes they do things.
> ANN: To you?
> GRAHAM: No, not to me, for me, for the camera.
> ANN: **I don't... why... why do you do this?**
> GRAHAM: I'm sorry this came up.
> ANN: **This is just... so...**
> GRAHAM: Maybe you want to go.
> ANN: **Yes, I do.**

CASABLANCA

> ILSA (*controlling herself*): Oh, Rick -- it's a crazy world -- anything can happen -- **If you shouldn't get away -- If -- If something should keep us apart -- Wherever they put you -- wherever I'll be -- I want you to know that I--** (*she can't go on; she lifts her face to his*) Kiss me. Kiss me as though -- as though it were the last time.

DOUBLE MEANING

Earlier in this chapter, we looked at double meaning for comic effect. Here, it can be used dramatically to convey a particular emotion. A character uses a line of dialogue which has two meanings. The first may be considered on the nose, while the second meaning is the implied emotion. The following examples illustrate this technique:

DOUBLE INDEMNITY

> NEFF: Know why you couldn't figure this one, Keyes? I'll tell ya. The guy you were looking for was **too close**. Right across the desk from ya.
> KEYES: **Closer than that, Walter.**
> NEFF: I love you, too.

SOMETHING'S GOTTA GIVE

> HARRY: What's with the turtlenecks? It's the middle of summer.
> ERICA: Now seriously, why do you care what I wear?
> HARRY: Just curious.
> ERICA: I like them. I've always liked them. I'm just a turtleneck kinda gal.
> HARRY: **You never get hot?**
> ERICA: No.
> HARRY: Never?
> ERICA: **Not lately.**

EMOTIONAL MASKS

This technique mirrors a common psychological truism: When we're embarrassed, we often try to hide the negative feeling by putting up an artificial front in order to maintain a façade of strength and pride. As Oscar Wilde once said, "A mask tells us more than a face." For example, when a teenage boy asks a girl out and she turns him down, the boy covers his shame by saying something like "No big deal, I had some stuff to do anyway." This deceptive front—tough on the outside, hurt on the inside, is an effective way to create subtext in a dialogue exchange, and to invite the reader to share what the character is feeling, as illustrated by the following examples:

UNFORGIVEN (DAVID WEBB PEOPLES)

> DELILAH: Alice an' Silky gave them... free ones.
> MUNNY (*understanding, embarrassed*): Oh. Yeah.
> DELILAH (*shy, timid*): You want... a free one.
> MUNNY (*looking away, embarrassed*): Me? No. No, I guess not.
> *And Delilah is hurt... crushed. She gets up and covers it by picking up the remains of the chicken and Munny is too embarrassed to look at her.*
> DELILAH (*covering her hurt*): **I didn't mean... with me. Alice and Silky, they'll give you one... if you want.**

CAROLINE IN THE CITY (TV)

> CAROLINE: Maybe we could catch a movie sometime.
> DEL: Yeah, when?
> CAROLINE: How about tonight?
> DEL: Ohhh, tonight's bad. I've got a thing.
> CAROLINE: A thing... like elective surgery?
> DEL: No. I've got an, am, a, a...
> CAROLINE: Oh, Del, I'm an adult. If you have a date, just come right out and tell me.
> DEL: Okay, I've got a date.
> CAROLINE: A date? A date?
> DEL: Hey, you're the one who said we should, you know, get on with our lives.

CAROLINE: **As we should. As a matter of fact, talk about coincidences, I just remembered, I have a date tonight, too.**

DEL: Really?

CAROLINE: **That would have been embarrassing, huh? Me making a date with you and then having this other big, hot date.**

IMPLY INSTEAD OF CONCLUDE

Remember the "2+x=5" equation, and how we automatically conclude that x=3? Readers like to be engaged by a script page when it implies things, rather than states them overtly, thus allowing the reader to come up with his own conclusions. Implying would be subtext; concluding would be on the nose. The choice is clear. It's your duty through craft and art to create dialogue that implies so that the reader gets to evaluate its meaning. This is how the pros do it:

BLADE RUNNER

DECKARD: Where do you get them, the memories?

TYRELL: In the case of Rachael, I simply copied and regenerated cells from the brain of my sixteen-year-old niece. Rachael remembers what my little niece remembers.

DECKARD: **I saw an old movie once. The guy had bolts in his head.**

THE APARTMENT (BILLY WILDER, I. A. L. DIAMOND)

FRAN (*explaining the cracked mirror in her compact*): I like it that way. It makes me look the way I feel. **When you're in love with a married man you shouldn't wear mascara.**

SOMETHING'S GOTTA GIVE

ERICA: So I can't decide if... you hate me or if maybe you're the only person who ever got me.

HARRY: **I don't hate you.**

REAL GENIUS

MITCH (*reading from notes*): There's a mistake all right, but I think you guys made it. Look, you inverted the last two steps.

CARTER (*grabbing the notes*): I don't make mistakes... (*reading*)... **Usually.**

METAPHORIC OR SYMBOLIC DIALOGUE

Just like in narrative description, you can use metaphors in dialogue to symbolize a character's thought or emotion, rather than spell it out in an obvious way.

THE APARTMENT

SHELDRAKE (*taking her hand*): I want you back, Fran.

FRAN (*withdrawing her hand*): Sorry, Mr. Sheldrake - **I'm full up. You'll have to take the next elevator.**

BUD: You know, I used to live **like Robinson Crusoe – shipwrecked among eight million people. Then one day I saw a footprint in the sand – and there you were.** It's a wonderful thing – dinner for two.

SIDEWAYS

JACK: No, see, I want both of us to get crazy. We should both be cutting loose. I mean, this is our last chance. This is our week! It should be something we share.

The older waitress comes over.

WAITRESS: Can I take your order?

JACK: But I'm warning you.

MILES: Oatmeal, one poached egg, and rye toast. Dry.

WAITRESS: Okay. And you?

JACK (glaring at Miles): **Pigs in a blanket. With extra syrup.**

AS GOOD AS IT GETS

SIMON: Do you still think I was exaggerating?

FRANK: **Definitely a package you don't want to open or touch.**

BULL DURHAM

SKIP: Look, men--you got a choice. You wanta be roasting your nuts off for Midas Muffler welding exhaust pipes up the assholes of Cadillacs... or-- (*beat*) You wanta be sitting in the Caddy while some other guy's crawling around in a monkey suit with a blow torch? (*beat*) **There's only two places you can be in life--in the Caddy or under it.**

And look at this classic Billy Wilder scene from *Double Indemnity*. Note how it avoids the clichés of pick up lines and typical seduction dialogue by using the metaphors of cars, police officers, and speeding tickets:

NEFF: I wish you'd tell me what's engraved on that anklet.

PHYLLIS: Just my name.

NEFF: As for instance?

PHYLLIS: Phyllis.

NEFF: Phyllis, huh. I think I like that.

PHYLLIS: But you're not sure.

NEFF: I'd have to **drive it around the block** a couple of times.

PHYLLIS (*standing up*): Mr. Neff, why don't you drop by tomorrow evening around 8:30? He'll be in then.

NEFF: Who?

PHYLLIS: My husband. You were anxious to talk to him, weren't you?

NEFF: Yeah, I was. But I'm sort of getting over the idea, if you know what I mean.

PHYLLIS: There's a **speed limit** in this state, Mr. Neff, **45 miles an hour.**

NEFF: How fast was I going, **Officer?**

PHYLLIS: I'd say **around 90.**

NEFF: **Suppose you get down off your motorcycle and give me a ticket.**

PHYLLIS: **Suppose I let you off with a warning this time.**

NEFF: Suppose it doesn't take.

PHYLLIS: Suppose I have to whack you over the knuckles.

NEFF: Suppose I bust out crying and put my head on your shoulder.

PHYLLIS: Suppose you try putting it on my husband's shoulder.

NEFF: That tears it...

PHYSICALIZE THE EMOTION

In another classic scene, this time from *On the Waterfront (Budd Schulberg)*, Terry and Edie walk through the park, exchanging small talk. As they walk, Edie accidentally drops one of her white gloves. Terry picks it up and cleans it off, but instead of immediately returning it, he holds it, and then puts it on his left hand. This is a great example of physicalizing an emotion. In this case, putting on the glove symbolizes his desire to get closer to her. This technique is similar to "Action as response" except here, the character is not responding to anything, simply physicalizing his emotion instead of verbalizing it on the nose. Here are more examples:

THELMA AND LOUISE

THELMA: I guess you haven't heard anything from Jimmy... yet?

Louise's jaw tightens. The car speeds up.

THELMA: ... never mind.

J.D.: Oh. I... where's Louise?

THELMA: She's off with Jimmy, that's her boyfriend.

J.D.: That's lonely for you, I guess. I always think of motel rooms as lonely.

Thelma pretends like she's had a lot of experience with this sort of thing.

THELMA *(letting him in the door)*: Oh, yes, well, they can be.

SIDEWAYS

*Pursued by Jack, Miles dashes down the hill, all the while **taking huge swigs from the bottle.***

*Miles slows down to a walk between rows of grapevines. **He polishes off the bottle and tosses it.** A panting Jack catches up with him in the adjacent grapevine corridor.*

Miles's face crumbles as though he were about to cry. Then he collapses to the ground and closes his eyes tight.

A HAND-PRINTED SIGN, attached to a STOP SIGN and decorated with balloons, reads: "RECEPTION THIS WAY!" with an arrow pointing RIGHT.

*One by one, CARS are making a right turn. But when his turn comes, **Miles turns LEFT.***

ANSWER A QUESTION WITH A QUESTION

This is a style of dialogue where a question is answered with a question. This is often a defensive technique when someone has something to hide or simply wants to play his cards close to the chest. It's the reason this technique was often used in film noirs where the clichéd response to a detective's inquiry was often "Who wants to know?" or "What's it to ya?" Here are more examples:

TOOTSIE (LARRY GELBART, DON MCGUIRE, MURRAY SCHISGAL)

RITA : I'd like to make her look a little more attractive. How far can you pull back?

CAMERAMAN: **How do you feel about Cleveland?**

CARNAL KNOWLEDGE (JULES PFEIFFER)

JONATHAN: When did you go to high school?

SUSAN: **What are you doing this summer?**

JONATHAN: **Why do you answer a question with a question?**

SUSAN: **Why are you dating your best friend's girlfriend?**

AS GOOD AS IT GETS

Melvin walks back into the apartment and is about to close the door when Simon has another burst of bravery.

SIMON: Did you... do something to him?

MELVIN: **Do you realize that I work at home?**

SIMON (*eyes downcast*): No, I didn't.

REVEAL EMOTION THROUGH TEMPO

As you saw earlier, tempo is the speed of dialogue affected by the character's emotional condition. For instance, when composed, he speaks normally; when angry, he speaks quickly, in short, jerky sentences; when happy, he speaks rapidly; and when sad, he speaks slowly and hesitantly, stopping and starting again. This is why contrasting tempos in a scene is a great way to individualize character voices. Here, you don't have to worry about contrast, just the tempo of a specific character whose emotion you want to convey. Once you figure out the emotion, you can vary the speed of dialogue to evoke their feelings and attitudes without stating them directly. In the following example from the TV show *Gilmore Girls*, Rory conveys her anxiety and insecurity not only through the speed of her dialogue but also the amount of words spoken in one clip:

DEAN: I'm Dean.

RORY: Hi. (*beat, then realizing*) Oh. Rory. Me. That's... me.

DEAN: Rory.

RORY: Well, Lorelai technically.

DEAN: Lorelai. I like that.

He smiles at her. She's melting.

RORY: **It's my mother's name, too. She named me after herself. She was lying in the hospital thinking about how men name boys after themselves all the time, you know? So, why couldn't women? Her feminism just took over. Although personally I think a lot of Demerol also went into the decision.** (beat) I never talk this much.

REVEAL CHARACTER TRAITS AND ATTITUDES

Another way to add subtext to dialogue is to suggest a character's personality through his speech, since it's implied rather than stated overtly by another character. For instance, if you have a funny or sarcastic character, let the reader figure out his traits through his dialogue, rather than have another character say, "Gee, you're a funny guy" or "Don't need the sarcasm." For more on this technique, you may review the "Revealing attitudes and traits" section on page 202. When your characters talk, the reader should learn who they are.

SCENE CONTEXT CAN PROVIDE THE SUBTEXT

Method-acting teacher Sandford Meisner had an exercise where two actors would sit face to face and speak four or more lines of trivial dialogue. The dialogue had to remain the same boring, insignificant chitchat. What changed each time was the context of the scene—what each of the characters felt toward each other, or just experienced before the scene started. Were they attracted to each other? Did they hate each other? Did one want to get money from the other, or hurt them? With each context, the same lines of "average" dialogue suddenly took on different meanings, each context giving a line a new subtext. Look at these examples and note how the simple words, "I hate you" take on a different meaning each time the context of the scene and the character's emotions change:

A grieving husband yells it at his dead wife:
HUSBAND: I hate you...
He breaks downs in tears.

An aspiring actress to her screen idol, who just won an Oscar:
ACTRESS: I hate you...
She smiles.

At the climax of When Harry Met Sally:
SALLY (*almost in tears*): I hate you, Harry... I hate you.
They kiss.

SILENCES

The "Less is more" principle discussed in the previous chapter is equally applicable with dialogue. Pick your cliché—*Silence is golden, silence speaks louder than words, a silent moment can be deafening.* The bottom line is that silence can be quite effective is conveying a particular thought or emotion without resorting to on-the-nose dialogue. Whether the silence is involuntary due to overwhelming emotion, or calculated to ignore a comment or question, it evokes an emotional response in the reader, as these examples show:

THELMA AND LOUISE
LOUISE: It won't work.
THELMA: Why not?!

LOUISE: No physical evidence. We can't prove he did it. We probably can't even prove he touched you by now.

They both pause for a moment.

THELMA: God. The law is some tricky shit, isn't it?

Then:

THELMA: How do you know 'bout all this stuff anyway?

Louise doesn't answer the question.

THE SHAWSHANK REDEMPTION

ANDY: I'm done. It stops right now. Get H&R Block to declare your income.

Norton lunges to his feet, eyes sparkling with rage.

NORTON: Nothing stops! NOTHING! Or you will do the hardest time there is. No more protection from the guards. I'll pull you out of that one-bunk Hilton and put you in with the biggest bull queer I can find. You'll think you got fucked by a train! And the library? Gone! Sealed off brick by brick! We'll have us a little book-barbecue in the yard! They'll see the flames for miles! We'll dance around it like wild Indians! Do you understand me? Are you catching my drift?

SLOW PUSH IN on Andy's face. Eyes hollow. His beaten expression says it all...

WHEN ON-THE-NOSE DIALOGUE IS ACCEPTABLE

At this point in my dialogue classes, I usually see students with a glazed look on their face, as they grasp just how much work is involved in crafting great dialogue. Some even wonder if they need to maintain this high level of excellence throughout the script. My answer is that it couldn't hurt. The more techniques you can apply to your dialogue, the better, as long as it remains honest to the scene's dynamics. However, when it comes to subtext, remember that characters often speak indirectly when there's a lot at stake psychologically. Subtext is a defensive mechanism to protect speakers from the emotional consequences of what they say. This means that when it's safe to say exactly what's on your mind, on-the-nose dialogue is okay.

There are actually three circumstances when on-the-nose dialogue is actually acceptable and believable:

WHEN IT'S EMOTIONALLY SAFE

Characters may speak directly when it's emotionally safe. Think of a first date when you use subtext to get what you want versus a happily married couple who's comfortable communicating without fears. The way to write on-the-nose dialogue in a believable context is to have your character speak to **a best friend, a confidante, a baby, a pet, a therapist, a priest** in a confessional, or **to himself.** When you're totally at ease with someone, you don't have to use subtext or walk on eggshells around them. You can be honest, relaxed, and direct. We see examples of this when **a character talks directly to us**, breaking the fourth wall, like in *High Fidelity* and *Annie Hall,* or through **a voice-over,** like in *Sunset Boulevard* and *American Beauty.* Here, we become the character's best friend, therapist, and confidante. There's a great scene in *Before Sunrise* where the two characters are in a restaurant and talk to their respective best friends on their cell phone. Only it's an imaginary conversation. They're just playing around with their hands being the phone, and telling their "friend" how they met on the train and how they feel about each other. Their dialogue is technically on the nose, but because they're sharing their deepest thoughts with their "best friend," not with each other, it works.

WHEN IT'S BEEN EARNED, AT THE CLIMAX

Ever wonder why you see direct dialogue in well-written professional scripts? It's because it often appears at the climax, after the character has kept his emotions in check, can't keep them bottled any longer, and they explode in a climactic scene. In other words, the right to be direct has been earned throughout the script. In the climactic moments of *American Beauty*, Angela asks Lester "What do you want?" and he answers "Are you kidding? I want you." You can't get more direct than this, and yet it doesn't seem on the nose because this feeling was conveyed through subtext throughout the script, thus earning the right to be direct.

WHEN IT'S SIMPLE AND TO THE POINT

Finally, there are times in a script when the most effective type of dialogue is the simplest, when all the bells and whistles are cut aside, and a character says exactly what he means. Writer-director James Cameron says: "Sometimes the hardest thing to do is be obvious, because that's not your impulse. Your impulse is to be more artful. You're trying to find a clever, elegant solution to a dramatic problem when probably the best thing to do is just have the guy say what's on his mind." Sometimes, when the thought is simple and to the point, it may not feel like on-the-nose dialogue, like with this moving example from *Notting Hill (Richard Curtis)*, where Anna says to William, "I'm also just a girl, standing in front of a boy, asking him to love her."

IT TAKES A LOT OF REWRITING

In John Brady's book *The Craft of the Screenwriter,* Paddy Chayefsky offers the following advice for crafting great dialogue: "I write laboriously worked-out dialogue... because I know what I want my characters to say. I envision the scene; I can imagine them up there on the screen; I try to imagine what they would say and how they would say it, and keep it in character. And the dialogue comes out of that. I think that goes for every writer in the world. Then I rewrite it. Then I cut it. Then I refine it until I get the scene as precisely as I can get it." The art of writing dialogue couldn't be conveyed any better. Effective dialogue is developed through trial and error. Don't expect your first draft to have sparkling dialogue.

The key is to write whatever comes to mind in the first draft, then come back to it in subsequent rewrites and apply any of the techniques presented in this chapter. Write it, rewrite it, cut it, hone it, refine it, and polish it until it shines enough to blind the reader.

TEST YOUR DIALOGUE

Another effective way to improve your dialogue skills is to test what you've already written. **Read your dialogue aloud**, or get others to read the dialogue aloud as if it were a conversation. This is done all the time with television shows, where the cast gets together for a "table read." Writers I know often arrange a staged reading of their final draft to test how the dialogue plays out. While the actors speak, the writer sits back and listens closely, making notes on the script. You can do this on your own. Read the dialogue aloud, and see if it "works." Does it sound like real people talking? Does it flow? Does it move the story? Does it reveal or create tension? Most important, does it have emotional impact? Does it move you in any way—make you laugh, cry, excite you enough to keep turning the pages and see what happens next?

STUDY THE MASTERS OF DIALOGUE

I can't stress this enough: **If you want to learn how to write a great screenplay, you have to read, study, and analyze great screenplays.** This is true for every element of the craft from concept to dialogue. In fact, the techniques in this book come from seeing them in action in great scripts. My method is simple: read a script; come across a moment that affects me emotionally—anything that has emotional impact; highlight it; then, analyze how it was created, thus discovering a technique that can be applied to my own writing. Anyone can do this. It's not rocket science, but you have to read scripts. When it comes to great dialogue, you have to read the scripts and plays written by the following: Paddy Chayefsky, Billy Wilder, David Mamet, Joel & Ethan Cohen, Robert Riskin, Quentin Tarantino, Robert Towne, Aaron Sorkin, Neil Simon, Joseph L. Mankiewicz, Ernest Lehman, John Sayles, Shane Black, Eric Bogosian, Kevin Smith, James L. Brooks, Woody Allen, Scott Rosenberg, Scott Frank, Richard LaGravanese, Nora Ephron, Kevin Williamson, and Elmore Leonard (novelist), among others. This is by no means an exhaustive list, just enough to get you started. You won't waste your time with any of these fine dialogue writers.

FINAL THOUGHTS
Painting on the Page

"I hear and I forget; I see and I remember; I do and I understand."
-CHINESE PROVERB

So here we are, at the end of this stimulating journey through the world of emotional impact and the kind of writing that makes the reader go "Wow!" I hope it's given you new insights and inspiration for ways to create great stories—most of the techniques in this book are equally useful in fiction, non-fiction, and playwriting.

Keep this book handy and refer to it any time you encounter a flat moment on the page. Think of it as your writing partner, of whom you can ask, "How can I make this page more suspenseful, or this dialogue crisper?" The answers will always be a few pages away. Keep in mind that these techniques are just that—tools designed to arouse an emotional response in the reader. You still have to add your magic to them to create great art—your unique vision, your originality and creativity.

These techniques are not rules, just examples of what has worked for thousands of years in the field of dramatic storytelling. The only absolute, full-proof, unbreakable rule, for which you'll never find an exception, is never be boring on the page. In today's Hollywood, with the staggering amount of screenplays competing for a reader's attention, you can't afford the luxury of a dull page. I know this may seem like an extreme standard to achieve, but that's what's expected among professional screenwriters. When you think about it, not only do they have to string words together on the page, but they'd also better have emotional impact so that talent can sign up on the project with passion and enthusiasm. To reach this level, you'll probably need to rewrite your script.

REWRITING TIPS

Only a mediocre writer is always at his best. -W. SOMERSET MAUGHAM

It's not about how many times you rewrite the material, but what you have to do to make it work, in other words, evoke the desired emotional response in the reader. The difference between a professional writer and an aspiring one is that the pro can recognize flat writing that has no emotional impact on the page and is willing to rewrite it as often as it takes.

The best part of this necessary step in the writing process is that no one knows how long or how many times you had to rewrite your script to make it brilliant. All that counts is what's on the page, and unless you're dealing with a production script where the rewrites are documented and dated, nobody has to know what you had to go through physically and emotionally to create that final draft. Richard Walter, co-chair of the UCLA Screenwriting Program, says, "Rewriting is like finding focus on the camera. You never hit clarity exactly on the first rotation. You rack from out of focus to focus and on beyond a touch, then rotate the lens back to the clearest possible picture."

First, you have to know what needs rewriting. This is where discriminating between good and bad writing comes in handy. Outside feedback from writers' groups and script consultants is also important. Most beginners think rewriting consists of tweaking a character here, changing some dialogue there, maybe adding a scene, or deleting another. In reality, rewriting is a massive task—sometimes as much work, if not more, than writing a first draft.

Just as professional scribes plan their scripts, most plan their rewrites, focusing on specific elements at every pass. For example, once you have a first draft and you know what needs rewriting, you focus, say, on your characters, making sure they're consistent in actions and dialogue. Then, you may concentrate on structure, making sure that the flow of the script works, that the scenes are in order and vital to the telling of the story. You may then do a pass on plot, making sure there are no holes, that the plot follows a clear cause-and-effect pattern, and that there aren't any inconsistencies. Finally, you do a polish, where you correct any formatting and spelling errors, pull everything together that might have changed in the previous rewrites, and finish with a pass at the dialogue.

The process is simple, but difficult: writing a first draft–getting feedback–rewriting–getting feedback–rewriting–repeat as often as necessary.

This is just one example of a rewrite plan. There are, of course, other ways professional screenwriters rewrite—many are shared in my *101 Habits* book. It's all about what works for you. You could either finish a first draft, and then rewrite it; or you could rewrite as you go along, like veteran UCLA professor Lew Hunter, who rewrites his pages as soon as he finishes them that day, and takes another pass at them before going to sleep. Then, he goes over them again in the morning before writing the next set of pages. This way it's like writing three drafts at the same time.

LEARN MORE BY READING SCRIPTS

Ernest Hemingway once said, "Find what gave you emotion, what the action was that gave you excitement, then write it down, making it clear so that the reader can see it too." Not only is this advice a great way to show and not tell, it's also the best way to learn new techniques from great writers. When you read a script, mark the sections that make you feel anything, whether it's laughter, fear, curiosity, anticipation, sadness, pity, like, or dislike, and analyze how the effect was created. A writer in my writing group has the habit of drawing smiley faces and check marks whenever she likes something on the page. It's all about analyzing your emotional reactions to the material. Whenever you realize you've forgotten where you were because you were so engrossed in the script, ask yourself why? What kept you on the edge of your seat? Equally, when you find yourself distanced from the story or distracted by amateur flaws, figure out the cause, and learn how not to make the same mistakes in your writing.

But you have to read scripts, not just watch movies. Reading scripts will force you to deal exclusively with the emotional response caused by the words on the page, which are your only tool to express your art as a screenwriter. Reading lets you discover the dramatic techniques and tricks of the trade of the professional screenwriter without being influenced by the acting, directing, editing, cinematography, set design, and music in a completed film.

YOU'RE A PAINTER ON THE PAGE

> *Tell me a story! Because without a story, you are merely using words to prove you can string them together in logical sentences.*
> -ANNE MCCAFFREY

Successful screenwriters always think of specific emotions, especially the visceral responses of their readers. You can do the same. You're a painter on the page, and emotions are the colors on your palette. Every word, every line, every moment in your script will create a response in the reader. It's up to you whether you want him to feel bored or exhilarated. A great artist has absolute control over those responses.

Never forget that you're in the emotion-delivery business. Emotion is everything in storytelling, and Hollywood is a business of selling emotions, carefully packaged and sold around the world. Get to know them, the way a painter gets to know the power of each color on the spectrum. If you keep emotion at the forefront of your scenes, your words will disappear, and readers will lose themselves in the script.

If you're just starting out, I recommend you set this book aside and read a few books on the basics of screenwriting so that you can get a solid foundation before honing your craft. Learn to build the skeleton before tackling the nuances of muscles, nerves, and skin.

And if you're still writing your first couple of scripts, be patient. Your focus should be on developing your craft, not worrying about marketing, getting an agent, or pitching. Take as many classes as you need, especially at UCLA Extension's Writer's Program, either on campus or online, read as many books and scripts as you can, and keep writing script after script until more than one reader, who's not a friend or family member, tells you they truly enjoyed reading it.

If you are rewarded by becoming a contest finalist, optioning or selling your script, or getting an agent or manager to champion your work, I hope you'll email me, or come up to me at any of my seminars, and share the good news. I wish you the best of luck, and happy writing.

INDEX

HOW TO GET A FREE GIFT WITH THE PURCHASE OF THIS BOOK

As you read on page 131, if you're purchased a copy of this book, you're eligible to receive a free PDF file of *The Emotional Thesaurus*, which not only lists all the possible emotions a character may feel in a scene, but also orders them by intensity. This is a valuable tool in creating the beats of a scene. For instructions on how to receive this free file, visit my website at **www.karliglesias.com** and click the free gift banner.

READER COMMENTS AND INQUIRIES

For reader comments, questions, or inquiries about script consulting services, speaking enagagements, writing workshops, and upcoming classes, you may contact me through my website at **www.karliglesias.com.**

Printed in the USA
CPSIA information can be obtained
at www.ICGtesting.com
LVHW050347180823
755546LV00002B/224